OUR
WOMAN
IN
HAVANA

OUR
WOMAN
IN
HAVANA

A DIPLOMAT'S CHRONICLE
OF AMERICA'S LONG STRUGGLE
WITH CASTRO'S CUBA

AMBASSADOR
VICKI HUDDLESTON

THE OVERLOOK PRESS
NEW YORK, NY

To the Cuban People

This edition first published in hardcover in the United States in 2018 by
The Overlook Press, Peter Mayer Publishers, Inc.

141 Wooster Street
New York, NY 10012
www.overlookpress.com
For bulk and special sales, please contact sales@overlookny.com
or write to us at the above address.

The opinions and characterizations in this piece are those
of the author and do not necessarily represent the views
of the United States government.

Cataloging-in-Publication Data is available from the Library of Congress

Book design and type formatting by Bernard Schleifer
Manufactured in the United States of America
FIRST EDITION
1 3 5 7 9 10 8 6 4 2
ISBN: 978-1-4683-1579-0

CONTENTS

FOREWORD 7

PROLOGUE 11

PART I 1989–1993:
Cuban Affairs, US State Department;
Presidents George H. W. Bush and Bill Clinton   17

1 I Am the Director of Cuban Affairs 19
2 The Legacy of Terror for Cubans and Americans 35

PART II 1999–2000:
US Interests Section, Havana; President Bill Clinton   47

3 Our Woman in Havana 49
4 A Provocation 61
5 Fidel Is Cuba 73
6 The Last Battle 85
7 Fidel's Last Hurrah 103

PART III 2001–2002:
US Interests Section; President George W. Bush   119

8 Regime Change: Ours 121
9 From Fidel with Love 135
10 Havana, My Afghan Hound 149
11 The Best of Enemies: Guantanamo Naval Base 167
12 Fidel's Charm Offensive 183
13 My Little Radios 201
14 The President and the Dissident 219
15 Mr. W. versus Mr. Castro 231

PART IV 2002 and Beyond   245

16 Myths, Contradictions, and Lies: Bush, Obama, and Trump 247
17 The Future Is Havana, Not Miami 265

EPILOGUE 287
NOTES 292
BIBLIOGRAPHY 302
ACKNOWLEDGMENTS 304

FOREWORD

I WAS BORN IN HAVANA IN 1953. SEVEN YEARS LATER, MY FAMILY LEFT Cuba for the United States, one of many families who fled Cuba's communist revolution. In 2006, when I first met Ambassador Vicki Huddleston, I was serving as US Secretary of Commerce, charged with implementing President George W. Bush's Cuba policy. Vicki and her colleagues at The Brookings Institution, who were developing a blueprint for restoring relations with Cuba, were convinced that as long as the US threatened Cuba there was no hope for positive change in the relationship. By the time Vicki and I next saw each other at the Meridian International Cultural Diplomacy Forum on Cuba in 2016, I had joined other Cuban Americans in supporting President Barack Obama's opening to Cuba. I felt strongly, after having visited Cuba for the opening of our embassy in Havana on August 14, 2015, that a policy of engagement was in the best interests of the American and the Cuban people.

In thirty years of doing business around the globe, I have found that a vibrant private sector often has an uplifting effect on communities and whole societies. Since Cuba was opening its own private sector when President Obama pursued normalization, it seemed that for once in almost sixty years the stars were aligning. When I visited Cuba again during President Obama's historic visit to the island in March 2016, it was clear to me that the time had come for a new relationship between the two countries. As Vicki reveals in this engaging book, policy towards Cuba is often not a product of the foreign policy process but of domestic politics. In 1991, with the Soviet Union imploding, many Cuban Americans were convinced that Cuba would collapse without the five billion dollar annual subsidy from the recently defunct Soviet Union. Yet it did not collapse. Both President George H. W. Bush and Bill Clinton, candidates for President in 1992, endorsed legislation that expanded and extended the embargo. When Bill Clinton defeated the incumbent Bush, gaining more votes among Cuban American voters than any recent Democratic candidate before him, the Cuban diaspora imagined he would carry out policies that were largely acceptable to them. He did so until the final years of his second term, when his administration returned Elián González—the five-year-old boy found floating on an inner tube in the Florida Straits—to his father in Cuba. This international imbroglio—described from Vicki's perspective from her experience on the ground in Cuba at the time, with valuable first-hand knowledge—contributed to Al Gore's pivotal loss of Florida in the 2000 presidential election.

When President Obama initiated his outreach to Cuba I hoped it would be the beginning of a long process of reconciliation among Cubans—those on the island and those abroad. But, powerful conservative Cuban-Americans have found in President Trump an ally; once again domestic politics have trumped US interests. The tightening of travel policies has had a devastating impact on new Cuban entrepreneurs. Furthermore, a health incident, caused by the strange and still unconfirmed term "sonic attacks" endured by US diplomats, has pushed the relationship back to almost Cold-War depths. In the meantime, China has stepped up trade and investment in Cuba, while Russia has moved to replace Venezuela as one of Cuba's strategic partners.

In Ambassador Huddleston's revealing memoir, which shows a resourceful diplomat at work, Vicki illustrates with stories and an insider's knowledge the myths, misunderstandings, and false statements that have characterized our relations with Cuba. For more than forty years, the US and Cuba have had diplomatic relations. It is a myth that diplomatic relations started with President Obama's push for normalization; the reader discovers that they actually began under President Carter. Although prohibited from flying the Stars and Stripes, the American diplomatic mission in Havana—known as the United States Interests Section—had long been influential.

Vicki is a realist and not naïve about the complexities of this relationship. In fact, she describes, in fascinating detail, her often-tense relationship with Fidel Castro. The Cuban leader denounced her and the US government, threatening to close the US Interests section, and then to underline his intent he organized a protest rally of 20,000 that she dared to attend. During her three years as the Chief of our diplomatic mission in Havana, Fidel seemed to have a competitive relationship with her. She describes how he seemed to be interested in her every move, from the dog show career of her prize-winning Afghan hound "Havana," to her collection of exile art that she displayed in the beautiful residence of our former ambassadors to Cuba. Their relationship, albeit complicated, had its benefits: after 9/11, Vicki persuaded the Cuban Government to decline to denounce the incarceration of unlawful combatants at Guantanamo base.

I lament the fact that relatively few women diplomats have written their memoirs. Vicki's approach to diplomacy is creative and courageous. She doesn't sugarcoat her own mistakes and writes very candidly about the challenges of representing the United States in Cuba. In reading Vicki's book, one can see that our relations with Cuba have too often been a story of what might have been.

This is a book for anyone interested in Cuba. Americans will find a comprehensive guide to what has happened to prolong the unrelieved animosity. Cuban Americans will be fascinated by the details of the Elian Gonzalez case and model relations worked out after 9/11 between our two militaries. Academics will discover never-before revealed accounts of espionage, alliances, and betrayals. Our European, Latin

American, and Canadian friends will come to better understand the influence of domestic politics on US Cuba policy.

As CEO of the Kellogg Company and then US Secretary of Commerce, I saw firsthand that our private sector is truly the best ambassador for American values, especially the power of free enterprise to raise living standards. I hope American entrepreneurs and companies will again soon have the opportunity to bring their best to Cuba. This important and personable memoir gives everyone invested in Cuba's success something to think about and aspire toward. It informs readers of much that they should know about US-Cuba relations, the unique beauty of Havana, and the graciousness and charm of the Cuban people, all through the eyes of a gifted diplomat.

Secretary Carlos Gutierrez
Washington, DC
January2018

PROLOGUE

I N THE LATE 1980S JAMES MICHENER AND JOHN KINGS WROTE A wonderful book titled *Six Days in Havana*, in which Kings noted, "I may go back again one day, but it will never be with the same feelings of exhilaration and utter surprise that this first visit engendered." I recall feeling this way during my first visit to Cuba's capital, and I imagine this sentiment was experienced by the hundreds of thousands of Americans who visited during President Barack Obama's short-lived opening to Cuba. That period began in December 2014 and ended in June 2017, when his successor, Donald Trump, announced that he had "canceled" Obama's national security directive, which had initiated a process of normalization between the United States and Cuba. President Trump's decision to reinstate a punitive policy advocated by a small group of Cuban Americans was nothing new. For over a half century, US policy toward Cuba has been dictated by Cuban Americans who were forced from their country by the triumph of the Cuban Revolution on January 1, 1959. Since the failed CIA-organized Bay of Pigs Invasion in 1961, the premise of this policy has been to bring about regime change, initially through the use of force and then through a comprehensive, unilateral economic embargo. Yet despite the successive hardening of sanctions against Cuba, we have failed to oust Cuban leaders Fidel and Raúl Castro or alter the course of Cuban politics. Nor has our policy enabled its advocates to recover their forfeited property or recover to their country.

The history of US-Cuba relations is filled with myths and contra-dictions that are principally designed to help Cuban Americans regain the country they lost. Latin America and much of the developing world watch, appalled that the most powerful nation on earth continues to isolate and castigate its small neighbor of eleven million people who live on an island that is smaller than the state of Florida. What they fail to understand is that our Cuba policy is actually domestic policy, not foreign policy. The Cuban American voting bloc in Florida has seduced Democrats and Republicans alike. In 2000, *el voto castigo* (the punish-ment vote) against Al Gore—in retaliation for President Bill Clinton re-turning a Cuban child to his father—pushed the Florida election as far the US Supreme Court, which then awarded the presidency to George W. Bush. Republicans have always bowed to the demands of the Cuban diaspora, but so too did Presidents John F. Kennedy and Bill Clinton, who aggressively courted Cuban American money and votes.

With Obama's opening of relations with Cuba it seemed that our country had finally given up this charade of a foreign policy and would bring Cuba back under our sphere of influence through a policy of ac-tive engagement. Over time, both countries would benefit from closer cooperation on terrorism, crime, and the environment, as well as from mutual trade and investment. As affinity started to grow, there was hope of reconciliation between Cubans in the United States and on the island. But with Trump's recent policy reversal, normalization is once again impossible. By treating Cuba worse than some of our most dan-gerous enemies, we are pushing it into the arms of the Chinese and the Russians, whose economic and military influence is steadily increasing.

I am writing this book because I believe we must put an end to this punitive policy and restart an opening that appeals to "the better angels of our nature." It is well past time that we stop making Cuba a glaring exception to the way we engage with countries around the world whose political systems we oppose. Cuba is the only country against which we maintain a comprehensive unilateral economic embargo and the only country in which we occupy part of its territory against its wishes. By doing so we undermine both countries' political and economic interests, deprive our country of a potential strategic ally, and create unnecessary division among our allies. Ironically, now is the best possible time to mend relations with Cuba. Fidel Castro is dead and his brother Raúl has announced that he intends to give up the presidency in February 2018. For the first time in fifty-nine years, a Castro will no longer rule Cuba.

My relationship with Cuba began as the Soviet Union curtailed its financial and strategic alliance with the island. It was then that I first encountered Fidel Castro, who feared that he might not hold on to power. But he did, even as the Soviets withdrew five billion dollars in annual subsidies and the US tightened its embargo. During my first four years working on Cuba policy within the State Department (1989–93), first as the deputy and then as the director of Cuban affairs, I endeavored to keep US policy from becoming overly confrontational. The powerful Cuban American lobby, led by the Cuban American National Foundation (CANF), seized every opportunity to denigrate Cuba in the hope and expectation that it would lead to a confrontation with Fidel Castro. I mostly succeeded at maintaining an even keel, but when I failed, US policy and I came under attack.

In 1999, I was delighted when President Clinton asked me to lead our diplomatic mission in Havana. (Despite the general perception that the United States and Cuba had no diplomatic relations, our two governments have in fact maintained diplomatic representation in each other's capitals—housed in our former embassy buildings, but called by different names—since President Jimmy Carter reestablished relations in 1977.) Clinton hoped that I might assist in building upon his initial opening with the island, but it was soon overtaken by the fevered custody battle between Cuban exiles and Fidel Castro over little Elián González, a five-year-old Cuban child, who was found floating on an inner tube in the Florida Straits. In this case the culprit for destroying the possibility of improved relations was Fidel Castro, who could not resist the opportunity to taunt Cuban Americans and walk the world stage yet again.

Surprisingly, for eighteen months (January 2001–May 2002) President George W. Bush continued the moderate policy of the Clinton administration, which permitted cooperation between our governments and "people-to-people" travel to Cuba for cultural, humanitarian, and religious purposes. At the US Interests Section my staff and I created an outreach program that supported Cuba's civil society and dissident movements. The result was the blooming of the so-called Cuban Spring of 2002—the most open period in Cuba since the revolution. But a hard-right lobby that had broken away from CANF, the Cuban Liberty Council, which had supported Jeb Bush's reelection campaign for governor of Florida, demanded that President Bush revert to a hostile policy. Bush did so after this lobby rejected his New Cuba Initiative, which he had laid out for them in a speech in Miami on May 20, 2002, the one hundredth anniversary of Cuba's independence from Spain. I left Havana in September 2002. Only six months later, on the eve of the US invasion of Iraq, Castro arrested and imprisoned seventy-five dissidents. The Black Spring of 2003 descended on Cuba, along with the strictest sanctions ever imposed on the island.

For three years, from September 1999 until my departure in September 2002, Fidel Castro and I competed for the hearts and minds of the Cuban people. Cubans loved our active policy of outreach and engagement, including the little AM/FM/shortwave radios that my staff and I distributed to the Cuban people, but Fidel did not, and he threatened to throw me out of the country. In diplomatic parlance, I would be asked to leave because I was no longer welcome, a persona non grata. At the same time, US-Cuba relations were improving: hundreds of thousands of Americans were visiting the island, Cuba was for the first time purchasing millions of dollars in US agricultural products, and it was even cooperating with us in the fight against terrorism.

Not only did Castro refrain from denouncing the US incarceration of "unlawful enemy combatants" at the Guantanamo Bay Naval Base, but his military cooperated with ours to ensure the safety and security of the base.

Havana still beckons to Americans who for nearly six decades have been denied the city's charms. Having spurned Spain and then the United States in the expectation of becoming truly independent, Cuba slipped into the arms of the Soviet Union. During the height of the Cold War, Cuba brought us to the edge of nuclear Armageddon with the Soviets, sent armies to Africa, and attempted to ignite revolution in Bolivia, Columbia, and Nicaragua. But Cuba had chosen poorly, the Soviets withdrew their subsidies, and the United States tightened its embargo. The Cuban people suffered great deprivation, but again were revived in the 1990s through the oil-fueled largess of Venezuela under the late Hugo Chávez.

When the United States again came courting in the form of an opening by President Obama on December 17, 2014, it seemed that our natural ally and third-closest and smallest neighbor would willingly, if not enthusiastically, accept our proposal of mutual respect and friendship. Most Cubans certainly desired this outcome. But many Cuban Americans who had watched Cuba's slow decline from across the Florida Straits remained stubbornly unwilling to accept reconciliation. In lingering bitterness, they found in President Trump a willing antagonist who slammed the door closed on Obama's opening. Rather than becoming a strategic ally through whom we might build closer and stronger bonds in the Caribbean, Central America, and across the Western Hemisphere, Cuba once again seeks a patron who will help it confront the United States and resist the tide of animosity coming from the north. Will the latest patron be China, or Russia? Or will both Americans and Cubans finally be convinced that we are too close and too linked by the bonds of family and friendship to continue this destructive relationship?

PART I

1989-1993: CUBAN AFFAIRS, US STATE DEPARTMENT; PRESIDENTS GEORGE H. W. BUSH AND BILL CLINTON

CHAPTER 1

I AM THE DIRECTOR OF CUBAN AFFAIRS

WHEN HE GLARED ACROSS THE ROOM AT ME, IT WAS A WARNING sign of things to come. The year was 1991, the place was the Palacio de la Revolución in Havana, Cuba, and my glowering interlocutor was Fidel Castro, one of the most consequential figures of the twentieth century.

A member of the US Foreign Service, I had recently taken a job to manage US government relations with Cuba. It was a politically sensitive position reserved for senior officers, but many of my fellow diplomats avoided it because a powerful lobby—the Cuban American National Foundation (CANF)—dictated a punitive US policy toward Cuba. If you got on the wrong side of exiles ousted by the Castro regime, they could ruin your career. During the past two years as the deputy in the US State Department's Office of Cuban Affairs, I had become adept at getting along with the lobby. Still, it wasn't going to be easy; there would certainly be critics and naysayers, I didn't have the rank required, and I would be one of a very few career women in an office director's job. What probably tipped the scales in my favor, however, was the ongoing legal challenge on behalf of women Foreign Service officers, which claimed that the State Department discriminated against women in awarding high-ranking jobs. Whatever the reason, I was delighted and thus seized the opportunity despite the risks.

To me it was a tremendously important job. In the early 1960s, US-Cuba relations had shaken the very foundations of world peace. Fidel Castro and his rebels' triumphal entry into Havana on New Year's Day 1959 turned Cuba—if not the world—upside down. President Dwight D. Eisenhower imposed a destructive unilateral embargo after the rebels seized American oil companies. In the early days of the administration of President John F. Kennedy, believing that Castro's revolution could be destroyed in its infancy, the CIA organized an exile invasion at the Bay of Pigs that became a disastrous failure when the administration refused to provide additional air support. A year later, in October 1962, the Cuban Missile Crisis with the Soviet Union brought us to the brink of nuclear Armageddon. In the 1970s and early 1980s, with the backing of the Soviet Union, Castro was at the peak of his power. A major player in Africa, he was admired by leaders of the developing world for standing up to rich, white governments—notably South Africa and the United States. In Ethiopia, Cuban troops helped defeat the invading armies of Somali dictator Siad Barre. In southern Africa, Cubans fought alongside Angolan and Namibian troops against South Africa, losing as many as five thousand troops over thirteen years. Nelson Mandela, one of the most admired men in the world, said, "The Cuban people hold a special place in the hearts of the peoples of Africa. The Cuban internationalists have made a contribution to African independence, freedom, and justice, unparalleled for its principled selfless character." He was right; it was Cuban generals, troops, and air power—all underwritten by the Soviet Union—that had defeated the South African Army at the Battle of Cuito Cuanavale in Angola.

Presidents from both parties had tried to improve relations. Jimmy Carter had briefly lifted the travel ban, but Ronald Reagan reinstated it again in response to Castro's African adventures. Nevertheless, Reagan authorized the State Department's head of African Affairs, Chester Crocker, to find a way to remove Cuba from Africa. He and his Soviet counterpart played a critical role in brokering the Tripartite Accords among Angola, Cuba, and South Africa. By the summer of 1991 Cuba had completed the withdrawal of fifty thousand troops from Africa.

President George H. W. Bush authorized a US delegation to attend the ceremonies in Havana that would recognize the completion of the accords. The head of our interagency delegation, Jeff Davidow, was a career diplomat from the Africa Bureau. I joined the delegation to reassure CANF that no insidious goodwill would creep into the two countries' antagonistic relationship. They were right to be concerned. The Africa Bureau—like most of the State Department—thought that our Cuba policy was a pawn of Miami's Cuban American community, who ardently believed that isolating the island would force Castro from power and allow them to return.

I was pleased to be on my way back to Havana. I enjoyed visiting the lovely but languishing city, and I liked to uncover its architectural treasures, ravaged by time and neglect—the beautiful lines of the cathedral darkened by mold, the lovely mansions overtaken by vines climbing up walls and over once-elegant entrances, and the Malecón—the seawall built by the US Corps of Engineers—where Habaneros sought relief from their constricted lives as they imagined life beyond the wall.

Our delegation's first and only meeting with Cuban government officials was at the Palacio de Convenciones de la Habana, an impressive conference complex built to promote Cuba's standing as a leader in the developing world. Our delegation met the Cubans in a small room, away from the principal building, a massive white structure in Havana's beautiful suburb of Cubanacan, where the country's former wealthy elite once lived, and where the revolution's hierarchy now dwelled. We exchanged greetings, and the Cubans seemed pleased that we were there. But nothing of importance was discussed. Perhaps there was little to be said, or the Cubans were under instructions not to raise their concerns about the economic disaster the country was facing with the breakup of the Soviet Union. It was all rather stiff; we smiled and shook hands, and there were no warm *abrazos* (hugs). The Cubans didn't know Davidow, the delegation lead, because a new team had replaced those who negotiated the agreement. Reagan had been replaced by President George H. W. Bush, who was in turn wary of the Cubans, in part because his younger son Jeb's political base in Florida was founded on the support of conservative Cuban Americans who wished to ensure that Castro's Cuba would not outlive the dying Soviet Union.

During the thirty months it had taken Soviet transport vessels to return the Cuban troops from Angola and Namibia, the Castro brothers had lost a little of their luster. General Raúl Castro had tearfully sentenced General Arnaldo Ochoa, the popular hero of Cuba's successful African wars, and three other high-ranking officials, to death by firing squad. Other officers were given long prisons terms for allegedly participating in drug trafficking. Their trials were part of a purge led by Fidel Castro to ensure the loyalty of the Revolutionary Armed Forces and the Ministry of the Interior's police and secret service. His timing was impeccable, as the trials occurred just a year before the Soviets began reducing their military and financial support to the Cuban armed forces and eventually terminated five billion dollars in subsidies to the Cuban economy.

Ochoa's crime was most likely that he was a young, handsome, and charismatic general who posed a potential threat to Fidel. Every Cuban leader who—if even briefly—was a possible replacement for Fidel had been demoted, exiled, imprisoned, and/or executed, beginning with Fidel's fellow revolutionary leaders. His two principal commanders died in the early years after the revolution. Camilo Cienfuegos, age twenty-seven, perished in the suspicious crash of a small plane, and Ernesto "Che" Guevara, age thirty-nine, was killed during an attempt to lead a peasant revolt in Bolivia. More recently, potential successors such as Ricardo Alarcón, Carlos Lage Dávila, and Felipe Pérez Roque had all lost power, though they had avoided imprisonment or execution.

Castro must have believed that relations with the United States might improve or at least that the administration of President Bush wouldn't punish him. He had complied with the Tripartite Accords and brought home fifty thousand Cuban troops from Africa. To celebrate the occasion, he invited delegations from Angola, Namibia, South Africa, the Soviet Union, the United States, and the entire diplomatic corps to celebrate the successful completion of the Tripartite Accords at the Palacio de la Revolución. The massive white building sat behind a huge four-sided tower and memorial dedicated to Cuba's national hero José Martí. Its 1950s style and the iconic visages of Guevara and Cienfuegos on the front of the two principal buildings gave the impression that this imposing complex, where Castro held massive rallies, had been built by the Communists. In fact, the dictator Fulgencio Batista had ordered the construction of the Plaza Civica, as it was initially named. Before it could be completed, Fidel's revolutionaries stormed into Havana, forcing Batista and his government to flee.

In Havana, I was staying with Alan Flanigan, the principal officer of our diplomatic mission, which was known as the US Interests Section. This rather cumbersome name was simply an artifice for what was in fact a small embassy. Use of the name began in 1977 when Carter and Castro reestablished diplomatic relations. American diplomats returned to Havana and began operating out of the old embassy building. The Cubans returned to Washington, DC, to install themselves in their old embassy building, which was located on Sixteenth Street. But to mollify the Cuban diaspora, the agreement stipulated that neither mission would fly their national flags and the level of representation would be less than that of an embassy. Thus, Alan's job was like that of an ambassador, but at a lower level. He represented our government's views to the Cubans and managed the work of the Interests Section. As the coordinator or director of Cuban affairs, my job was to back him up and provide policy direction from the State Department. This made me the bad cop, the overseer of our policy of isolating Cuba.

As Alan and I neared the Plaza de Revolución in his official car, we were directed to a narrow road that circled behind the hill on which stood the tower and statue commemorating Martí. There, partially out of view, was the palace from which Castro and his aides ran the country. Once inside, we were directed to take the elevator to the first floor, where Ricardo Alarcón, then the presumed number four in the Communist Party hierarchy, and president of the National Assembly, greeted us in a spacious ballroom.

Among the two hundred guests there were only three women: Castro's young, beautiful interpreter, the Soviet ambassador's spouse, and myself. It seems surprising now, with women in all spheres of diplomacy, but in the early 1990s there were very few senior women diplomats. There were no women ambassadors present, which implied that there were none in Havana. Spouses had not been included, except for the Soviet ambassador's wife. It seemed as if Africa and Europe weren't doing any better than the State Department when it came to placing women in high positions.

This was my first in-person view of Fidel. He fit the legend, with his green fatigues and beard, but this night had no cigar—a cancer scare had persuaded him to give up smoking. I'd read about him, of course, and knew some of his secrets—his affairs and vanities—as well as the bizarre methods the CIA had deployed to attempt to assassinate him, which included the Mafia dousing his scuba suit with poison powder, and even recruiting a former lover to do the deed (though she was found out by Fidel).

Castro stood behind the ministers from Angola, Cuba, and South Africa as each signed three documents, one for each government. As the signing dragged on, he began to fidget, adjusting his fatigues, and occasionally making a funny face. He didn't like being a bit player because he was accustomed to a starring role. It was then that we made eye contact. Fidel, recognizing who I was, glared at me, then frowned slightly. I smiled but, not wanting to be caught staring, quickly looked away. I was surprised to note that he was wearing a bulletproof vest. I couldn't imagine that there was any danger from these diplomats. Could he be worried about his own people, or was it that the vest appealed to his vanity because it made him appear even bigger? He was certainly larger than most Latin men, possibly one reason why Cubans referred to him as El Caballo (The Horse).

With the signing finally over, the guests relaxed, sipped drinks, and nibbled canapés. I had been warned that Castro would chat with the delegations in a booming voice so that all his guests could admire his clever repartee. Sometimes he embarrassed his guests by pointing out their ignorance of some obscure topic or by denigrating their government. I wasn't worried. After all, Castro had never even spoken to Alan Flanigan, who led our mission. If he wanted to talk to an American, it would be Jeff Davidow, our delegation head. I should have known better. I was the diplomat primarily responsible for American policy, and Castro preferred female interlocutors, assuming his formidable charisma would always work in his favor.

Fidel made a beeline for me. I thought I looked good, and younger than my forty-nine years, in my favorite cream-colored chiffon dress with long sleeves and a skirt that fell just above the knees. Even so, I was relieved that Jeff, our delegation head, intercepted him. Fidel simply looked him up and down and moved on toward me. I might claim that he ignored Jeff because he was so anxious to talk with me. More likely he didn't want his image spoiled by having to look up to the tall, heavyset American who was bigger than him. Castro intended to present himself as the biggest and most powerful man in the room, an image that would be abetted by talking down to a petite woman.

Fidel made an erudite observation about Mexico's agrarian reform program. He didn't address himself to anyone in particular in our delegation, and one of my colleagues provided a reasonable response. I certainly didn't have a ready reply. Then Fidel turned toward me. In retrospect, I should have been better prepared, because it made sense for him to target me. I was the "enforcer"—the American official who represented the hated Cuba policy. I could take a message back to Washington or advocate for or against him. What I didn't imagine was that I'd become a foil for amusing his guests.

Castro smiled, clearly enjoying a moment where he could hover over the representative of the "empire," as he called the United States. He then asked in English, "Who are you, someone's spouse?"

I was furious. Fidel knew exactly who I was. He knew everything about those of us who managed US policy toward Cuba. I had visited Cuba several times before when I had served as deputy in the Cuba office. He might have missed the fact that I had been promoted to director, but he absolutely knew I was not "someone's spouse."

As I drew myself up for an appropriately outraged reply, I realized that the entire room was listening. No matter. I stood as tall as possible—at five feet, five inches—and announced boldly, "No. I am the director of Cuban affairs."

Fidel, now purring with pleasure, surveyed the room to ensure that no one would miss his next words. He boomed, "Oh? I thought *I* was!" My delegation was speechless; I was angry and embarrassed. Fidel moved on, having skewered me.

I took a glass of something, smiling ruefully at my colleagues. As I stood sipping the drink, I was relieved to no longer be the center of attention. Just as I was thinking that perhaps this job wasn't the right fit, security guards asked me to accompany them. Fidel was waiting at the entrance to the buffet. He offered me his arm. I swallowed my pride and took it. The other diplomats gasped.

Fortunately, this was 1991—there were no media on hand and no cell phones to record Fidel and I arm in arm. Diplomacy still took place largely behind closed doors, in private. Diplomats still lived in a world where personal relations counted for a lot—where an angry word from John Foster Dulles in Cairo had been strong enough to push an ally into the arms of the Soviet Union, and a smile from Jackie Kennedy could charm the hearts of Parisians. Had the ever-wary Cuban diaspora seen this, I would have been fired instantly. They were always on the lookout for a friendly smile or handshake that might indicate some lessening of hostilities.

A few minutes earlier, Fidel had mocked me; now we were leading the diplomats into dinner, in the tradition of rulers leading their subjects to a banquet table. In this case, I hoped that I wasn't being led to something worse. I realized that, without intending to, I'd become Castro's foil. I desperately wanted to say something clever so that I could redeem myself, but before I could think of anything, Fidel gave a slight bow, indicating that I should lead the guests in filling their plates with Cuban delicacies. I hesitated, then walked along the long table, which was covered by a sparkling white tablecloth. I took a few shrimps from the scrumptious display of lobster, roast beef, ham, and traditional Cuban delicacies that included *Moros y Cristianos* (Moors and Christians, the name for beans and rice), *platanos* (fried plantains), and *ropa vieja* (sautéed beef). I felt a bit uneasy knowing that Cubans, who were already suffering from the diminishing Soviet subsidies, did not have enough to eat. They weren't allowed to traffic in lobster and shrimp, even if they had harvested the catch themselves; these delicacies were reserved for the government and its guests. Cubans were jailed if caught selling shellfish. There was little fresh produce available in the open-air farmers' markets, and none in the tiny, dingy, stores with unhappy clerks, where the people used their government-issued ration cards to buy tinned meat and root crops. Their lives were hard. Some were so desperate that they raised pigs in their apartments, cutting the animals' vocal cords to avoid problems with the neighbors.

As I moved away from the buffet table, a security guard again appeared, this time to escort me to Fidel and his interpreter, who were standing alone on the far side of the room. Even if I yelled, the diplomats would be unable to hear me say something clever that might redeem my earlier blunder. The long buffet set up to fete the diplomats had become a buffer against eavesdroppers or even my colleagues attempting to rescue me.

Fidel, still handsome at sixty-five with a long face made even longer by his heavy gray-black beard, was talking rapidly in Spanish rapidly and passionately, throwing up his hands. The American *bloqueo* (blockade)—Castro's name for the embargo—was cruel to Cuba's children. They were suffering, and it was the fault of my uncaring government. How could we treat Cuba so unfairly? It was unprecedented that any government would impose a harsh and unilateral blockade against the purchase of food and medicines. When would we stop hurting the Cuban people?

The delegations on the other side of the room (mine included) were keenly watching this pantomime. They couldn't hear Fidel, but they could see his passion. They must have been wondering whether he would humiliate me again. His calculating brown eyes scrutinized me, like a cat toying with a mouse. Would I meekly listen to his tirade, or would I stand up to him? With plate, fork, and napkin in hand, I felt at a distinct disadvantage. I felt trapped. I was on my own. I detected a fleeting smile cross Fidel's lips as his security guards blocked Jeff's attempt to join us. This moment would determine if I were up to the job.

Fidel pushed closer to me, forcing me to take a step back. "Your *bloqueo* is killing our children. Not one aspirin to stop their suffering. How can you be so cruel?" I took a deep breath. In fact, I disagreed with American policy on exactly this point. Our embargo hurt the Cuban people far more than its Communist leaders.

However, as much as I disliked the embargo, I wasn't going to be Fidel's patsy. It was my job to defend US policy, regardless of my personal feelings. I looked him squarely in the eyes. "That's not true," I almost shouted. "The embargo is not a blockade. Cuba can buy aspirin from any country it wishes, except the United States." It had been almost thirty years since the Cuban Missile Crisis, when the United States and the Soviet Union came to the edge of a nuclear showdown over Soviet missiles located on Cuban soil. So, I added, "Despite the embargo, other countries can trade with you. And, if a child needs a medicine that is only made in the United States, we will sell it to you."

Fidel scoffed. "You know it takes years to get permission."

Castro turned to the issue that was bothering him, the survival of his island nation. Communism was under attack. The Berlin Wall had fallen two years earlier, and Russian president Mikhail Gorbachev had since introduced Perestroika reforms, with which the Cuban hierarchy disagreed. Soviet subsidies had been sharply reduced and would soon be terminated. Without aid, Castro's vaunted revolution was in danger of collapsing. Fidel seemed to be trying to find out whether there would be any change in the Bush administration's policies. He had lived up to the Tripartite Accords, and brought his troops home from Africa, removing a major irritant in US-Cuban relations. I knew that some diplomats thought we owed Cuba something, and perhaps had even promised better relations in return. Presumably, we had no reason to gratuitously further punish Cuba. But Castro and I both knew that the Cuban American lobby wanted to further tighten the embargo.

"When Cuba holds free and fair elections with international observation, we will lift the embargo," I said. My statement was policy, and I believed in it. Fidel protested that Cuba did hold elections. He was elected as one of the representatives to the National Assembly from the eastern province of Oriente, where he, his siblings, and his Cuban mother, Lina, had lived with Angel, his Spanish father, on a prosperous farm in Birán. But Castro and I both knew that Cuban elections were unlikely to meet our criteria or that of international observers.

Castro moved closer; he was intense, and seemed to be searching for a sign of softening in my position. I stood my ground. "No, there is no change in US policy. Cuba must change, first." Fidel fumed, "You will never give up the *bloqueo*; the *gusanos* won't allow it." *Gusanos*, meaning worms, was the spiteful image he used to describe Cuban exiles in America. Turning away, he stomped off, his interpreter in trail.

The encounter was over. As I walked back to the other side of the buffet table, chatter resumed among the diplomats. Our talk seemed to have lasted hours. Jim Smith, the Department of Defense representative, came over and much to my relief said, "You did well." Alan reminded me that I'd better have a cable reporting on the conversation ready to send to the State Department first thing in the morning. If not, rumors would spread and Cuban Americans would be sure that they had been betrayed. Washington also would want to know that Castro was worried about the future. But I was sure that Castro's concerns would only reinforce our expectation that the loss of his Soviet benefactor would be his undoing. I did not imagine that we would respond to Fidel's overture, if indeed that was what it had been.

I looked over at Fidel as a waiter appeared with a tray on which was centered one dry martini with a green olive in a very large glass with a long crystal stem. Castro took it and quickly drained it; the conversation must have rattled his nerves as well. Jim pointed to Cuba's finest old rum on the buffet table. I set down my still full plate and poured myself a glass. I had made my points and defended our policy. I had not succumbed to Fidel's forceful personality; I had stood up to him and proven to myself and my delegation that I could handle my new position. I didn't like the embargo, but I loved the job. Fidel was the most powerful and charismatic man I had ever met. It was no wonder he preferred female interlocutors; he undoubtedly thought that against a female adversary his formidable size and personality would work in his favor.

When I returned to Washington a few days later, everyone wanted a firsthand account. I happily told and retold my story. I credited Fidel with talking during two-thirds of our conversations, but pointed out that I had forcefully interrupted him to insert my one-third. My boss, Bob Gelbard, the principal adviser to the assistant secretary of state, asked, "What do you think it was all about?"

"Bob, I am not sure," I replied, "but one thing is clear: Castro is worried about whether we will tighten the embargo just as Cuba loses its Soviet subsidies." I explained that Havana was bleak, apartment houses along the Malecón were collapsing from lack of repair, and tall grass was pushing up through the cobblestones in the streets surrounding the principal square, the Plaza de Armas. It seemed as if the island's infrastructure, from peeling paint to crumbling buildings, was in free fall. The picture that stayed in my mind was a stray, mangy, and hungry dog in the deserted Plaza de Catedral, where Cubans once gathered to meet and socialize.

Possibly believing he owed Castro for removing fifty thousand troops from Africa, President Bush so far had refrained from endorsing Representative Robert Torricelli's Cuban Democracy Act. Torricelli, a small, pugnacious Democrat from New Jersey, was at the behest of CANF pushing legislation that would prevent American subsidiaries in foreign countries from selling their products to Cuba. If passed, it would cut off a large portion of Cuba's food and medicines. I disliked the proposal; it seemed mean-spirited to further punish Cuba's people.

CANF's president and driving force, Jorge Mas Canosa, was absolutely determined to see the legislation enacted. He believed that victory was finally at hand. Once the Soviets removed their troops, personnel, and money from the island, Castro would be vulnerable. Fidel would fall, and Mas Canosa thought he himself might even become Cuba's next president. All he had to do was convince President Bush to endorse Torricelli's legislation, which would deliver the final blow. Mas Canosa was a man with a mission. He seemed an unlikely power broker: a rotund man of little political pedigree but great persuasion. He was a peddler of dreams who owed his success as the preeminent leader of the Cuban American community to his determined campaign to restore power, position, and property to Cubans who had fled Castro's island. He wielded power in Miami as completely as Castro did in Havana. He and CANF believed that Cubans made desperate by the loss of Soviet subsidies and an even stricter embargo would rise up and throw off Castro's shackles.

Cuban Americans had voted overwhelmingly for Republican presidential candidates, in retaliation for President Kennedy's refusal to provide US air power to save the exile invasion. In return, all Republican presidents have loyally supported the embargo, ensuring the favor of the influential Cuban American voting bloc in the key state of Florida. President Reagan set up Radio Martí, which broadcast news, information, and a variety of programs to Cuba. At the behest of President George H. W. Bush, Tony Navarro, a Cuban American political appointee, and I spent months putting TV Martí on the air, at considerable cost to US taxpayers. Now Mas Canosa wanted Bush to stop dragging his feet and endorse the Cuban Democracy Act. He wasn't going to let Bush—even if he'd provided excellent support to CANF in the form of TV Martí and had been a good friend—stop him from getting what he wanted. He wanted Castro out so that he and the diaspora could return to Cuba. Now, 1991, was the time to ensure the revolution's downfall. Mas Canosa and the diaspora absolutely believed that they would celebrate the coming Christmas in Havana—without the Castros.

When Bush didn't act promptly, Mas Canosa betrayed him. He made a deal with Bill Clinton, the Democratic presidential candidate. Badly in need of campaign funds and suffering from the Gennifer Flowers sex scandal, Clinton agreed to a hard line on Cuba. In exchange, Mas Canosa told Cuban Americans that any fears that he might have had about Clinton's attitude toward Fidel Castro "have dissipated." Much to the consternation of Florida Republicans and the Bush family, Clinton endorsed the legislation and told cheering Cuban Americans at a dinner where he raised $125,000 that "I think the Administration has missed a big opportunity to put the hammer down on Fidel Castro and Cuba." This was all political theater, but it forced Bush to endorse the legislation and allowed Clinton to make inroads into the Cuban American vote.

President Bush must have been appalled by Mas Canosa's treason. His son Jeb Bush, who was close to Mas Canosa and the Cuban Americans, hadn't even been informed. Still, Bush acted quickly to staunch the potential hemorrhage of Cuban American support. Deputy Secretary of State Lawrence Eagleburger received from the White House a copy of the Cuban Democracy Act with a note from the president in the margin: "What the hell is going on?"

My office on the third floor of the State Department had a map of the world that covered an entire wall. Somehow Cuba was right in the center of the map, reflecting the belief of many Cubans and Cuban Americans that their island was at the center of the world. At that time, of course, Cuba was the center of *my* world. President Bush had decided to endorse the bill, and Deputy Assistant Secretary Gelbard and I were told to negotiate with Mas Canosa. We eliminated some of the rhetoric and reduced the bill's impact on the president's authority to make foreign policy, but the key provisions that made it illegal for US subsidiaries and companies in foreign countries to sell products to Cuba remained.

The day that Bob informed the House of Representatives Foreign Affairs Committee that the Bush administration supported Torricelli's legislation, a jubilant Mas Canosa stopped me as I exited the hearing. "Vicki, I've got something I want you to see," he exclaimed. Balancing his briefcase on his knee, he pressed open the locks and extracted an editorial cartoon. Uncle Sam, sitting at a table with Mexican president Carlos Salinas de Gortari and Fidel Castro, is passing bags of dollar bills to Salinas, who in turn is passing them under the table to Castro. The blurb over Castro's head said, "I love NAFTA"— the North American Free Trade Agreement. Mas Canosa crowed, "Vicki, if Bob hadn't come up here today and endorsed our bill, every major newspaper in the country would have carried this cartoon." Had CANF escalated its opposition to the trade deal, the Senate might not have ratified NAFTA, which eliminated tariffs among Canada, Mexico, and the United States. Several months later, President Bush signed the Cuban Democracy Act into law.

For the first time, in the 1992 presidential race a Democrat made inroads into the once-monolithic Cuban American support for Republicans. Bush still won Florida, but Clinton won the presidency. His deal with Mas Canosa meant that he was tied to a hardline approach to Cuba, and when he later tried to improve relations, Castro wasn't interested.

There was no Christmas in Havana without the Castros that the Cuban diaspora so much longed for—neither then nor at this writing twenty-six years later.

CHAPTER 2

THE LEGACY OF TERROR FOR CUBANS AND AMERICANS

WEEK AFTER HURRICANE ANDREW STRUCK MIAMI, I BOARDED A small Cessna aircraft at the Kendall-Tamiami Airport about fifteen miles from the center of the city. My pilot José Basulto was the founder and manager of Brothers to the Rescue. Basulto, as most people referred to him, welcomed me with a warm *abrazo* (hug). He was delighted that I—the director of Cuban affairs in Washington, DC—had asked to join his search for Cubans lost at sea because it would validate his mission. His hands flew about his lanky frame as he described the rescue mission. We would fly over the Caribbean, where fleeing Cubans were likely to be found in leaky boats and inner tubes in which they had escaped the island. If we spotted anyone, he would contact the US Coast Guard, which would bring the migrants to safe harbor in Florida. This was August 1992, when no Cuban migrants were ever returned to Cuba; wherever found, they were paroled into the United States. The Cuban Adjustment Act would allow them to become a legal resident alien—a green card holder—after a year and a day.

Basulto spoke Cuban Spanish, swallowing vowels and spitting out words in a rapid staccato. When he detected that I was having trouble keeping up he would switch to halting English. A veteran of the failed CIA-backed exile invasion of the Bay of Pigs, he was passionately anti-Castro. Tall, pugnacious, and absolutely committed to the rescue mission, he was a man of action who was self-confident to a fault. His brown eyes flashing with indignation, he accused Castro of destroying his country by imposing a brutal dictatorship that drove Cubans to attempt to cross the ninety miles of the Caribbean Sea that lie between the Florida Keys and Cuba.

I knew that flying with Brothers to the Rescue was risky. Although they were engaged in a needed and valid humanitarian activity, I couldn't be sure that Basulto wasn't a member of one of the militant exile groups that operated in South Florida. These groups, like Alpha 66 and Comandos L, were tolerated by law enforcement because it was legal to train their members in military tactics. But it was illegal to conduct attacks against Cuba or Cubans, and some of their members had done so in the past and would do so in the future.

I had decided to take a chance and fly with the Brothers because it would be an adventure, and it would give me an opportunity to see firsthand whether they were carrying out a valid rescue mission. The Cuban government would not appreciate my flight with them, however; it would consider such a journey irresponsible because it would highlight our immigration policy, which the Cuban government believed tempted Cubans to leave the island. People of other nationalities who attempted to enter the United States without documents were deported. But in this, as in many things, Cubans were an exception. I knew life was difficult, and partially because of the embargo, but I agreed with the Cuban government that our policy of allowing all Cubans into the States encouraged them to risk their lives in flimsy boats or to pay smugglers to bring them here. But this policy, like the embargo, was what that the Cuban diaspora wanted; and what the diaspora wanted, the Cuban American National Foundation (CANF) often got given its political muscle.

Basulto was typical of exiles who remained focused on their former homeland rather than integrating into American life. I suspected that he, like other exiles who could not let go of their past, would return to Cuba if the Fidel and Raúl Castro ever lost power. He was passionate, even obsessive, about overturning the Castro regime. But rather than forming another militant exile group, he had founded Brothers to the Rescue, a humanitarian organization dedicated to saving lives. It also gave exiles a chance to do good by helping their compatriots rather than practicing commando skills in the Everglades. The Brothers was a popular organization that received in kind and financial donations from the Cuban diaspora. Volunteers manned the phones, looked for homes for newly arrived migrants, and dealt with logistics; all of this was a more productive use of their time and money than buying weapons and ammunition for an assault on their former homeland.

Strapped into my seat in the small gray Cessna, I nodded that I was ready, and we were off. Looking out the window as we headed toward the coastline I could see the destruction left behind when Hurricane Andrew had stormed through South Florida a week earlier. The skies were still gray and windy when our aircraft reached the coastline and headed out to sea. The usually green Caribbean was dark and choppy. It wasn't a good day for Cuban migrants who might be attempting to survive on a flimsy craft. Days like this made the Brothers' work particularly valuable. It was better to be flying above the choppy sea than cruising on it. Basulto had begun his lifesaving mission from his boat, but realized that an aircraft would be quicker, safer, and provide a far better vantage point—especially when, like today, visibility was limited by weather conditions.

The Brothers had saved many lives. The *balseros* (rafters), as they were called, were habitually unprepared to cross the open sea. Too often they risked everything for the chance of starting a new life in the States. They would set off on a large inner tube, or lash planks together to form a makeshift raft, or make, borrow, or steal a boat. If the Brothers spotted them from their aircraft, they would likely survive. If not, their chances of making landfall were slim. The longer the *balseros* were at sea, the more desperate their plight. Few seemed to have had access to weather forecasts. Most were wise enough to avoid setting sail in the winter months when the Atlantic became colder and storms more frequent. They seldom set out with sufficient water, food, or gasoline (if the boat even had a motor); they rarely had life preservers, warm clothes, or protection from the wind and sun. All too frequently their boat would be caught in the North Atlantic Current and pulled away from the Florida coast and farther out to sea. Basulto told me that some migrants reached uninhabited atolls in the Bahamas where, if the Brothers didn't find them, they would slowly die for lack of water and food. Others would be caught in squalls or major storms. The number of dead was unknown; neither Cuba nor the United States recorded those who didn't make it. Migrants left Cuba clandestinely and US immigration recorded only migrants who reached our shores. Over a four-year period, the Brothers rescued forty-two hundred migrants; if one-fourth of that number lost their lives, that would be over a thousand souls, or about 250 annually. In the end, only Cuban and Cuban American families know the full extent of their losses.

The fortunate ones would realize their dream of a new life in the States, and it was mostly a matter of luck. Perhaps their crafts were sounder, or the weather was good, or they were better prepared, but most of all they were lucky. Often family and friends in Florida who knew about the migrants' plans would notify the Brothers and the US Coast Guard that loved ones had fled. With both the Brothers and the Coast Guard searching, they had a better chance of being located, especially if the informants could provide the time and place of their departure.

Our aircraft followed the Florida Keys as they curved southwest toward Cuba. We descended, continuing southward until we were twenty or thirty miles off the Cuban coast, then began making wide clockwise circles. After about two hours flying low over dark and monotonous sea, Basulto shouted, "¡Mira! ¡Mira!" (Look! Look!). In the distance I could barely make out a small dot on the horizon. As our plane drew closer and circled, I saw a bare-chested young man on a raft. He waved jubilantly. Basulto tipped a wing to acknowledge him. It was an emotional moment. We were all excited—even Basulto and his copilot, both of whom had done this hundreds of times before. The man was in the middle of a choppy sea on a flimsy raft, and with no land in sight. Very possibly we would save his life.

Basulto picked up the hand microphone and called the coast guard, providing the rafter's coordinates. Soon the Coast Guard would be steaming toward him. We circled again, waved, and left, knowing that he'd likely be in Florida before nightfall. I was impressed and began straining my eyes to possibly catch a glimpse of another rafter.

Suddenly the receiver squawked. A harsh voice demanded in Spanish that we identify our coordinates and ourselves. An ominous silence descended in the tiny cockpit. Basulto whispered, "It's Cuban Air Control."

"Are we in Cuban airspace?" I asked.

"No, no. But we must be very careful." Basulto then answered the query, "This is *Seagull One*, Hermanos al Rescate [Brothers to the Rescue]," and gave our coordinates. We waited. Then, "Gracia, gracias. Está bien," from the Cuban air controller. The tension lifted, and we could proceed with our search. Basulto said that we were perhaps within a mile or two of Cuban airspace, but not in jeopardy of slipping over the line.

Still, it was clear that Basulto and his copilot were worried, even though we really were in international airspace. Perhaps, intent upon letting the rafter know that help was on the way, we had come closer then we intended. And I suspected that Basulto had not wanted me to know how close we'd come. Yet what remains with me to this day is the palpable fear in the cabin. Clearly, crossing into Cuban airspace—intentionally or not—was dangerous.

Four years later, on February 24, 1996, Cuban MiGs shot down two of three Brothers' aircraft that were flying above international waters. Basulto was flying one of the aircraft with Silvia Iriondo and her husband on board. They had briefly entered Cuban airspace, but quickly departed. I knew Silvia, a sensible and strong woman who certainly wouldn't have been part of any illicit activity. Having turned back, all three aircraft were flying above international waters when a Cuban MiG screeched past Basulto's aircraft. It fired and brought down one of the Brothers' aircraft. Seven minutes later, as Basulto was searching for the downed plane, a second MiG destroyed the other aircraft. Recordings of the tragedy from US air traffic control indicate that the MiG's pilots gave no warning prior to shooting down the unarmed planes. The pilots did ask for and obtained permission from their superiors to destroy the two Brothers' aircraft. Castro later claimed that he had approved the shoot-down.

With two MiGs on his tail, Basulto turned his aircraft north toward home. Flying low and weaving to avoid the MiGs, he and his passengers landed safely. The four men piloting the other two aircraft did not. They died in a senseless act of terror, motivated by animosity between the Cuban government and the Cuban diaspora in the United States. A more humane and prudent plan would have been for Castro to order the MiGs to escort the Brothers' aircraft to Havana; once there, he would have had a major propaganda victory. But for unfathomable reasons, Castro seemingly ordered the planes shot down.

I also found it strange that the Cubans who knew about the Brothers' rescue mission would destroy their aircraft. But things had changed. The US State Department had sent me to Haiti and then to Madagascar. In the interim, thirty thousand Cubans had taken to the sea to escape the dire poverty brought about by the loss of Soviet subsidies, the embargo, and the policies of the Cuban government during the period Castro labeled the Special Period in Time of Peace. Hoping to reduce future undocumented migration from Cuba, President Bill Clinton announced that Cubans found at sea would be returned to Cuba; only those who made it to US soil would be allowed to remain. This new policy, which became known as Wet Foot–Dry Foot, meant that the migrants no longer wanted to be spotted by the Brothers or picked up by the coast guard. To realize their dream of living in Florida, they had to make it to US soil on their own. Unless in dire straits, the *balseros* sought to avoid the Coast Guard because if they were interdicted, they would be returned to Cuba.

The Wet Foot–Dry Foot policy also meant that the Brothers' mission was considerably diminished. No longer was Basulto simply spotting Cubans lost at sea and informing the US Coast Guard. He had on several occasions entered Cuban airspace; not just on the day of the shoot-down, but several times in the past. The Cubans accused him of dropping a smoke bomb, and on two occasions he had dropped leaflets over Havana that contained the words of the UN's Universal Declaration of Human Rights. Predictably, the Cuban government was furious and protested the Brothers' incursions to the US State Department.

I still find it incomprehensible that Castro would be so foolish as to commit an act that could possibly result in a war with the United States. Since the Missile Crisis, he had taken care not to give us any excuse for mounting a military strike or an invasion. He had terminated Cuba's brief flirtation with drug trafficking with a public trial and the execution and incarceration of the accused. Since then, to my knowledge, Cuba has not trafficked in drugs or engaged in other criminal activity that might give the United States an excuse to use force against Cuban territory. The Cuban Border Guards cooperate with the US Coast Guard, passing on information about suspect aircraft and vessels using Cuban airspace and waterways. Castro also began returning some criminals who had fled US justice. I have long suspected that Castro didn't give the order to shoot down the Brothers' planes, but had to take responsibility to show that he was fully in charge. The order might have come from Raúl Castro, who at the time was chief of the armed forces, or the head of the Cuban Air Force.

The consequences of the midair shoot-down were severe for both countries. Secretary of State Madeleine Albright reflected the public's distain for the Cuban MiG pilots. US air controllers had recorded the two MiG pilots praising each other; they mentioned having *cojones* (Spanish slang for "balls"—that is, testicles) when celebrating their victory. Albright announced that "Frankly, this is not *cojones*. This is cowardice," Public outrage—especially among the Cuban diaspora— demanded more than words. Many believed Cuba had to be punished for its reckless and illegal actions. Clinton considered and rejected a military response, instead signing into law the Cuban Liberty and Democratic Solidarity Act, a legislative proposal crafted by Senator Jesse Helms (R-NC) and Representative Dan Burton (R-IN). Clinton did so even though the legislation contained language that dictated how and when an opening with Cuba could take place. It was designed to prevent any president—Clinton included—from engineering an opening with Cuba until both Fidel and Raúl Castro were no longer in power.

CANF and the Cuban diaspora had for some time pushed for the punishing legislation. But until the tragedy, Clinton had successfully refused to consider it because it was so draconian. It removed the president's discretion in conducting US foreign policy toward Cuba, replacing it with a law that codified the embargo and demanded that both Castros must be out of power before the United States could establish normal relations. Still, for some in the diaspora the punishment was insufficient. They regretted that they were prohibited from using arms—theirs or the US government's—to destroy Fidel and Raúl Castro. Others in the diaspora took matters into their own hands.

Cuban paramilitary groups like Acción Cubana, Alpha 66, and Comandos L have, since the revolution, attacked or planned to attack Cuban targets (initially with the backing of the US government—notably, in the Bay of Pigs invasion—and later on their own). In 1975 Rolando Otero—a former troop member in Brigade 2506, which carried out the CIA-organized Bay of Pigs invasion—bombed a police station, banks, and an airport in Miami. In 1976, exiles placed a bomb aboard Cubana

Airlines flight 445 that killed seventy-three people, including the Cuban national fencing team; all the evidence indicated that Cuban exiles Orlando Bosch and Luis Posada Carriles were the perpetrators of the atrocity. Posada even admitted to the crime, but later recanted. Bosch, Posada, and their accomplices were tried in Venezuela; all were found guilty except Bosch, who was acquitted on a technicality. Before Bosch could be retried, he fled to Miami, where he was arrested and jailed. Cuban Americans demanded his release. Seeking to remain within US law and respond to CANF's demands to free Bosch, the State Department sought to find a country that would accept him, but no government wanted anything to do with him. President George H. W. Bush interceded. Bosch was released from jail and granted residency in the United States. Bush's actions were likely taken to enhance his son Jeb's political career in Florida, which was based on his close relationships with prominent Cuban Americans, including CANF leaders and Representative Ileana Ros-Lehtinen (R-FL), who urged Bush to pardon Bosch. Attorney General Richard Thornburgh described Bosch as an "unrepentant terrorist." Some years later Posada slipped into the United States and managed to avoided prosecution for the airline tragedy. Today he is a free man.

Many in the Cuban diaspora considered these terrorist acts legitimate. CANF's Jorge Mas Canosa was accused by his detractors of sponsoring violence against those in Florida who opposed his anti-Castro views as well as supporting attacks against Cuba. But no evidence was presented to validate these claims. Attacks against Cuba continued well into the 1990s, including firing on tourist hotels and tourists (1992, 1993, and 1997), firing at a Greek tanker (1993), killing a Cuba national in Cuba (1994), and an attempted assassination of Fidel Castro (1994–2000) led by Posada. Although the perpetrators were often known within the Cuban diaspora, few were arrested, tried, and convicted.

When I was leading the Office of Cuban Affairs in 1992, I discovered that these paramilitary groups had a writ of immunity that extend to the highest levels of government. I told a reporter from the *Sun Sentinel*, a South Florida newspaper, that if US law enforcement encountered militants about to attack Cuba, we would inform the Cuban government. I was responding to an attack by militant Cuban exiles who had fired machine gun rounds on the Hotel Melia, located at Cuba's Varadero Beach Resort. I hoped that my comments would discourage copycat attacks without getting me into too much trouble with CANF and Mas Canosa. Knowing that it would be unlikely, I had prudently avoided saying they would be arrested and tried for terrorism.

The next day articles appeared in both the *Sun Sentinel* and the *Miami Herald* quoting an unidentified State Department official who denounced the attacks and claimed that they would be punished. CANF was furious. Jeb Bush complained to the White House, which in turn demanded that Bernie Aronson, head of the State Department's Bureau of Western Hemisphere Affairs, punish the offending official. Although the *Miami Herald*—a larger and more important newspaper than the *Sentinel*—appeared to have embellished my remarks, I had no choice but to take responsibility for both articles. The gist of the message reflected in both papers was that the US government did not condone and would seek to prevent terrorist activities directed against Cuba.

The Cuban American community was outraged. They felt betrayed. How could a US official claim that attacking Cuba was illegal when Castro was the United States' enemy? Many in the diaspora considered it unacceptable, even immoral, to inform the Cuban government about terrorist acts because those involved in carrying them out might be killed or jailed. It didn't matter that these acts were contrary to US law and could result in the deaths of innocent people.

CANF wanted the culprit fired. Governor Bush complained to the White House about the callous American official who had dared to confront the militants, if only through the print media. Aronson demanded to know if I was the guilty party. I told him I was. His assistant,

Bill Brownfield, called to warn me that the White House wanted me fired, and he advised me to keep out of sight for the next couple of weeks. I knew there wasn't much Bernie could do to save me. Bernie was entirely focused on resolving the civil war raging in Central America, and he left Cuba issues to his principal assistant, Bob Gelbard, and me. Now I was in trouble, and Bob happened to be out of town.

At home that evening, I imagined that I had lost my job. I didn't even think about appealing to my Cuban American friends. Yet Tony Navarro, with whom I had worked to put TV Martí on the air, reached out. When he asked if I were the guilty party, I explained that I had given the *Sentinel* interview and assumed that the *Herald* had used it for its own article. Much to my surprise and delight, he told me not to worry. He would tell Mas Canosa that it was I—not some unknown State Department official—who had made the remark. Since Mas Canosa considered me a friend, he would stop the calls for my dismissal. With Mas Canosa on my side, the story faded from view in the Florida media. I was lucky: Tony and Mas Canosa stuck by me. But the militants now knew that they could act against Cuba with impunity.

It took me several weeks to solve the mystery of the article in the *Miami Herald*. Mimi Whitfield, a *Herald* reporter, told me that my boss, Bob Gelbard, was responsible for the *Herald* interview. Bob was one of the State Department stars, clearly destined for leadership roles. He was also extremely outspoken and throughout his career would find himself in trouble over being too candid. Given Bob's larger-than-life personality and the way he stood by his positions, I wonder what would have happened had he been there when the White House threatened to fire the guilty party. Some years later, when he was the American ambassador to Indonesia, Bob criticized the Indonesian government for failing to provide adequate security for the American embassy when Al-Qaida threatened to blow it up. Paul Wolfowitz, then the deputy secretary of defense, objected, and Bob was fired. But when the stories broke in the *Miami Herald*, Bob was already in Latin America. He had stopped briefly in Miami for the interview and continued on his way. Since these were the days before cell phones, he didn't learn about the furor until he returned a week later.

I've often wondered what Bob would have done. Would he have forced the issue and convinced our government to take a stand against attacks on Cuba? Had he been in town, we might both have stood up to the criticism. But he was not, and I simply followed Bill's advice to disappear into the corridors of the State Department. But this was the essence of the issue. No one, from presidents to bureaucrats, was willing to challenge the power and authority of CANF. And the terrorist acts by militant exiles continued.

In 1997 Luis Posada Carriles, the alleged co-conspirator with Bosch in the downing of the Cubana Airlines jet, carried out a bombing of a Havana hotel that killed an Italian tourist. In 2000 a Panamanian court found he and his accomplices guilty of attempting to kill Castro while he was attending the Ibero-American Summit in Panama. But the Cuban diaspora managed to convince the president of Panama, Mireya Moscoso, to pardon the perpetrators just before she left office. Although Posada told Ann Louise Bardach, who was writing a story for the *New York Times*, that he was the perpetrator behind the Cubana Airlines downing and the bombing that killed the Italian tourist in Havana, his lawyers successfully argued in a Texas court that he should not be tried for any crime other than illegal entry. Although the US Justice Department described him as "an admitted mastermind of terrorist plots and attacks," today Posada remains a free man living in Miami.

PART II

1999-2000: US INTERESTS SECTION, HAVANA; PRESIDENT BILL CLINTON

CHAPTER 3

OUR WOMAN IN HAVANA

I T WAS SEPTEMBER 1999, AT THE US INTERESTS SECTION, HAVANA,
Cuba. Standing on the fifth-floor balcony of the steel and glass
building that shines like iridescent obsidian, I wondered how a girl
from Hungry Horse, Montana, could have been so fortunate. President
Bill Clinton had sent me to Havana to lead our diplomatic mission, the
US Interests Section, which had once been the called the US embassy.
From the balcony I had a panoramic view of the Malecón, the city's es-
planade and seawall; the elegant Hotel Nacional, built on a bluff over-
looking the green waters of the Caribbean; and, further on, the white
columns of the USS *Maine* Monument, dedicated to sailors who died
when their ship blew up in Havana Bay in 1898. In the distance I could
see the great old fort, the Castillo de los Tres Reyes del Morro, that
once guarded Havana Bay and the gathering of Spanish galleons bursting with Inca and Aztec plunder.

After working on US-Cuba relations from 1989 to 1993, I had become ensnared by the two countries' dysfunctional relationship and developed a deep and abiding interest in the issue. But I couldn't continue in
the same job. At the State Department four years was a long time to work
on the same country, so for the good of my career it was time to move
on. I served in Haiti, then Madagascar, and then returned to Washington,
DC, as a senior policy maker for Africa. But I kept dreaming and watching
for an opportunity that would bring me back to Cuba, an island nation
lost in time but so close to our southern shore and our national psyche.

During the next three years of my assignment, I would have an opportunity to see what I could do to heal the wounds left by Fidel Castro's failing revolution and our destructive policy, which together managed to deprive the island and its people of their future. I loved the magic of Havana, the spirit of its people. I hoped that I might begin to untangle the contradiction, lies, and myths that from the beginning had been too present in our unhappy relations.

The contradiction that haunts our relationship with Cuba is that the United States has always coveted the island. And perhaps this foundational contradiction is what makes the US-Cuba relationship so fractious. In 1805, President Thomas Jefferson considered annexation, while Secretary of State John Adams believed that, like "a ripe fruit," Cuba would fall to the United States when severed from Spain. The Monroe Doctrine was very much directed at keeping European nations out of Latin America, and especially the Caribbean region, which we have long considered our backyard. If even a friendly foreign power gained influence in the region, it would be at our political and economic expense. Cuba, the biggest island in the Caribbean, only ninety miles from Key West and thus our closest neighbor after Canada and Mexico, was the greatest prize. In all likelihood, Cuba would have become a US state or territory had Henry Teller, a senator from Colorado, not persuaded his colleagues to vote for an amendment to the War Powers Act that prohibited annexation while authorizing the conflict with Spain on the eve of the twentieth century.

One of the first lies or myths (whichever you prefer) was the sinking of an American warship, the USS *Maine*, in Havana Bay. The United States, inflamed by the yellow press and a new sense of nationalism, blamed Spain. The rallying cry "Remember the Maine, to Hell with Spain," convinced Americans that Spain blew up the ship, but it was a malfunction in its boilers that actually sank it. Spain lost its "Ever-Faithful Isle," as well as Guam, the Philippines, and Puerto Rico in the Spanish-American War of 1898, which began in Cuba. Lieutenant Colonel

Teddy Roosevelt and Colonel Leonard Wood, who led the Rough Riders' victorious charge up San Juan Hill, strongly advocated for the war that belatedly made the United States a colonial power. In turn, Cuba gave Roosevelt fame and the opportunity to claim the vice presidential spot in the 1900 election. A year later William McKinley was assassinated and Roosevelt became president of the United States. Both Roosevelt and Wood continued to play outsize roles in Cuba's history. Together they initiated a process that pushed the United States into becoming the predominant political and economic power in Cuba. Roosevelt insisted that Cuba cede the lower half of Guantanamo Bay and allow the United States to control its foreign policy. His superior officer during the battle outside Santiago de Cuba, Leonard Wood, became a general officer and our first military governor of Cuba.

The influence of the United States in Cuba was overwhelming, first through our occupation and then through vast amounts of American investment. Over time Havana and, to a lesser degree, the whole island became a playground for Americans. Havana's casinos and nightclubs were run by the American Mafia and Fulgencio Batista, Cuba's corrupt dictator. Income inequality, corruption, and state-sponsored violence resulted in young, idealist Cubans confronting Batista in Havana. Castro was better organized and better funded than the urban opposition, which supported him as his military campaign in Cuba's eastern provinces gained momentum. But few suspected that Castro would ally Cuba with the Soviet Union and transform the island into a communist nation, the first in the Western Hemisphere.

Cuba, while geographically close, became shrouded in mystery. The first crack in the island nation's isolation didn't occur until fifteen years after the Cuban Missile Crisis. In 1977, President Jimmy Carter and Fidel Castro reestablished relations under another name. A bilateral agreement set up the US and Cuban Interests Sections, rather than embassies, in one another's capitals, which were overseen by "principal officers" rather than ambassadors. By the terms of the agreement,

American and Cuban diplomats worked in their former embassies, but were prohibited from flying the flag of their respective countries on the other's soil. There was a good reason for this sleight of hand: Cuban Americans vehemently objected to diplomatic relations with Cuba. Had an American flag been raised outside the former embassy building, it would have appeared as if the United States had reestablished its embassy and normal diplomatic relations.

Most Americans and even the media believed that we didn't have formal relations until December 17, 2014, when President Barack Obama announced that the United States had reestablished diplomatic relations with Cuba. Without the Stars and Stripes flying, Americans—even those who watched on television as Fidel Castro led massive marches past the Interests Section in 2000, demanding the return to his nation of a Cuban child—didn't think we had relations. This impression was further enhanced by the fact that the Swiss government was our official diplomatic representative in Cuba. Most Americans—even those who visited Havana—had the impression that if American diplomats were in Cuba, they were working from a back office within the small Swiss embassy located on the Avenida de las Americas. In fact, the tiny Swiss embassy did little more than provide us with stationery that proclaimed, "Embassy of Switzerland" at the top and, below, "The US Interests Section." This added an extra layer of illusion to the myth that the United States didn't have a presence on the island when, in fact, ours was the largest diplomatic mission in Cuba.

The Interests Section in Havana is unique. It is a hybrid of the American Institute in Taiwan and our consular missions in Hong Kong and Jerusalem. The American Institute is a de facto embassy representing US interests in Taiwan through a private corporation run by US diplomats. But unlike the Interests Section it does not have diplomatic status. Our Interests Section in Havana is also similar to our consulates in Hong Kong and Jerusalem, which represent the United States at a lower level than an embassy would. But Cuba is neither a large urban area like Hong Kong nor a disputed city like Jerusalem. Rather, it is a country that is recognized by every other nation in the world. The contradiction was maintained simply to appease the Cuban American community, which had the political clout to force the US government to pretend that the United States and Cuba didn't have diplomatic relations.

When I arrived in Havana in September 1999 to lead the Interests Section, Clinton was making his second attempt to improve relations with the island. But his efforts were only the latest in a series of secret and not-so-secret talks with Castro on the part of Democrats and Republicans alike. These behind-the-scenes negotiations were sometimes wrecked by divergent views, and other times by fear of political retribution by the Cuban American National Foundation (CANF) or by Castro himself. Secretary of State Henry Kissinger had hoped to open up to Cuba as he had China, but the initiative stalled. President Richard Nixon never trusted Castro, and his successor Gerald Ford was considerably less interested in Kissinger's project.

Clinton's second attempt to open up relations began with an exchange of information on possible terrorist attacks in the United States and in Cuba. (His first attempt had crashed with the downing of two civilian aircraft by Castro in 1996.) The Colombian author Gabriel García Márquez was sent by Castro to serve as a liaison, and his mission resulted in a visit by the FBI to their counterparts in Havana. Cuban officials hoped that the information they provided would be used to stop exiles from carrying out attacks on the island. To their dismay, soon after the exchange the FBI arrested five Cuban agents who had been working in the United States to expose and infiltrate exile organizations such as the militant groups Alpha 66 and Comandos L as well as Brothers to the Rescue and CANF. The Cuban Five, as they came to be known—either spies or heroes, depending on your point of view—were convicted in a Florida court and received long jail sentences for espionage. This brought about an impasse between the US and Cuba that continued over the next fifteen years, ending only with the Barack Obama–Raúl Castro opening when the Cuban spies were exchanged for an American spy and a USAID contractor, Alan Gross, who had been jailed for providing communications equipment to members of Cuba's Jewish community.

The Interests Section's size and location on Havana's seafront made it stand out from other embassies and reflected the fact that it had been the American embassy until President Dwight D. Eisenhower broke diplomatic relations in 1961. One of New York's premier architectural firms, Harrison and Abramovitz, had designed it shortly before the Cuban Revolution. The building looks like a smaller version of the United Nations headquarters in New York City, also designed by Harrison and Abramovitz. Only Russia's embassy—an ugly, gray brutalist concrete tower in the Miramar suburb of Havana that was constructed in the 1970s—rivaled our building for prominence, though not for beauty.

I was the first woman to lead the Interests Section. Fidel referred to me as the *jefa* (chief). My official title was principal officer, but Americans and Cubans alike called me Ambassador Huddleston because I had previously held that title in Madagascar. The Cubans liked the idea, and began calling Fernando Remírez de Estenoz Barciela, the chief of the Cuban Interests Section in Washington, DC, Ambassador Remírez. It gave the illusion of relations at a higher level. My staff consisted of about fifty Americans representing several US agencies and about two hundred Cubans. But officially—yet another contradiction—we had no Cuban employees. Like all other foreign entities in Cuba, we did not directly employ our Cuban staff; a Cuban government corporation provided us with local personnel. But we treated them the same as our local staff in embassies around the world; we paid them fair salaries based on their responsibilities and helped fund pensions to which they were entitled when they retired. This confused status of our local employees meant they had two masters: the Cuban state employment agency and the US Interests Section. Moreover, in a few cases our local staff had three masters; some were spies, employed by the Cuban Ministry of the Interior, which is responsible for the internal security of the Cuban state. To protect our secrets, Cuban employees could only access the first two floors of the Interests Section. All of our local employees were forced to report on our activities to the Cuban government if they wished to keep their jobs. If a Cuban employee failed to report on our activities, he or she would be fired and we would find out when that employee didn't show up for work. On several occasions I protested to the Ministry of Foreign Affairs, but the employees were never reinstated. The best I could do was to extract a promise that the person in question might be sent to work in another diplomatic mission.

Our American staff was much like that at any embassy: foreign service officers worked in the political, economic, administrative, and public diplomacy sections. An Immigration and Naturalization Service annex a few blocks away operated out of a smaller building on the Malecón, the seafront. Its sole purpose was to provide refugee visas to qualified Cuban applicants. Our consular staff of Americans and Cubans issued thousands of visas to Cuban visitors and migrants to the States. By the terms of the 1994 migration agreement, we issued twenty thousand immigrant visas annually. Still, this did not stop the exodus of undocumented Cubans.

The consular section, which took up most of the ground floor, also provided citizen services to Americans visiting Cuba, both legally and illegally. Initially those who were illegal were reported to the US Treasury's Office of Foreign Assets Control (OFAC), which enforced the embargo. I changed this policy because it prevented Americans in need of medical, financial, or other help from coming into the consular section. The new guidelines were simple: consular officers wouldn't ask the status of American visitors, and by not knowing would not be obliged to report to OFAC. It worked well during my time in Cuba, but I assume my "don't ask, don't tell" rule was reversed as relations deteriorated after I left Cuba in September 2002.

Additionally the Interests Section cooperated with the Cuban government on environmental research to ensure the health of Cuba's coral reefs, which are the principal fish hatcheries for the North Atlantic. We also exchanged information to thwart narcotics trafficking. The Cuban Border Guard informed the US Coast Guard when traffickers used Cuban airspace or waterways. The Coast Guard officer on my staff had excellent relations with his counterparts at the Cuban Border Guard. Occasionally, Cuba returned to US authorities criminals wanted by the FBI.

I expected the Cuban government would be pleased that I was the new American representative. This was the first time that a woman and a former ambassador had been sent to Havana as our chief diplomat. I knew that Castro preferred to deal with women, and a bonus was that I had a title that conferred a higher status on the job. Therefore, I anticipated that I would be able to build a relationship that could lead to improved relations. It turned out that this was not the way the Cuban hierarchy viewed me. In fact, they were wary because a former head of the Cuban Interests Section who didn't like me—or in my opinion, any woman in an official position—told the Cubans that I was a hard-liner. Still, I wasn't overly concerned. I planned to build a relationship of trust with Ricardo Alarcón, Castro's principal adviser on the United States, whom I knew from my years managing Cuban affairs at the State Department.

One of my principal jobs was to meet with Cuba's human rights activists, an activity that the Cuban government particularity disliked. Concerned about our relations with the dissidents, Castro and the hierarchy monitored these meetings closely. I often wondered why he was so obsessed with the dissident community, given that they had little power or influence within the country. Perhaps he just didn't like the fact that there were Cubans who were willing to contradict his vision of how the country should be ruled.

I came to know the dissidents very well. There were many small groups that regularly attempted to form a united coalition, but the most conservative dissidents invariably refused to join. The best-known conservatives were the Group of Four (the regime called them the Gang of Four), which comprised Felix Bonne, Rene Gomez Manzano, Vladimiro Roca Antúnez (son of Blas Roca Calderio, a founder of the Cuban Communist Party); and Marta Beatriz Roque. In the 1970s and 1980s, they had held important positions in universities and the military, but their views led to confrontations with the political commissars and dismissal from their positions. They were jailed for publishing a pamphlet, *La Patria es de Todos* (The Homeland is for All), which urged Cubans to boycott elections and asked foreign investors to avoid Cuba.

Roque, who was the leader of this group, was as tough as Fidel. Her reputation as one of the country's leading activists was well earned; she never stopped confronting the government, despite persistent illness that occasionally forced her into the hospital. When I worried about her outspoken comments, she brushed off my concern: "They will jail me no matter what I do or say." Bonne was my favorite dissident. One of the few major dissidents of African descent, he had been a brilliant electrical engineer until the regime forced him out of his university job. The most militant of the Group of Four were Roca, a Social Democrat, and Gomez Manzano, a lawyer who represented dissidents and then joined them in opposition to the government. In their view, there could be no compromise with the Castro regime. Roca, who had been an elite MiG pilot in the Cuban armed forces before becoming a dissident, was deeply mistrusted by the Cuban hierarchy. In their eyes, he was not only a dissident but a traitor because he had initially fought for the revolution but then dared to defy it.

The best known of the liberal group of dissidents were Oswaldo Payá and Elizardo Sánchez. Sánchez was well known for his human rights monitoring group and Payá would become famous for his Project Varela—named for a Spanish priest and advocating for Cuban independence—which was designed to modify the Cuban Constitution rather than completely reject it. Project Varela was successful in garnering worldwide attention, but it did not—nor did any other dissident activity—pose even the slightest threat to Castro's rule.

The Group of Four and the liberals from Project Varela faced overwhelming odds. None of them had the charisma of Fidel Castro. They did have forceful personalities, but they lacked followers. The overall lack of communication and transportation made it difficult to spread their beliefs around the country and rivalries further eroded their potential influence. Cuba's network of neighborhood block committees, Committees for the Defense of the Revolution, monitored and reported on their activities. More injurious still was the fact that the omnipresent state security had infiltrated the entire dissident community. No one could be sure if one of their own was a double agent.

A few weeks into my tenure I thought I was making progress when we received an invitation to attend the "old-timers" baseball game between the Cuban and Venezuelan teams. Generally the Cubans did not include the Interests Section when they extended invitations to the diplomatic corps, nor did the State Department invite Cuban diplomats to their functions. Sometimes I was pleased not to be included because I was spared from attending Fidel's interminable speeches on July 26, the anniversary of his attack on Moncada Barracks. But I was pleased to have received this unexpected invitation. I hoped—definitely more optimistically than realistically—that perhaps this was a small gesture reciprocating my friendly round of introductory calls on Cuban officials.

Castro was coaching the Cuban old-timers, while Venezuelan president Hugo Chávez was pitching for his national team. We entered the stadium just as iron bars were descending across the entry, blocking thousands still waiting to get in. Every Cuban loves baseball; the players are excellent, and often pursued by US major league teams, which pay them salaries that are unimaginable in Cuba. Those who defect either hire a human smuggler, attempt to cross the Florida Straits in a small craft with friends or family, or quietly defect when their team is playing in another country.

With our invitation in hand we approached the section reserved for diplomats. A cross-looking official examined it, then asked what country we represented.

"Estados Unidos" (the United States), I told him.

Without any hesitation, he exclaimed, "No hay espacio."

"If there is no space here, then where should we go?" I asked. He simply shrugged and walked away. Maneuvering among the excited crowd, we were about to sit on a bench in the right-field section when a rather haughty man announced "No, *señores*, this is not the place for you." I was beginning to wonder if there was *any* place for us when we spotted the international media staked out on top of the Venezuelan dugout. We squeezed in, and they didn't mind sharing space with some cast-off diplomats.

From the roof of the dugout, we had a good view of Chávez, whose paunchy frame didn't prevent him from getting the ball over the plate with enough zip to strike out Castro's old-timers. We could see Fidel sitting in the Cuban dugout, chatting happily, possibly remembering the days before the revolution, when he had a fastball good enough to get him a tryout with the old Washington Senators. By the fifth inning, Fidel's old-timers trailed the Venezuelans, until some even older old-timers, with long gray beards, began getting hits that put players on base. It turned out that these recent additions were younger players from Cuba's national team who had donned false beards. Castro wasn't going to lose to his protégé, Chávez, even if the game was just for fun.

We might have escaped notice had I not run into Chávez's wife, Nancy Colmenares, an attractive peroxide blonde, who was approaching the dugout as I was leaving. We literally ended up toe-to-toe. I excused myself, beyond which there seemed to be no appropriate comment. But the incident did not escape the eyes of the ever-sensitive

Cubans. The following day, the official newspaper, *Granma*, reported that the Cuban old-timers had won—no surprise there. Inside, however, was another article that lamented the poor security practices of the Venezuelans. This was directed at my little encounter with Colmenares. The Cubans did not like the idea that their number one enemy had somehow managed to gain entry to this friendly game. And rather than behaving, I had the nerve to call attention to myself by supposedly sidling up to and greeting the wife of their honored guest.

I told myself that this was a minor incident; surely, we would make up. Yet the auguries were not good—my first several weeks in Havana seemed to indicate that Castro was not reciprocating Clinton's attempts to improve relations. Certainly I wasn't going to become a trusted go-between.

CHAPTER 4

A PROVOCATION

UCH TO MY DISMAY, I REALIZED THE CUBANS WERE CONVINCED that I had been sent to Havana to lead the Cuban human rights activists—or dissidents, as I referred to them. I had gotten to know some of the older dissidents when I had been director of Cuban affairs at the State Department. But what poisoned my relations with the Cuban hierarchy was a meeting that Charles Shapiro, the newly appointed officer responsible for Cuba policy in Washington, DC, had with dissidents at the American residence prior to my arrival. The Cubans had either monitored the meeting with listening devices or had received reports from a dissident who was in their service. In any case, the meeting between Charles and the dissidents convinced the Cubans that I would encourage and possibly help them to disrupt the upcoming Ibero-American Summit.

Fidel Castro was delighted that for the first time Cuba had been given the honor of hosting the summit, and he wanted everything to go smoothly. Not only would his peers be present, but also Spain's King Juan Carlos and Queen Sofía. This would be the first time that a Spanish king had set foot in Cuba; it was a momentous occasion, and Castro wasn't going to let the dissidents or I spoil it. It was unfortunate that he didn't know that I had absolutely no intention of advising the dissidents or helping them protest the summit. It would have avoided a lot of ill will.

The week before the Ibero-American Summit, which would be held on November 16, 1999, I was focused on the visit of Illinois governor George Ryan. I was concerned that Ryan, in an effort to please his hosts, might avoid the Interests Section. In most countries, American diplomats greet high-level American visitors at the airport and accompany them to the embassy, where they are briefed about local conditions. This was not always the case in Cuba where, to please their hosts, American officials sometimes avoided meeting with us. This meant that they were only exposed to Castro's version of Cuba; it also made us diplomats feel as if we were being scorned. Intent on keeping members of the US Congress from meeting with us, state security would switch air terminals at the last minute, so we would be unable to locate our visitors.

I didn't like being treated as a pariah. Since Governor Ryan's visit was important, I called him and we agreed that I would host meetings for him with foreign ambassadors and Cuban dissidents. He would come alone, leaving behind his delegation and his Cuban "minder." (All VIPs are assigned a minder whose job is to take care of their every need.) Ryan's minder would serve as a guide, friend, and confidant, later reporting back to the Ministry of the Interior. As planned, on the second day of Ryan's visit, a black Mercedes provided by his Cuban hosts dropped him off at my residence in time for breakfast with the British, French, Italian, Spanish, and Turkish ambassadors. I immediately liked him. He fit my vision of a typical Chicago politician: big, with a booming voice, gregarious and charismatic.

I welcomed him to the lovely mansion built as the residence for our ambassadors and now for the chiefs of our Interests Section. I told him that the residence had been constructed in 1942 with the idea that President Franklin Roosevelt would visit. But World War II had intervened, and Roosevelt missed staying in the Rose Room that looked out over the formal gardens and the magnificent bronze eagle that had once adorned the two columns of the monument to the sailors who went down with the USS *Maine*, its wings outspread. This sculpted eagle had taken flight many years ago in one of the frequent hurricanes that hit Havana. Prominent Cuban business leaders had repaired it and given it to the American ambassador as a token of Cuban and American friendship. A new eagle was placed atop the seafront monument, but it didn't nest there for long; Fidel's rebels tore it down shortly after the revolution.

Located behind our great bronze eagle were lovely mansions that once belonged to Havana's elite. Gabriel García Márquez, the author who figured as Castro's liaison with Clinton, lived nearby in a house given to him by Fidel. But no one lived in three large houses that faced 146th Street; they had other uses. One was used as a set for a local soap opera broadcast on Cuban television. The other two were strategically located with video and listening devices pointed at my residence; the windows in the back of these houses looked directly into the garden, where the eagle stood watch.

I introduced Ryan to the ambassadors, who would not have mentioned the listening devices pointed at our breakfast party from the neighboring houses if they had noticed them. It was simply impossible to evade Cuban surveillance. None of them had any illusions, as they knew that every word they said would be recorded and possibly videotaped. The British ambassador relished telling a story about how a basket of potatoes magically appeared at his door. He was hosting a high-ranking British official and his cook wanted potatoes for this special dinner. But none were to be had on the local market. Frustrated, the ambassador decided to send a message to his Cuban watchers. He walked into his garden and announced that he needed potatoes. His watchers—or their listening devices—heard him and the next morning a basket of spuds was on his doorstep.

As a VIP visitor Ryan could expect that his limousine, hotel room, and wherever he dined would also hold the omnipresent listening devices. Diplomats and businessmen knew that if they misbehaved, Cuban security would know. An illicit affair could be used by security to ensure that the diplomat reported favorably on Cuba or that a businessman arranged a favorable contract.

Ryan was delighted to be in the company of ambassadors and impressed that they were willing to talk frankly with him. Over a typical American breakfast, they gave him their candid views on US policy (unfavorable) and on the Castro government (also unfavorable). As the discussion ended, Ryan summarized his understanding by commenting to the group, "You might say the trouble with Cuba is Castro." We laughed, ruefully, aware that it was true but that no one would dare say so publicly.

Next I introduced Ryan to Cuba's leading human rights activists. They were waiting for him in the spacious dining room on the ground floor, where two palm trees in large planters framed the curved French doors that looked out on the tennis court and swimming pool. This room, too, was under audio surveillance—both human and nonhuman. Our security officer warned me that he did not bother to look for the video and audio devices because if he found them, they would soon be replaced. The dissidents knew this. They also knew that my Cuban staff would report on who attended; they had no choice if they wished to keep their jobs. I waited until the coffee and cakes had been served and the Cuban staff left the room before beginning the discussion.

Each dissident told his story. Some had spent years in prison, suffering physical abuse at the hands of the Cuban government or its sympathizers. Gustavo Arcos Bergnes, one of Cuba's first and most eminent dissidents, told the governor that in the early years he had been one of Castro's militants who had attacked the Moncada Barracks. But after the revolution succeeded, he and Fidel had had a falling-out. Arcos was imprisoned, served his term, and then became a prominent dissident. Elizardo Sánchez, a former professor, explained to Governor Ryan that he kept in contact with several hundred political prisoners and dissidents. Two independent journalists, who had recently formed their own group of dissidents, told him that if they were well known abroad, they would be less likely to be jailed. Cuban security was more hesitant to scorn, abuse, or jail a well-known dissident, whose story would be reported by the international media. Sánchez spoke for everyone present when he told Ryan that even though his life was difficult, he would remain and fight for his beliefs. He lamented that the entire island was like a company that belonged to Castro, though he didn't dare utter Fidel's name. Instead, he made a motion with his hand to show he was stroking an imaginary beard. Ryan was shocked. He seemed touched, and thanked the group profusely.

Ryan was upset. He strode out the front door, across the driveway, and out the entrance gate to where a gaggle of reporters was waiting. There along the narrow partially paved road across from one of Castro's principal residences he held an impromptu press conference.

Ryan did not mention what he had told the journalist, so when I reached my office the next morning, my staff was waiting to show me an article in the *Diario de las Americas*, Miami's oldest Spanish-language newspaper. It proclaimed that Ryan had concluded, "The trouble with Cuba is Castro!" No one ever criticized Castro, and certainly not an important guest like Ryan. Fidel was furious, and canceled Ryan's invitation to dine with him. Ryan and his delegation were devastated; the late-night dinner with Castro was to have been the high point of their visit.

Neither Ryan nor his delegation wanted to give up their dinner with Fidel. What would they tell friends and family when they returned home? The major event for every VIP visitor was a meeting with the legendary Castro. The next day the *Diario* published a correction: Ryan hadn't said uttered the sentence of his own volition but had simply repeated what the dissidents he met at the residence had told him.

This was an unforgivable disservice to the dissidents. I was appalled, and feared that they would be rounded up and jailed for criticizing Castro to such a special visitor. Those had been Ryan's words, not the dissidents'; none of them had criticized Castro or even spoken his name. I didn't know whether Ryan, a member of his delegation, or even a Cuban official had changed the story. In the hope that Ryan would exonerate the dissidents, I sought him out at his hotel, the Golden Tulip.

When I arrived, Cuban security was waiting for me. Usually the door to the room where Cubans monitor their guests' conversations is tightly shut. But the room next to Ryan's suite was open to make sure that I could see that security officials were going to listen to our every word. Given the omnipresent listeners, I wasn't about to talk to the governor in his room. As we headed out, Ryan's minder, who accompanied him to his meetings, caught up with us as we entered the elevator. Thinking we were headed outside the hotel, he got out on the main floor. I pushed the up button, giving us just enough time to find a strategic location on the terrace where we could see the minder but he could not overhear us.

I told Ryan that what he already knew, that he—not the dissidents—had said "the trouble with Cuba is Castro." But he wasn't about to change his story. The new version—possibly made up by the Cubans themselves—blaming the dissidents had mollified Castro, who had reissued his dinner invitation. The governor's visit and Fidel's prestige had been rescued by the timely, if false, retraction. I consoled myself with the thought that Castro surely knew that it was Ryan who had unthinkingly blurted out the truth. It was all part of the media show. Ryan had messed up his role, but his visit was now back on track.

I drove home thinking that there would be no more difficulties with Ryan's visit. But I was wrong. I was awakened at about two o'clock the next morning. It was one of Castro's aides, calling to tell me that Governor Ryan would like to have visas issued for a child who had suffered a serious head injury when he fell from a second-story window. During dinner at the Palacio de la Revolución Castro had agreed to allow the boy and his parents to accompany the governor to Chicago for urgent medical care. Neither Ryan nor his aides had told my staff or me about the injured child or their plan to bring him to Chicago. Annoyed, I replied that the parents should apply for a visa at the consular section in the morning.

By late morning neither the Cuban government nor the child's parents had applied for visas. Fearing that the family might be denied entry or be forced to remain at the Chicago airport, US consul general Patty Murphy suggested that we find them and issue the visas. The couple was sitting forlornly on a bench at the airport in Havana with their child in their arms. We were both saddened, but Patty was relieved that now they wouldn't encounter difficulties with US Customs. I was furious. Ryan had simply ignored the rules, apparently assuming that US immigration authorities wouldn't give him any difficulty, even though he intended to bring with him three undocumented Cubans.

I remained at the airport, determined to tell Ryan that he had acted unwisely. I waited impatiently until a black limousine pulled up in front of the VIP waiting rooms. I marched over to the VIP room and was about to knock on the door when one of the security guards stopped me. "No es permitido," he said. I ignored his "It's not permitted" and banged on the door, which swung open away from me and into the room. Unbalanced, I fell forward into the arms of Ricardo Alarcón, the man I had hoped would be my advocate with the Cuban government. He was speechless. Foreign Minister Felipe Pérez Roque was white-faced with anger. Neither realized that I had tried to knock. Both assumed that I egregiously barged into a meeting of senior Cuban officials. There was a long silence. I disengaged myself, apologized, and made a hasty exit. Alarcón, who later got his voice back, condemned my *falta de respeto*; the next edition of *Granma* also rebuked me for my "lack of respect."

I got in my car and headed back to the US Interests Section. I had been in Cuba for all of two months and everything seemed to be falling apart. Cuba's highest officials thought that I was in the country to encourage the dissidents to wreck the Ibero-American Summit. If that wasn't bad enough, now they would blame me for wrecking Governor Ryan's visit. Worse of all, they would in the future refuse to deal with me because I had been—so they believed—very rude.

That evening I learned that the situation was even more dreadful than I had imagined. Apparently I had supposedly insulted Castro as well. For well over two hours, Castro warned his radio and TV audience to beware of the dangerous woman in their midst. Staring at my television, I could hardly believe that Fidel was accusing me, an American diplomat, of being a threat to the tightly controlled Cuban state. Sure, I had made a mistake, but most of the fault was on the Cuban side; they had used Ryan shamelessly. And now they were blowing the incident at the airport out of all proportion. It was unfair and unprecedented. And if they thought I was going to be intimidated, they would soon find out they were wrong.

Holding up a red folder, Castro snorted, "that woman—Oodolstone—la jefa [chief] of the SINA, is a problem." He couldn't get the *H* quite right and tried again, slowly pronouncing each letter: "H-U-D-D-L-E-S-T-O-N." Then he triumphantly proclaimed "Hoodlestone" and announced that I, the new chief of the US Interests Section, was "putting on a show to undermine the revolution." Rather than referring to the US Interests Section by its correct title, Castro called our mission the Sección de Intereses Norte Americano (North American Interests Section) so that he could make a play on the Spanish initials, SINA, which almost rhymed with CIA in Spanish. With that clever twist, it sounded as if the Interests Section was itself the CIA. This clever name change allowed Castro to create the impression that I was in charge of—as he would often say—"a nest of spies."

I had to admire his strategy and performance. Castro paced about the stage, talking about my misdeeds and those of my country, beginning with the embargo, the Cuban Adjustment Act, and our occupation of Guantanamo. Then he retreated to a small desk where he flipped through a dossier recounting my actions—which one would have thought were directed at him, since he seemed personally offended. Uncle Sam, he said, had sent him a "troublemaker." He wagged his finger, and then laid out the case against me. Holding high in the air the red folder that held the supposed incriminating evidence, he charged that I was instilling bad ideas in the minds of human rights activists. I had arranged for them to meet publicly with Ryan and had encouraged them to disrupt the upcoming summit. It seemed that an even greater sin than my barging into a meeting of Cuban officials was the fear that I was organizing a demonstration that would take place during the summit. This apparently had incited Castro's very personal and spiteful public condemnation of me.

Castro warned Cubans to avoid me, telling them that he kept track of every visitor to my residence. Cubans who visited might miss the cameras strategically placed along the wall that protected one of Fidel's principal residences, but they would certainly see the Cuban military guards taking notes from a guard house adjacent to my front gate. And most Cubans would not be visiting, anyway, because they were already barred from the beautiful Cubanacan neighborhood where diplomats and foreign businessmen lived and where Cuba hosted important visitors in government "protocol houses." Only Cuban diplomats, dissidents, and artists visited my residence. The diplomats were there on business, the dissidents were already outcasts and had nothing to lose, and Cuban artists were allowed to visit, most likely because they were trusted by the government. Castro's ploy was to emphasize that official Americans—not just me but my staff—should be avoided. I did wonder what Castro had in mind by spelling out my name, until some months later when I signed a hotel register, the clerk turned pale and quickly picked up the telephone—undoubtedly to report the presence of "that woman, Hoodlestone."

I found Fidel's overreaction troublesome and disappointing, especially as it was directed solely at a few members of my staff and me.

Fidel had thought that Ryan's visit would be a great coup for Cuba. The first US governor to visit since the revolution, a Republican from an important state who could persuade his peers to weaken the embargo and normalize trade with Cuba. Instead Ryan had stumbled, telling the media that "the trouble with Cuba is Castro." But rather than blaming Ryan, Castro blamed me because I had arranged the meeting with dissidents. Despite that one moment of truth, Ryan—like so many others before him—had been awestruck. The most important event for him and those with him was the dinner with Fidel, and the box of cigars each had been given that had Castro's autograph scrawled across the lid. They could go home and tell their stories, but I would have to stay here and clean up the mess.

The *Diario de las Americas* headlines shouted, "Gobierno de Castro Amenazas Sección de Intereses de EEUU" (Castro Government Threatens the US Interests Section). The spokesman for the Foreign Ministry accused us "of sabotaging, torpedoing, and attempting to ruin Governor Ryan's visit" and accused five staff members and me of mounting a *escaramuza provocativa* (provocative skirmish) because we had arranged for the dissidents to meet with Ryan in public. This wasn't true; it was just another mistake, but it indicated how paranoid Castro was about the dissidents. We unexpectedly ran into the Ryan party when we took the dissidents to lunch in a nearby restaurant, thereby sparking Castro's anger for violating his prohibition on public meetings with the dissidents. It seemed that everything I touched in Cuba turned to ash.

Two of my staff members who were mentioned by name were fearful that Cuban security would play nasty tricks on them. Their concerns were valid. In the past, some staff members' pets were purposely killed and left on their doorsteps. Others found feces smeared on doorknobs or a cigar burning in an ashtray in their supposedly empty house.

Cuban Americans were ecstatic. They loved that I was standing up to their archenemy. President Clinton's point person on Cuba, Wendy Sherman, wanted to know why Castro had reacted so strongly. I didn't make excuses and she refrained from criticism, but I felt that she was disappointed. Lino Gutierrez, a Cuban American career diplomat and senior officer, was delighted. "Way to go, Vicki," he exclaimed.

Ryan's visit had been a total disaster for me. It had confirmed the worst fears of the Cuban hierarchy, giving the impression that I didn't respect them, the vilest of all faults in their eyes. If I were to succeed at my job, I would have to overcome this calamitous first impression. I did not have any regrets about arranging for Ryan to meet the dissidents privately—not publicly, as Fidel claimed was wrong of me to do. And I still chuckled about Ryan's initial and frank observation that Castro was the trouble with Cuba. I thought that it must have amused a lot of Cuban Americans and Cubans; it certainly delighted me, though Castro managed to have the record corrected in his favor by blaming the dissidents.

A few days later, the Ibero-American Summit went off smoothly. The dissidents did not protest or appear anywhere near the summit, as Castro had so feared, but some of the visiting foreign ministers did meet with a few of them, and this too annoyed him.

I would never have advised the dissidents to act against their government. I felt strongly that they must take responsibility for their actions. I did not want to lead them into danger. I was happy to listen to them, arrange for them to meet with American officials, and bring them together so that they could network and protest when they were mistreated. These activities would boost their status with visitors and help keep them safe. But I never told them what to do, and never suggested what actions they might take.

A fitting epilogue to the governor's visit and Castro's charade came a few weeks later, just as life appeared to be returning to normal. At a party I had held for Ryan's delegation, the governor had presented me with a bust of Abraham Lincoln that was to be displayed in the residence. As I descended the circular stairway carrying the bust, I tripped. Lincoln dropped from my arms, shattering on the black marble steps. It couldn't have been more appropriate, as Ryan had deleted from his speech at the University of Havana a quote from President Abraham Lincoln, "Do not silence those who are not in agreement with you. No man is sufficiently good to govern another without his consent."

I had a lot of pieces to pick up, not only of Lincoln but in repairing the damage inflicted by the Ryan visit. And it turned out that life was not about to return to normal, because on Thanksgiving Day 1999 a five-year-old child named Elián González was found floating on an inner tube in the Florida Straits.

CHAPTER 5

FIDEL IS CUBA

F
IDEL CASTRO RUZ, A PUGNACIOUS LAW STUDENT WHO CAME FROM
a prosperous if unimpressive farm, exploded into Cuban history
on July 26, 1953. His ill-planned attack on the Moncada Barracks in the eastern city of Santiago de Cuba was an unmitigated failure;
Fidel and a handful of comrades were captured and imprisoned, the
others rounded up and executed. Two years later, hoping to quell popular discontent against his rule, Fulgencio Batista freed Castro and his
rebels who then went into exile in Mexico City. Cuban congressman
Rafael Díaz-Balart, Castro's former friend and onetime brother-in-law,
warned the Cuban dictator that if he pardoned Castro it would result
in "Many days of mourning, of pain, of bloodshed, and of misery."

The Díaz-Balart family became the nucleus of Cuban American
opposition to Castro's revolution. Rafael's son Lincoln—born on August 13, the same day as Fidel—and his brother Mario both became US
congressmen and undying enemies of their uncle Fidel. Thus, the Cuban
Revolution is not simply a story of overturning a dictator, forcing out
the elite, and imposing a new order; it is also a family clash between
the Castro Ruz and Díaz-Balart families. Nor is this the only family
feud. Many of those who left in the 1960s and 1970s never again contacted their relatives, who in their eyes had become collaborators with
the regime by remaining in Cuba.

In 1956 Fidel Castro and eighty rebels sailed from Mexico in an overloaded secondhand yacht named *Granma*—in honor of the former owner's grandmother—to the isolated province of Niquero, Cuba. By the time they had reach the Sierra Maestra, where they established their base, most of the rebels had been killed by Batista's army. Yet in just over three years Fidel and his key aides Raúl Castro, Camilo Cienfuegos, Che Guevara, Celia Sánchez, and Haydée Santamaría had accomplished the unimaginable. On January 1, 1959, the rebels entered Havana and Batista fled. Two years and two days later, President Dwight D. Eisenhower, convinced that Cuba was becoming a beachhead for communism shuttered the American embassy. Three months later, President John F. Kennedy approved a CIA-organized invasion by Cuban exiles at the Bay of Pigs, but he withheld air and sea support to the exile invaders in a doomed effort to preserve the myth that the operation was not the CIA's handiwork. Commanding the new Cuban Army, Castro repelled the attack, blocking the only road that led out of the exiles' beachhead at Playa Girón (Bay of Pigs). Today billboards and a small museum at the Bay of Pigs proclaim this battle to be the "first defeat of imperialism in North America." Castro's surprise victory reinforced his revolution. The Cuban people rejected the idea of what might become yet another US occupation, and this in turn undermined the internal armed resistance, which Castro's forces soon rounded up and jailed. The exile invasion also triggered the Soviet Union's decision to supply Castro with advanced weaponry.

The Cuban Revolution succeeded and endured because Fidel Castro proceeded to mold the country to reflect his vision and desire for international acclaim as the leader of the developing world. To accomplish this he turned Cuban society upside down, throwing out Batista and the American Mafia, while at the same time obliterating Cuba's elite and professional classes. In exchange for providing the resources for Castro's overseas military and diplomatic adventures, he transformed the country into a satellite of the Soviet Union.

Castro was always intolerant of dissent. In the early years, he jailed two of his closest allies, Gustavo Arcos Bergnes and Jesús Yáñez Pelletier, each of whom had raised money and bought arms that supported the rebels in the Sierra Maestra. Arcos, a true hero of the revolution, had been with Castro when he and his audacious militants attacked the Moncada Barracks on July 26, 1953, the date celebrated as the beginning of the Cuban Revolution. Arcos served Cuba's new government as its ambassador to Belgium. But Castro turned against him for objecting to the killing of Batista's supporters and the revolution's turn toward communism. Released from prison in 1979, Arcos and his brother Sebastián joined Elizardo Sánchez, a former university professor, to establish the Cuban Committee for Human Rights, which has been a steadfast advocacy of democracy, freedom, and human rights.

I first met Arcos—a wiry man with intense and sad eyes—in 1989 at the home of the deputy chief of the US Interests Section. Photos of my visit were taken by Cuban security and distributed to the dissidents, a not-so-subtle warning that their visit with an American official had been monitored. In 1999, when I became chief of the Interests Section, I visited Arcos at his home, where he was surrounded by the pet birds he loved. On one visit, he described an *acto de repudio* (act of repudiation) to which he had been subjected: as he approached his home he was pushed, punched, and scorned by a group of people he didn't know. But Cuban officials claimed that these acts of rejection were spontaneous demonstrations by neighbors disgusted with dissidents' criticisms of their revolution. As we both knew, the perpetrators were regime thugs ordered to intimidate and frighten the dissidents into more submissive behavior.

Yáñez Pelletier is known as the man who "saved Fidel Castro's life." He was the supervisor of the Boniato Prison on the Isla de los Pinos, where Castro was jailed after his attack on the Moncada Barracks. When Yáñez Pelletier received orders from the Batista government to poison Castro, he publicly denounced the plot. In retaliation, he was expelled from the Cuban Army and later became one of Castro's security personnel. But it wasn't long before he was incarcerated for being "pro-Mafia and pro-American." Although he died a year after I arrived in Havana in 1999, I remember Yáñez Pelletier as a man of absolute integrity.

Since the revolution there had been successive waves of dissidents, but none have threatened or weakened Castro and his government. The first wave of dissidents emerged from the rebel movement and its new institutions. One of the most impressive was Raúl Rivero, a poet and journalist. As Cuba's chief correspondent in Moscow during the 1970s, he discovered that "Russia was dogmatic, schematic, and secretive." In 1991, after returning to Havana, the man who had become known as the poet of the revolution resigned his position and signed a letter to Castro asking him to release political prisoners. He summed up his feelings about Cuba as a "fiction about a country that does not exist." In 1995 he formed Cuba Press, one of the first—and certainly most impressive—groups of independent journalists.

The earliest dissidents, like Arcos, Rivero, and Yáñez Pelletier, had been participants in or strong partisans for the revolution. The first time I visited Rivero, Cuban security was ostentatiously removing a portable antenna from the roof of a car parked next to his apartment. This was their not-so-subtle way of warning me that they would be keeping track of my visits. It also reflected their belief that Rivero's writings could embarrass if not undermine the regime. Yet it seemed to me that all Rivero wanted was to live quietly, write, and remain in Cuba. The next time I met with him, a black sedan—undoubtedly Cuban security—remained parked outside the gate of my residence.

Castro had no rivals of any importance for power; he removed all those from within the hierarchy who potentially would have been most threatening to him sometime before they even knew they were his rivals. In 1989 General Arnaldo Ochoa was executed; in 1992, Carlos

Aldana, the regime's number three official, was forced from power; and in 1999, Roberto Robaina, a foreign minister, was accused of corruption. Raúl Castro, like Fidel, continued to purge high-level party members who'd loyally served for years, including Carlos Lage, vice president of the Council of State, and Felipe Pérez Roque, a foreign minister, and Ricardo Alarcón, president of the National Assembly.

The Cuban hierarchy controlled every aspect of the political process through the parallel structures of government and the Communist Party. Women, youth, and labor groups determined those who were fit to be candidates for the Municipal Assemblies. Members of these groups not only knew each other but knew who was a good communist and deserving of a political position. Generally, no more than two candidates were selected and the voters would decide between them, both having been vetted. Those elected to the local Municipal Assemblies then elected from their members those who would represent them in the Provincial Assemblies, and they in turn selected the members of the National Assembly, the principal legislative body of which Ricardo Alarcón—my regular interlocutor—was president. To complete the picture, the National Assembly in turn selected the members of the Council of Ministers and the Council of State. Fidel was president of both government councils and the first secretary of the Central Committee of the Communist Party until Raúl assumed these positions in 2008. Most elected government officials were party members, and many, like Fidel and Raúl, held positions in both state and party organizations.

The only independent institution in Cuba is the Catholic Church. The Archbishop of Havana, Cardinal Jaime Lucas Ortega y Alamino, was an independent thinker who stuck by his belief that he could best help the people of Cuba by slowly and cautiously creating within the church a place for reflection and independent thought. The Catholic Church was an important part of Cuban life, providing solace, entertainment, and medicine and care to the ill and the elderly. Bishops and priests throughout the country were allowed to determine the degree to which they would support dissidents and independent thinkers. Ortega himself did not encourage dissent, but a number of his bishops and priests provided dissidents sanctuary. He never took a stand against Castro or the government; if he did, Castro might have shuttered the Catholic Church. The Cuban hierarchy tolerated religion, especially the Baptist Church, which Castro used to undercut the Catholics. Still, Castro enjoyed the papal visits, which provided a measure of protection to believers and dissidents alike. Ortega had to shoulder the disdain of the diaspora who disparaged him for not advancing the cause of human rights. But had he done their bidding, he would have incurred Castro's wrath, which inevitably would have diminished the church and its ability to comfort its adherents.

The cardinal told me that Fidel respected the church because of his Catholic education by Jesuit priests in Santiago de Cuba. Ortega felt that he had limited ability to influence the way Fidel governed. Their conversations were principally related to issues regarding the reestablishment of the Catholic Church. He had to tread carefully; after the Bay of Pigs fiasco, over a hundred Spanish priests were forced to leave the country. Believers of all faiths were discriminated against and prohibited from joining the Communist Party or holding important government posts. After the collapse of Soviet subsidies, the government could no longer provide social services. The desperate situation of the young and the elderly forced Castro to permit the gradual revival of religion and the reopening of Catholic and Protestant churches throughout the country. By distributing medicines and food, and caring for children and seniors, the churches helped to ameliorate the poverty and deprivation that were widespread during the Special Period in Time of Peace. When I occasionally attended services at the cathedral or other churches, there was always a warm and welcoming atmosphere; they were oases of silence far from the eyes of neighbors and the security forces.

Castro made sure he was safe from attack; it was not an unwise maneuver given the numerous assassination attempts directed at him. His principal residence was located in front of the American residence, although he had several more houses across Havana. According to the Canadian ambassador whose residence was located across the street from Raúl Castro's house, this was a tactic copied from the Soviets, who believed that it was prudent to keep your enemies close. Any attack against the Castros would spill over and harm the Americans and the Canadians as well. In today's world of drones and precision bombing, the tactic is outdated, but there are still advantages to the arrangement, like enhanced opportunities for surveillance—with guards at the Castros' residences keeping watch on ours as well.

Fidel's compound was part mansion and part military barracks. The barracks, which faced the American residence where I lived, was enclosed by a crumbling mud wall and big trees. Along the wall cameras recorded all those who dared to approach either residence. Next to the gate of my residence, a Cuban guard stood duty in a small hut, rather like an outhouse. In a small building on Castro's side of the pitted, half-paved, lane between our houses, cameras peered out of small, dirty windows.

Fidel's compound was approached on a paved road in good condition along the far side of my residence; he didn't use the alley between our houses. As his black limousine approached, a guard raised and lowered a flimsy wooden barrier. When my official car drew near, a spotlight flashed, warning me to turn right toward my residence. I could always tell when Castro was home because the guards were reinforced and considerably more nervous, repeatedly blinking the spotlight as I approached. When I myself was driving (my driver would not have dared this), I sometimes taunted Castro's guards by driving up the road fast, making it appear that I had no intention of turning. Then the spotlight would flash, an alarm would blare, and soldiers would appear.

In June 2000 when Fidel collapsed in front of television cameras while giving a speech in one of Havana's barrios he was taken to this residence. Security was immediately tightened, so much so that when the Turkish ambassador—the only other diplomat permitted to live on the same street—stopped his car to discuss the drama with me as I was walking my hound dog named Havana, several spotlights went on and a loudspeaker blared instructions to move on, even though the ambassador's car was headed away from Fidel's house and Havana and I couldn't possibly pose a danger. Once, when I was turning into the principal avenue, Fidel's motorcade came whizzing by. I followed, as his security detail frantically waved at me to back off, almost falling out of the windows of their small Ladas.

Castro's residence could not be seen from the principal streets. It was hidden from view by a once-elaborate and elegant mansion that had formerly been the home of Brazilian ambassadors but was now vacant, having fallen into an advanced state of decay. Before the revolution it had been one of the most elegant homes in Havana, even rivaling and perhaps surpassing the American residence, where I now lived. After those opposing the revolution in the early years had taken refuge in its vast gardens, Brazilian and Cuban relations deteriorated. The counterrevolutionaries were freed—among them my friend Tony Navarro, with whom I had worked on TV Martí—but the mansion lay neglected for the next three decades until the famous author James Michener visited Havana. He lamented the beauty and tragedy of this great house in the book *Six Days in Havana*, which apparently inspired the Cuban government to begin the massive repairs required to make it again livable. It was under construction when I first arrived in Cuba, and I kept track of the progress by sometimes sneaking on to the grounds with my special assistant, Peter Corsell. A few months later, when it was finally restored to its full glory, it was used to house Venezuelan president Hugo Chávez on his frequent visits to Cuba.

The Portuguese residence, which was considerably more modest than Brazil's, also abutted the grounds surrounding Castro's compound. The Portuguese ambassador, a trusted friend of Castro's sons, could walk from his residence to Fidel's. But this relationship turned perilous when the allure of the revolution contributed to his falling in love with one of Che Guevara's daughters. His beautiful wife left him, and some months later both the affair and his diplomatic tour ended. He was sent away to Africa, presumably for his sins.

As the principal representative of the US president and Cuba's number one enemy, I received special attention from Fidel himself. And with good reason: the eleven American presidents that served during Castro's rule represented the only serious threat to his absolute power in Cuba. Had any one of them succeeded, the Cuban diaspora would have returned to the island, restoring itself to power and replacing Castro, his revolution, and the communist system he had put in place.

I knew that if I misbehaved, Fidel would be the first to know. I would be the second—I would be confronted with "evidence," which would be used to blackmail me. Our marine guards were targeted by beautiful Cuban women; if they succumbed, they were sent home. Cuba was the only country where the US government still had a nonfraternization rule in effect. But I wasn't worried; I was well ensconced in my life. My husband, Bob, lived with me in the residence and my children, Alexandra and Robert, visited often. We all enjoyed observing the mystery of Fidel's residence across the street and his occasional comings and goings. Nor were we especially bothered by surveillance, which was a part of life in Cuba. I liked the code name the Cubans gave me— Golindrina (the swallow). Although a swallow isn't a very impressive bird, I liked the sound of the name and took note of the fact that swallows are known to return.

Initially I think Fidel enjoyed targeting me, and perhaps he thought I might be easily intimidated. When the Cubans learned that I would be selling American cake mixes at the ambassadors' wives' Christmas bazaar, they informed the group's president—the wife of the ambassador from India—that either I must stand down or the bazaar would be canceled. Like everyone else, the wives had no choice but to do as they were told. I didn't mind; it seemed to me that the Cubans had made fools of themselves by stooping so low. I kept in mind what the Polish ambassador had told me. He believed that the Cuban government's control of every aspect of life on the island exceeded that of the Soviets in Eastern Europe. I didn't doubt him. The smallest detail seldom escaped the notice of state security who kept my minders at the Foreign Ministry apprised of my every action and various misdemeanors.

Like the three chief diplomats who preceded me, I did not formally meet Castro while living in Havana. I didn't know what he thought of me, but I was impressed by his overwhelming charisma and struck by his need to always win and to be the center of attention. He expected to be the unequivocal overseer of everything that took place on his island. Everyone, including foreign diplomats, were expected to follow his rules. He didn't appreciate my boldness in confronting him on his turf, and he made me aware—through proxies—that he was unhappy about it. But I wasn't about to stop. Initially I had been appalled at his reaction to our confrontation over Governor George Ryan's visit, but even then it seemed to me a good thing that someone in the country was willing to challenge Fidel's absolute control.

Our next confrontation took place because I dared to promote Cuban exile artists. The State Department's Art in Embassies program allows every chief of mission to select works of art to decorate the American residence. I asked that they provide me with paintings and photographs produced by Cuban artists living abroad. The collection was impressive, and included works by the photographer Arturo Cuenca and the painter José Bedia. One painting that I personally selected was by Suzanne Lago, whose mother had been my Spanish teacher at the State Department. Suzanne printed below her painting of two young boys, "I cannot return to the house of my childhood," which perfectly expressed her feelings and those of many Cuban Americans. I realized that the collection might be considered a political statement about those who had been forced or had chosen to leave. But I liked to point out that it also included a photograph of Che Guevara; certainly no other US government building displayed his image.

To celebrate this extraordinary collection I invited diplomats and local Cuban artists to view it at the residence. The local artists had never seen the works of their contemporaries who had left the island—some of whom had become famous. I was very pleased until the next morning, when I was summoned to the Foreign Ministry. It was a Saturday, and most Cuban bureaucrats didn't work over the weekend, so I knew that once again I had committed yet another diplomatic violation of the unspoken and unwritten rules. When I arrived at the Foreign Ministry I learned that my transgression was to have disrupted the treasured Biennial Art Festival by creating a counter exhibition of exile art. Smilingly, my composure unshaken, I reassured my interlocutors that my exhibit was meant to complement the Biennial. But I knew that Fidel wouldn't be fooled.

The best description of Castro's mania for absolute power was provided by Arthur Miller, author of *Death of a Salesman* and *The Crucible* and onetime husband to the actress Marilyn Monroe. In an article titled "My Dinner with Castro" he wrote that "[Fidel's] endless rule seemed like some powerful vine wrapping its roots around the country and while defending it from the elements choking its natural growth. And his own as well." Then Miller in one line caught the essence of the Cuban Revolution: "The focus of these contradictions was Castro himself; the man, in effect, was Cuba."

CHAPTER 6

THE LAST BATTLE

O N NOVEMBER 25, 1999, THANKSGIVING DAY, PRESIDENT BILL Clinton's hopes for an opening with Cuba were shattered by five-year-old Elián González, who was found floating on an inner tube in the Florida Straits. The ensuring custody battle between the Cuban diaspora and Fidel Castro had as momentous an impact as the failed CIA-backed exile invasion at the Bay of Pigs. In that earlier debacle, Castro captured twelve hundred American-backed exile invaders, whom he then ransomed back to the United States for $53 million in baby food and medicine. And in its wake, the Soviet Union sent missiles to Cuba, leading the world to the edge of a nuclear crisis.

In 2000, with the help of President Clinton, Castro handed a humiliating defeat to the Cuban diaspora when Elián was sent home to Cuba and his father. In return, the Cuban diaspora extracted revenge by denying Al Gore the presidency in the closely contested 2000 election. Their *voto castigo* (punishment vote) and protests cost Gore the crucial state of Florida and ultimately played a decisive role in the election of George W. Bush, whose victory underscored the electoral power of the Cuban American community.

From the deck of their cabin cruiser, fishermen Sam Ciancio and Donato Dalrymple spotted a child tied to an inner tube floating in the open sea on Thanksgiving Day 1999. Ciancio jumped into the water, rescuing the five-year-old boy from Cárdenas, Cuba. The US Coast

Guard rushed Elián to the Joe DiMaggio Children's Hospital in Hollywood, Florida, where he was found to be in amazingly good health and able to provide his father's phone number in Cuba. When told of his son's plight, Juan Míguel González contacted his uncle Lázaro who lived in Miami's Little Havana and asked that he care for Elián until he could arrange to come to the United States and pick up his son. But within hours, Lázaro (who was under pressure from the Cuban American community) had changed his mind, deciding that he and his family would keep the child. A pro bono attorney stepped forward to represent Lázaro, and claimed with great bravado that Elián was "perhaps the last hero in the twentieth century battle against totalitarianism." It turned out he was half right. To Cubans on the island he would become a hero of the revolution, but to the Cuban diaspora he would become yet another stinging reminder of their losses.

On Saturday, November 27, Dagoberto Rodríguez Barrera, the Cuban official responsible for dealing with the Interests Section, called me at home to inform me that a Cuban child had been rescued at sea and was now in Miami. He emphasized, "This is a very important issue. President Castro is interested." I told him I hadn't heard anything and probably wouldn't because this was the Thanksgiving holiday weekend. He insisted, "You must inform Washington. We want the child returned immediately." Although surprised that Dagoberto was so pushy, I promised to let the State Department know. "Please do it today," he said.

I had taken the call from Dagoberto in my wood-paneled study, where the photos of former ambassadors and principal officers lined one wall. At the far end of the room stood a beautiful Chinese partition with a long golden dragon painted on black lacquer across three panels; it had been given to the last US ambassador for safekeeping when a Cuban family fled during the early days of Castro's revolt. Prior to my arrival, Charles Shapiro, the new director of Cuban affairs at the State Department, had met with dissidents in this room. It was his meeting that convinced the Cuban government to mistakenly believe that I would lead the dissidents in disrupting the Ibero-American Summit; their information was gleaned from listening devices implanted in the room. One or two of the dissidents, along with the residence staff, undoubtedly supplied additional and probably contradictory reports. Cuban dissidents liked to say that if two people met, one would inform the government. It was perhaps a slight exaggeration, but in any group, there was bound to be an informant. Now, one month later, I was still trying to repair the damage created by Castro's misinterpretation of Shapiro's remarks, and by my own missteps during Governor George Ryan's controversial visit.

Hoping to convince Dagoberto that I was taking his concerns seriously, I called the State Department's seventh-floor, twenty-four-hour, Operations Center in Washington, DC, which monitors messages from our embassies around the globe. If there is a crisis anywhere, our diplomats can send the latest information along with their analysis to the secretary of state at any time, in a matter of minutes. But this wasn't a crisis—at least not yet. The Operations Center connected me to Shapiro, who agreed to contact the Immigration and Naturalization Service (INS). I wasn't surprised when I didn't hear back. He would have found it difficult to find anyone who could answer his queries over the weekend, and by Monday it was too late; the curtain had risen on the Elián saga.

Elián should have been playing with his classmates, not drifting in the sea. He lived in Cárdenas, about an hour's drive east of Havana. It is the closest port in Cuba to the United States, but no ships docked at its long wooden ramp because bilateral trade with Florida had vanished decades ago. The substantial homes and offices that bordered the principal street had fallen into a state of disrepair. An occasional horse and buggy rambled by, and perhaps an ancient American Ford, its original motor likely replaced by one from a small Lada. Elián's father, Juan Míguel, lived in a small house on a quiet backstreet a mile or two from the port. He worked at a modest and very plain Italian restaurant, patronized principally by visiting Cuban exiles who would treat their relatives to dinner. Elián was fortunate not to live in the large Soviet-style concrete-block housing project where clothes dried on the small, walled-in balconies and rusting climbing bars sat in a field of dried weeds.

Elián's mother, Elizabet, had divorced Juan Míguel, her childhood sweetheart, because he was said to be a *mujerago*—a man with many romantic dalliances. She worked in a hotel at the Varadero Beach Resort that was reserved for foreign tourists. Although Elizabet and Juan Míguel both earned the government-dictated peso salary equivalent to ten to fifteen dollars a month, she could count on tips in dollars and cast-off clothing or other items left behind. These hotels, built in the early 1990s, catered to the low-end Canadian tourist market. The rumor was that an all-inclusive two-week package for a vacation in Varadero was equal to a Canadian unemployment check for the same period. Cubans could work in these hotels but not stay in them; it would be another ten years before Raúl Castro's reforms allowed Cubans to be permitted as guests at hotels visited by foreign tourists. But it wasn't the lifestyle of these tourists, their clothes, and ability to travel that pressured Elizabet to leave. According to neighbors, Elizabet fled Cuba because she was madly in love with Lázaro (Rafa) Munero, a handsome man with few skills, no job, and little prospect of finding one. He, like so many other young men, had no future in Cuba. His greatest desire was to make his way to a new life in Miami. Elizabet was willing to go with him, but didn't want to leave her son behind.

It was a dilemma. If she left Elián with Juan Míguel, she would not see him for years—perhaps never again. She would not be with him as he grew from a child into a man. If she took him, they might create a new and better life with a good job, money, and perhaps a house and a car of their own. If they were lucky, the fifty-horsepower motor on Rafa's clandestinely built boat of aluminum and rusty scrap metal would deliver them to the beaches of South Florida in about thirty hours. Once they reached American soil, they would be allowed to remain and build new lives.

Having made her decision, Elizabet and Elián squeezed into the overloaded boat. This was a family affair, of which Rafa was the organizer: on board were Rafa's father, mother, brother, uncles, and a young couple Nivaldo Fernandez and Arianna Horta who had brought along her baby daughter. A half hour after setting sail, the boat's motor quit, forcing Rafa to return to Cárdenas. This gave the passengers a last chance to reconsider setting out in an overcrowded boat with a bad motor. Arianna took her baby daughter home, returning to make the journey with her lover Nivaldo. Thirteen souls set out once more; if the seas were calm, they would reach Florida within a day and a half. Then they could begin to live their dream.

All went well at first. They traveled smoothly throughout the night and next day, but when they were within thirty miles of the Florida coast a storm blew up. The boat's motor failed. A cold driving rain swamped their small craft, causing it to overturn and sink. The survivors clung to two inner tubes. Elizabet and Rafa tied Elián to one of them. As the day dragged on, Rafa's brother became delirious, suddenly swimming for shore. Rafa followed; neither was ever seen again. The others, tired, thirsty, and discouraged, disappeared one after another into the water, leaving only Elizabet to protect Elián as best she could on one inner tube while the lovers hung on to the other. During the night, the inner tubes broke apart. In the morning, Elizabet was gone. Elián was alone, floating under an azure sky in the vast Caribbean Sea.

Of the those who set out, only three survived; Arianna and Nivaldo washed up on a Florida shore sunburned, battered, and exhausted on Thanksgiving, the same day that Elián was plucked from the sea. Elián had floated for two days without water or food, exposed to the sun, the wind, and the cold of the dark night, but he had companions: he said that dolphins watched over him and nosed him toward the distant shore. Fate had surly destined him to live. But where would he live—with his relatives in Florida, as the diaspora demanded, or back in Cuba with his biological father and his ersatz father Fidel Castro?

Many Cuban Americans had themselves arrived alone in the United States. The Catholic Church organized an airlift, known as Pedro Pan, that lasted from 1960 to 1962 and delivered thousands of children—principally boys between the ages of twelve and eighteen—to the United States. The parents of these children sent them alone to the States because they feared that Castro's communist regime would send them to work and be indoctrinated in camps in the Soviet Union. When they arrived in the United States, they were placed with relatives or lived in temporary shelters. Their parents imagined or hoped that the revolution would fail and their children would return to Cuba. But they did not return to Cuba. Rather, as Castro consolidated power, their parents joined them in the States.

Having experienced coming to America alone, these former Pedro Pan children were confident that Elián would be better off with his Miami relatives. Former US senator Mel Martinez, who was President George W. Bush's principal Cuba adviser at the time, had been a Pedro Pan child. The Pedro Pan adults with whom I have spoken all told me that their parents did the right thing by giving them up, at least temporarily.

By Sunday, November 28, the Cuban American National Foundation (CANF) had circulated four thousand posters with a photo of Elián above a caption "Another Child Victim of Fidel Castro." CANF had a new cause and a new leader. It was now the turn of Jorge Mas Canosa's son to validate his leadership. The campaign to keep Elián in the United States would be Jorge Mas Santos's first initiative since his father had died in 1997. A brilliant political strategist, the elder Mas Canosa had used his political clout to convince American presidents to impose successively tougher sanctions on Cuba. Although the embargo wreaked economic havoc on the island, it did not overthrow the hated Castro regime. Now his son Jorge Mas Santos had a chance to humiliate Castro and give the Cuban American community a significant public relations victory.

The Cuban government moved quickly. Over the weekend they announced in a press release that they were demanding the return of a small Cuban boy whose mother had drowned at sea. The Cubans provocatively added that Elián's mother's death, along with other rafters, was due to the United States' "stupid" migration policy. On Monday morning Jamie Rubin, the State Department press spokesman, indignantly retorted, "It is reprehensible that anyone would suggest the United States is responsible in any way for these tragic events." But in truth, our policy of allowing Cubans to remain did encourage them to attempt the risky voyage across the Florida Straits.

Had the issue been simply a question of legal custody, Elián would have been immediately returned to his father. US and international law make it clear that a child belongs with his parent before anyone else. But during the Thanksgiving holiday, the INS had given temporary custody of the boy to his great-uncle Lázaro, who lived in Miami's Little Havana neighborhood with his wife Alina and twenty-year-old daughter, Marisleysis. The Cuban diaspora believed that Elián had a right to remain in the United States because his mother had given up her life to bring him to the "land of freedom." My phone call to my colleague Charles Shapiro and his attempts to engage with the INS had been ignored because no one wanted to gratuitously anger the Cuban American community. Elián had been entrusted to his relatives by Florida immigration authorities who undoubtedly believed that they were doing the best thing for the child. If the INS were to suddenly take back Elián, the Cuban diaspora would have been outraged, resulting in tremendous negative publicity for the Clinton administration, which might even impact the Democratic presidential candidate; the election was only a year away, and the likely candidate, Vice President Al Gore, would lose any chance of replicating Bill Clinton's relative success with the traditionally Republican Cuban American voting bloc.

Castro, however, was not about to oblige the Clinton administration. He seized the opportunity to embarrass the Cuban diaspora and reinvigorate his revolution. On December 6 (Elián's sixth birthday), and with Elián's father and classmates at his side, Castro threatened the United States, saying "They should be prudent, and before 72 hours, because if not, there are going to be millions of people in the street demanding the freedom of the boy." He then announced, "We will wage a worldwide battle, we will move heaven and earth." The administration took the threat seriously, worrying that my staff and I might be in danger, and fearing that Castro might be contemplating sparking yet another mass migration, announced that the United States would retaliate if Castro allowed Cubans to set sail or congregate on beaches. But that was just bravado. There was little we could do to stop a mass migration. President Clinton could close Florida ports, but Cubans would still set out to sea, and those rescued by the US Coast Guard would have to be brought either to Guantanamo Naval Base or to Florida. Neighboring countries would be hesitant to set up temporary holding sites or resettle the Cubans. They resented the fact that undocumented Cubans could remain in the United States when their nationals were returned home. In their view, if we wanted to end illegal Cuban migration, our government should send the migrants back to Cuba.

Castro's threat unnerved the Clinton administration. The president, the State Department, and the INS were now fully absorbed in finding a solution. But there was no good solution. Either way Clinton decided—to send the boy home or allow his Miami relatives to keep him—there would be severe consequences for the United States and for Cuba. Clinton certainly didn't want to risk another mass migration like the 1980 Mariel boatlift when over 128,000 Cubans fled, and again in

1994 when almost 30,000 Cubans were resettled in the United States. But Clinton also feared angering the Cuban Americans and diminishing Gore's chance of becoming president. He understood the consequences of denying their demands. Had President John F. Kennedy accommodated the diaspora's demands at the Bay of Pigs, the United States would have gone to war with Cuba, which the world would have condemned as a blatant example of a larger nation coercing a small neighbor. But by allowing the exiles to be captured and killed, Kennedy incurred the wrath of the Cuban diaspora, which punished the Democratic Party by voting Republican in every election until Clinton finally began to make inroads by currying the community's favor.

Two days after Castro's threat, Clinton responded. But it was neither the answer I was looking for nor was it a clear-cut decision. Clinton said, "The question is, and I think the most important thing is, what would be best for the child, and there is a legal process for determining that." Clinton was buying time, giving both sides hope. Most courts would award custody of Elián to his father in Cuba, but perhaps not Florida courts. The diaspora saw Clinton's remark as an opening, and attorney Spenser Eig filed a petition requesting political asylum for Elián.

It was my job to convince Ricardo Alarcón, the man I had so angered during Governor Ryan's visit, that our governments should move ahead with the previously scheduled migration talks. Doing so would demonstrate to the breathless media that as long as we were talking, Castro was unlikely to unleash a mass migration. Several days later Alarcón, a small, wiry man with wisps of gray hair and oversize plastic-framed glasses that continually slipped down his nose, informed me that Castro had agreed to proceed with the talks. We now had the situation back under control, or so it seemed.

On December 12, 1999, the deputy assistant secretary for the Western Hemisphere, Bill Brownfield, and I met with Alarcón. Brownfield, who was leading the US delegation to the talks, told Alarcón that

President Clinton had decided to return Elián. I thought that Alarcón would be surprised and delighted; I certainly was. Instead, Alarcón demanded to know when Elián would return. Brownfield explained that Clinton had decided to allow our judicial system to decide the custody case. But, he assured Alarcón, he was confident that our courts would return the boy to his father. Alarcón wasn't convinced, and asked, "How can you be sure that the US courts will decide in our favor?" Brownfield attempted to reassure him, pointing out that in almost all cases involving a minor the parent is awarded custody. He added that even if the verdict were appealed, the process shouldn't take longer than two or three months. Brownfield didn't mention the US Supreme Court because, like Clinton, he probably didn't imagine that the legal battle would be long and drawn out, eventually reaching the highest level. Alarcón was skeptical doubting that the Florida courts would decide in Cuba's favor; and besides, he noted, "Castro wants Elián home now." With his patience fraying, Bill responded, "If you had wanted Elián back immediately, you should have allowed Juan Míguel to travel to Miami and pick up his son." Annoyed, Alarcón snapped back, "Juan Míguel will only go to the States when we are certain that he will bring Elián home." Bill and I believed that if Juan Míguel had gone to Miami a few days after Elián was placed with his relatives, the Cuban American community would have had no choice but to allow father and son to be reunited. But Castro nixed the visit, undoubtedly worried that Juan Míguel might be convinced to stay in Miami with promises from CANF of money and position.

The meeting with Alarcón was inconclusive. He promised to brief Castro. We would resume the conversation the next morning, when our delegations met at the Palacio de la Convenciones, a large convention center located among the plush residences of diplomats and foreign businessmen in the Cubanacan suburb. The American delegation sat behind a long table covered with a white cloth, facing an unsmiling Alarcón and the rest of his unhappy delegation. Brownfield opened the talks and then asked each of us to present our agency's positions. A State Department representative raised concerns about the excessive cost of Cuban documents—physical exams and exit visas—that intending immigrants needed to complete. I pointed out that Cuba's policy of firing returned migrants from their jobs in the tourist industry made it more likely that they would flee again. The Coast Guard representative raised issues relating to drug and human trafficking.

Now it was the turn of the Cuban delegation. Rather than share their views, Alarcón announced, "There will be no further talks until Elián returns to Cuba." We watched in shock as Alarcón and the Cuban delegation pushed back their chairs and filed out of the room. A few minutes later, Alarcón repeated his statement at the press conference: "There will be no migration talks until Elián returns to Cuba." His announcement put the threat of a mass migration back on the table. My hope that the talks would dampen speculation about a mass migration had instead been used by Castro to create more conjecture and unease.

Still, I wasn't as worried as I might have been, Alarcón had assured me at a lunch he had hosted for our delegation that he and his team would be joining us for dinner that evening at my residence, giving us a chance to find a solution. I suspected that Alarcón would get Castro's agreement—if he hadn't already—to allow the American judicial process to settle the Elián case. After all, Clinton had decided in Castro's favor, even if it seemed to be a typical Clintonesque maneuver in which he attempted to escape blame by handing the decision to the courts. Castro might have been irritated that Elián wouldn't return home by the turn of the millennium, but he would be coming home at some point. Perhaps he was disappointed that he would miss celebrating his victory together with Elián's at the beginning of the twenty-first century. But I didn't think Castro's irritation would prevent him from agreeing to Clinton's plan for returning the child. Some days later, after our delegation left Havana, Castro (knowing that Elián wouldn't be home to celebrate the new year) announced that Cuba would celebrate the new millennium next year, on the "real" date, January 1, 2001.

I went home early to oversee preparations for the dinner in order to ensure that the event would provide the perfect backdrop for reaching an agreement. In the large dining room, tables were adorned with candles and white linen, as well as china and crystal embossed with the Great Seal of the United States. I set the place cards so that the American and Cuban specialists were seated together at round tables. At my table I placed Bill Brownfield (the head of our delegation), Ricardo Alarcón, and José Arbesu, Cuba's principal spy for the Western Hemisphere. This would give Bill and me a chance to convince the Cuban officials that Castro should await the decision of the US judicial system before taking any precipitous action.

The atmosphere was positive, aided by scotch whiskey, Alarcón's drink of preference, and my birthday cake. The residence staff in their black-and-white uniforms served the four-course dinner beginning with a shrimp appetizer and a main course of steak Béarnaise, which were paired with excellent French white and red wines. As the dinner progressed Brownfield explained the judicial process, pointing out that US Department of Justice lawyers would advocate for returning Elián to his father. By the time the champagne and my birthday cake were served, Alarcón and Arbesu had agreed that Cuba would await the decision of the American courts. But, Alarcón emphasized, "We want Elián back this year, not in 2000." By "we" he clearly meant Castro. But even then, he and Castro knew that would be impossible.

As our guests departed, Brownfield and I stood on the residence porch and waved cordial goodbyes as our guests stuffed themselves into the small, white Russian-made Lada vehicles that the government provided for its officials. I was pleased. Castro had made his move. There would be no mass migration, at least for so long as he believed that Clinton was acting in good faith. I told Brownfield that he had done a good job.

The first step in the process was to provide proof that Juan Míguel was a good father. The initial INS interview was positive, but CANF complained that it had not been informed. Still seeking to pacify the diaspora, the administration asked me to arrange a second interview. Suspecting a trap, Alarcón was annoyed, but after a few days he agreed. The second interview took place in Miramar, a pleasant Havana neighborhood where trusted Cubans were allowed to live. Castro had moved Juan Míguel's family there, most likely to keep control of who visited them and to gain a better sense of their loyalty. This interview, conducted by the same officers as before, reached the same conclusion that Juan Míguel was a loving father. The INS then ordered Lázaro González, the great-uncle who was caring for Elián, to hand him over so that they could return him to Cuba by January 14. The Cuban American community was beyond furious, feeling that Clinton and Attorney General Janet Reno, who hailed from Florida, had betrayed them. In their view Juan Míguel wasn't fit to be the child's father; no good father would want his child back in Cuba.

The first major setback occurred just weeks later; it was an early warning that the courts weren't going to be as helpful as Clinton had anticipated. On January 11, Rosa Rodriguez, a Miami-Dade circuit court judge of Puerto Rican heritage and a Yale Law School graduate, defied the order issued by the INS to turn the boy over to federal authorities. She ruled that Elián's relatives should have an opportunity to present their arguments for why his great-uncle Lázaro should be given custody. She gave the parties until March 6 to prepare their arguments, warning that her final decision could "be averse to the father's interests" if Juan Míguel did not appear in a Miami court. Janet Reno angrily retorted to this slap in the face by a local court that Judge Rodriguez's ruling had "no force or effect." She moved the case out of the Miami court and into the federal district court. But she also postponed the January 14 deadline for turning Elián over to the INS.

Worried that sooner or later the federal courts would uphold the government's decision to return Elián, Cuban American legislators sought to pass a law making him an American citizen. Representatives Ileana Ros-Lehtinen (R-FL) and Lincoln Díaz-Balart (R-FL), a member of the family of Castro's former wife, Mirta, led the effort. Senate Majority Leader Trent Lott (R-MS) and House Speaker Dennis Hastert (R-IL) supported the initiative. If they succeeded, it would complicate, if not void, INS's authority over the case. It was one thing to rule that a Cuban child must return home, but quite another to send an American child to Cuba. If Elián became a citizen, Clinton and Reno might give up the fight. Already it was becoming evident that this dispute with the Cuban diaspora was going to be costly for the administration.

I was convinced that the bill making Elián a citizen would pass unless his father came to Florida to retrieve him. But Castro had not budged from his decision that Juan Míguel wouldn't travel to the States until he could bring his son home. Then it occurred to me that a visit by Elián's grandmothers might also prevent the citizenship bill from becoming law. And, I knew just who I should contact! I had met Joan Brown Campbell, the first woman to lead the National Council of Churches when she had visited Havana at the request of the Cuban Council of Churches. Joan, an imposing woman with gray hair, sharp blue eyes, and a kind smile, was on a mission to reunite Elián with his family. I was impressed when she came by my residence on a Saturday. She had no obligation to keep me informed, especially as the State Department was concerned that she might make the already messy case messier. When she asked if I would be willing to issue visas to Elián's grandmothers, I realized that this was the real the purpose of her visit. I assured her that I would recommend that they be approved. In return, the president of the Cuban Council of Churches who had accompanied Joan to the meeting commented, "You are a nice woman; I thought you had fangs or something." This was a sure sign that Castro's public diatribe against me, over my meddling in Governor Ryan's visit and my support for Cuban dissidents, had indeed had an impact on the true believers.

To my surprise the grandmothers had not requested visas, as I had anticipated. Yet I was certain that if they traveled to the United States, they would stop the campaign to make Elián a citizen. I called Joan to encourage her to arrange the visit. I told her that it was the only way to stop the US Congress from passing a bill that would make Elián a citizen. If the grandmothers visited Elián, it would demonstrate to the American people that the child had a loving family in Cuba with whom he belonged. It would be even better if Juan Míguel would go, but Castro didn't seem ready to take that chance. She promised to talk with the Cubans—probably Alarcón—to determine if Castro would allow the grandmothers to travel. A few days later we received the request and the State Department told us to issue the visas.

On January 21 Mariela Quintana and Raquel Rodríguez landed in cold and gray New York. Shouting reporters immediately besieged them, demanding to know when they would see Elián, and if they would take him back to Cuba. Mariela, Elián's paternal grandmother, bravely announced, "No one has a right to make him an American citizen. He was born in Cuba. He lives in Cuba. He's a Cuban." In Washington, DC, they met with Janet Reno and congressmen who supported Elián's return to Cuba. Then they flew to Miami for a meeting with Elián, which had been arranged by Reno. Elián arrived in a black limousine, sitting between CANF's leader Jorge Mas Santos and Marisleysis González, the daughter of Elián's great-uncle, who was his young caretaker. Outside the home of Sister Jeanne O'Laughlin, president of Barry University in Miami, where the meeting was to take place, protestors chanted "Libertad! Libertad! Libertad!" Some signs even gave Elián's rescue a religious aura by declaring, "Three kings, three children, Jesus, Moses, and Elián." Older exile women seemed to give Elián's ordeal at sea a religious significance; in their eyes, he was a miraculous child who would bring about Castro's downfall and give them back their country.

The grandmothers meeting with Elián did not go well. The encounter was full of tension for all sides—perhaps most of all for Elián.

Raquel and Mariela later said they found their grandson "changed"—undoubtedly because he was dressed like a Cuban American boy with a baseball cap on backward and a gold chain around his neck. Sister O'Laughlin, who hosted the meeting at the behest of Attorney General Reno, came to the conclusion that Elián should stay in Miami. She explained that the atmosphere during the meeting was oppressive. She told the media that the Cuban government was somehow behind the meeting, and that one of the grandmothers bit Elián's tongue, apparently, to get him to talk to them. She also revealed that the grandmothers looked at Elián's penis to see if he'd grown.

If Castro was Elián's ersatz Cuban father, CANF's Mas Santos was his substitute Cuban American father. Mas Santos was orchestrating a show in Miami that was almost equal to Castro's in Havana. After the meeting with Elián's grandmothers, the media caught a small voice saying, "Tomorrow I become an American citizen." Elián was referring to the bill that Cuban American and Republicans legislators were hoping to pass. But Elián was wrong. The grandmothers' visit had reinforced the American public's view that the child should be returned to his father. Democrats, led by Charles Rangel (D-NY), blocked the initiative in the House. In the Senate, Republican Chuck Hagel (R-NE) persuaded Trent Lott to back away from pushing the legislation.

The seesaw of emotions didn't end when Congress dropped the idea of making the boy an American citizen. To Reno's evident dismay, the Federal Circuit Court for the Southern District of Florida did not, as she anticipated, confirm that Elián must be turned over to the INS as ordered. Rather, William Hoeveler, an experienced and respected judge, gave CANF's lawyers until February 24 to disprove the Department of Justice's contention that Juan Míguel had the sole right to determine where and with whom Elián would live. It suddenly seemed less certain that the courts would return Elián to Cuba.

It also was clear that Clinton's ploy of deflecting blame by turning the decision over to the courts had misfired. The judicial process had served only to highlight the courts' reluctance to enforce Clinton's and Reno's decision to return Elián to his father. In hindsight, it would have been better had Reno forced Elián's relatives and the diaspora to comply with the January 14 deadline to turn the boy over to the INS rather than extending it. At that point it still could have been done peacefully. There would have been a considerable outcry, but it would have been hardly a ripple in comparison to the drama three months later when US marshals forced entry into Lázaro's home and took the child at gunpoint.

CHAPTER 7

FIDEL'S LAST HURRAH

IDEL CASTRO PERSONALLY STAGE-MANAGED THE "ELIÁN SAGA," IN which he was the director and his compatriots were the audience. It played for seven months, ending when Castro escorted Elián González and his family on a victory lap of marches and speeches across the island. But the victory was not Castro's alone. Had President Bill Clinton and Attorney General Janet Reno not been committed to returning the child to his father in Cuba, Castro's theatrical production could have ended in disaster.

Castro's decision to await the outcome of American justice turned out to be brilliant. It gave him months during which to mobilize and revitalize his revolution, providing it with a much-needed, much younger hero. The other heroes were either old (like Fidel and his brother Raúl) or dead (like the father of the country, José Martí, and Castro's comrades in arms Camilo Cienfuegos and Che Guevara. Huge billboards once reserved for revolutionary heroes now displayed Elián, a captive of the "evil empire."

Castro declared that he was leading a "battle of ideas" in which the kidnapping of a Cuban child was only the latest in the series of evils perpetrated by the United States. Even better, this battle allowed him to once again walk the world stage as a David defending his people from the monstrous misdeeds of the Goliath to the north. Still, Castro had a lot at stake, and he couldn't afford to lose. Cuba's *babalus—*

priests of the Afro-Cuban Santeria religion, which has African and voodoo roots—predicted that he might fall from power if he didn't bring back Elián.

On December 22, 1999, Castro dressed in his customary fatigues and white athletic shoes, led the first in a series of protest marches. Hundreds of thousands of Cubans paraded from Havana Bay down the Malecón, past the USS *Maine* Monument and the Hotel Nacional. When they arrived at the Interests Section waving little blue, white, and red Cuban flags, they chanted and held up homemade signs declaring, "Salvemos a Elián" (We will save Elián). Hundreds of schoolchildren in their red and white uniforms surrounded the Interests Section. Holding hands, they completely encircled the long seafront block on which the building is located. Some looked scared, and others were stern, but all were determined to fight for the return of their schoolmate. I was embarrassed. My powerful country seemed to be a Lilliputian giant emasculated by a small child that we feared to return, despite knowing it was the right thing to do. Castro said he had sent the children to protect us. But he was merely exploiting the public declaration of a State Department press spokesman who had foolishly claimed that we would hold the Cuban government responsible for "the safety of our diplomats." Castro always named his marches; this one was Salvemos a Elián, but I thought of it as the March of the Protecting Schoolchildren.

Castro organized a second massive march on January 14, 2000, the day Elián should have returned to Cuba. Although Judge Rosa Rodriguez's decision had "no force or effect," Reno still hoped to persuade the Cuban American diaspora to accept the fact that the child belonged with his father. Had she not been a Florida native who wished to preserve her good standing with the Cuban American community, Reno might not have been so determined to find an amicable solution. But it was not possible. As she and Clinton belatedly realized, compromise was unbearable for a diaspora that fervently believed that this was their chance to defeat Castro.

Fidel labeled this second event the March of the Combatant Mothers. Much to my relief, he did not send schoolchildren to protect my staff and me from Cuba's mothers. Nor did Castro himself attend. This parade of Cuban women was led by Vilma Espín, Raúl Castro's wife and the head of the Federation of Cuban Women; Mariela and Raquel, Elián's grandmothers; and Nelsy, Elián's stepmother, pushing the stroller of his half-brother. An estimated 100,000 women, some pregnant and many accompanied by young children, slowly marched along the long sun-filled Malecón. They rested on the seawall and then, revived, continued to the US Interests Section where they chanted "Bring back our son."

Despite the fact that Clinton had agreed to return Elián, the US government—in the form of the Interests Section—was the focal point of the protests. In addition to the usual cameras and listening devices pointed at my office in the Interests Section, the adjacent three-story building displayed a translucent flag featuring Che Guevara. Since the first days of the crisis, in addition to the marches, several hundred Cubans gathered outside the Interests Section every day. But one morning in March they were replaced by heavy machinery and construction workers. Castro was building what he called a Tribuna Abierta (Open Court) that consisted of a large amphitheater with an open stage and a vast concrete courtyard spanned by large metal beams that formed a dome. When it was completed the amphitheater would be used by schools and community organizations to stage protests in song and dance that demanded Elián's return. At the far end of the Tribuna Abierta there was a statue of Cuban hero José Martí holding a very small child and pointing toward the Interests Section. It was rather incongruous, because the child in his arms was considerably smaller than Elián. Nevertheless, Cuban wags opined that Martí was telling a small Elián, "That is where you get your visa."

One morning when I arrived at the Interests Section, a Cuban guards whom we employed presented me with a large bronze tablet he had found among the rubble where construction had begun. On the tablet, which must have lain in the dirt for years, was inscribed the words "Fourth of July Park." This prime property that had stood vacant and neglected since the revolution had likely been named in honor of the US Army Corps of Engineers, which had designed and built the Malecón seafront promenade during the early 1900s, when the United States occupied Cuba. I placed the bronze plaque on the decorative wall bordering the steps leading into the Interests Section; it wasn't an American flag, but it was a reminder that friendship between the United States and Cuba might someday be resurrected.

It seemed as if Cuba breathed Elián. Every evening, television and radio broadcast the *Tabla Ronda* (Roundtable), in which experts discussed Elián's psychological health and the various evils inflicted on him by the Cuban diaspora and the United States. The Cuban media dissected the dysfunctional family with whom Elián now lived, pointing out that his guardian Lázaro was unfit, an alleged alcoholic with three citations for driving while intoxicated under his belt. His daughter, Elián's principal caretaker, was in their opinion an emotionally immature twenty-year-old whose name, Marisleysis, sometimes came out as "Mary-sleeze" by those who wished her ill. Castro denigrated Cubans in the diaspora by claiming that they thought they could buy anything, including Elián. He claimed that although they showered him with toys, they could never buy his affection because he did not belong to them. According to Castro, these deserters from the island could never replace a loving family, complete with father, stepmother, half-brother, and grandmothers. Cubans didn't share all of Castro's views, but most of them did believe that Elián should be with his father and grandmothers.

Castro's theater reached its peak with the Million Man March, the largest, longest, and most colorful demonstration, featuring Cuban flags, Elián T-shirts, and lots of foreign media coverage. Articles in *Granma*, *Juventud Rebelde*, and *Trabajadores*, Cuba's major newspapers, pressed every citizen to attend. Even the disillusioned young, who formed bands and rap groups and tested the patience of the police, had something fun to do. It didn't seem to matter that after the march these same young people, who had been zealously waiving their Cuban flags, would hang out on the Malecón and plot how they might reach La Yuma, Cuban slang for the United States that comes from the 1957 film *3:10 to Yuma*, a Western about Yuma, Arizona.

To cheer my staff and myself, I had my own form of defiance. I placed large papier mâché Haitian carnival masks of a lion and a giraffe on the Interests Section balcony. It was a silly gesture, but it made me feel good. I could at least respond, even if a bit foolishly—and, I assumed, harmlessly. Still, Fidel noticed. Raúl looked up as he marched passed, surprised to see a lion looking down at him, he stumbled. Fidel caught his arm and on they went. The next day *Granma* published a two-page photo spread featuring a few of my staff and me gazing at the marchers from the balcony. *Granma* scolded us for our perfidy and instructed its readers to just ignore the diplomats watching from their "glass palace," a most appropriate label for our beautiful glass building.

Most of the time my staff and I enjoyed the show from my fifth-floor balcony and retreated inside when the blaring music from the Tribuna Abierta was too much. The marchers were organized into groups of those from local barrios, youth and women, and government ministries. As they passed by the Interests Section each group was announced. It was discouraging to see the officials from the Ministry of Foreign Affairs march by, despite the fact that we were in fact on the same side, as we both were working to bring Elián home to Cuba.

Several of my staff wanted a firsthand look. They joined the marchers, sometimes persuading young men to exchange their Elián T-shirts or small Cuban flags for a few dollars. At times they would spot among the crowd an American movie star or even the infamous Joanne Chesimard, who had fled to Cuba after escaping from prison in the United States after being convicted of the murder of a policeman in

New Jersey. There was a circus-like atmosphere, and everyone had the day off. Missing work hardly mattered given that the country hadn't completely recovered from the devastation of the Special Period in Time of Peace, a term that described Cuba's economic free fall after the Soviets withdrew their annual five-billion-dollar subsidy and the United States tightened its embargo. To lessen the misery, Castro had permitted small family-run businesses to open small restaurants and rent out rooms, and farmers were allowed to sell a portion of their produce at local markets. The government owned and managed all other businesses. Another result of the Special Period was that the military took over the management of the economy—most notably the agricultural and tourism sectors. Essentially there was no private sector in Cuba until Raúl Castro's reforms ten years later. But to this day, no Cuban owns a business that employs more than a few hundred people.

Castro orchestrated so many marches—there were six between January and June, when Elián finally came home—that parents worried that their children were missing too many school days. But even Cuba's impressive universal education system was becoming less valued. It wasn't doctors and lawyers who lived well; they had the same government-mandated peso salary, equivalent to ten to fifteen dollars per month. Better-off Cubans were those who had access to dollars, either because they worked in the tourist industry or received remittances from friends and family abroad. It seemed foolish to spend years becoming a physician when taxi drivers, waiters, maids, and prostitutes earned more. Moreover, medical professionals were expected to leave their families and serve abroad in Haiti, Venezuela, and many African countries.

Cuban youth were beginning to look down on professionals. They were not rewarded for their education, dedication, and long hours. An attractive Cuban doctor in her thirties who lost her job because she ran afoul of a political commissar told me a story that illustrated the power of the dollar, even in this communist country. To support herself the doctor sold her television and other items of value. She often spent her long days in a friend's apartment watching television. Over-hearing the doctor lamenting her bad luck, the friend's daughter admonished her: "You shouldn't sit around. You should do as I do and pick up foreigners. They pay me in dollars." Her friend laughed, unconcerned that her daughter had become a prostitute. The sad fact was that the doctor's choices were limited: she could become a dissident and live on the margins of society, attempt to leave Cuba with smugglers or in an unsafe vessel, or—as her friend's daughter suggested—become a prostitute.

Castro took his Elián crusade on the road. It was an ideal cause around which to mobilize the countryside, which was poorer and more isolated than Havana. In every town and city and along the principal highways, Elián—like the other heroes, Fidel, Raúl, Cienfuegos, Guevara, and Martí—was featured on large billboards similar to those in the States that advertise presidential candidates, tires, and restaurants. All admonished Cubans to be vigilant, to sacrifice, and most of all to dedicate themselves to the revolution. Among my favorites was a large cutout of Castro, standing about two stories high, that was located on one of the few traffic circles leading out of Havana. From most angles the cutout was impressive, but approaching from behind, it seemed as if a shadowy Castro was being propped up. Often Americans would point out that Castro must be modest because he wasn't featured on many of the billboards. I explained that if they visited the poorer barrios or drove around the island, they would find that Castro was displayed on more billboards than any other hero—even Martí.

Another of my favorites was a homemade sign featuring the yacht *Granma* in the small village of Niquero in the southwest where Castro and his rebels had come ashore in 1956. But it was Guantanamo City, on the highland above the American military base in the southeast, that had the most impressive billboard. Entering the town, the road ran down to an intersection where three billboards joined together depicted the heroes and major events of the Cuban Revolution.

I suspected that Castro, in his campaign for Elián, enjoyed traveling around the island, his motorcade speeding down the almost deserted Carretera Central (Central Highway) and at every stop thousands of people waiting to hear him tell them about Elián, the embargo, the Cuban Adjustment Act, which in Castro's mind depicted our unfair immigration policy, and our occupation of the naval base at Guantanamo. His rallies brought news and excitement, which enlivened the dullness of daily life. The head of each block committee—the Committees for the Defense of the Revolution (or CDR)—ensured that everyone in her neighborhood showed up. Those who were good revolutionaries were rewarded by having their names placed on lists for jobs or for opportunities to buy scarce appliances like rice cookers or even refrigerators. Those who failed to show up, or engaged in other "unsocial" behavior, were warned and penalized. The CDR heads knew the secrets, desires, and misbehavior of every resident because neighbors and even family members informed on each other. I still believe that the pervasive snooping of the CDR is a major reason for the longevity of the revolution. It is impossible to plot even the small protest when your neighbor, friend, or child might report you.

The CDR leader was often a middle-aged, heavyset woman with short orange hair. Perhaps I exaggerate about the hair color. Even considering the scarcities in Cuba, the hair dye available to Cuban women seemed to be of a particularly poor quality. I met quite a few of these women in my travels, and I did not like them. One of the worst was the political boss at the regional hospital in Pinar del Rio who seized the opportunity to blame me—and the embargo—for deaths she said were caused because of lack of medicines and equipment. Although the hospital doctors, using Soviet-era equipment, provided unparalleled preventive health care, they meekly deferred to the orange-haired tyrant. They didn't want to lose their jobs, homes, or the education received by their children. The revolution provides, and the CDR leader takes away.

Everything that happens in Cuba goes up or down the Carretera Central, whether a visit from Castro or the transport of huge Soviet missiles that rumbled throughout the night to deposit their cargo in specially built silos around the island. The missiles, discovered in 1962 by an American spy plane, were trundled back up the Carretera Central to vessels that took them back to the Soviet Union in accordance with the agreement reached between President John F. Kennedy and Prime Minister Nikita Khrushchev.

Castro's rallies also were staged up and down the Carretera Central, first demanding Elián's release and then triumphantly celebrating his return. Yet, in the end, the Elián theatre created only a momentary commotion that quickly dissipated. The somnolent countryside soon returned to its isolation and poverty, remaining lost in time, rather like the country Gabriel García Márquez describes in *The Autumn of the Patriarch*, written with his friend Fidel in mind.

Despite turning the island into a vast theater, Castro seemed to be losing the battle. Three months had slipped away, but contrary to our promises the American courts had not sent Elián home. Each judicial decision gave the lawyers for Elián's relatives another chance to present their case. Finally, President Clinton decided to intervene. He sent his personal lawyer, Greg Craig, to Havana. I had met Craig in the early 1990s, when I was in charge of Cuban affairs at the State Department. He told me then that he was fascinated by Cuba and would love to visit. But I didn't imagine that ten years later we would be sitting in my Havana residence discussing an out-of-control child custody case, in which he had signed on to be Juan Míguel González's lawyer.

Craig was either amazingly persuasive or Castro—like Clinton— had already concluded that the only way to break the impasse would be for Elián's father to travel to the States to retrieve his son. On April 3, 2000, Castro read a letter from Juan Míguel in which he promised, "I am willing to leave tomorrow, absolutely alone, and transport myself to where the child is." He added, however, that if he couldn't immediately bring his son back to Cuba, he would come with his family and remain until Elián was turned over to him. On April 7, Juan Míguel, his family, and Elián's classmates arrived at Andrews Air Force Base, outside Washington, DC. Now all that was left to do was to reunite Elián with his family.

On April 12, Janet Reno again tried to broker a peaceful transfer of Elián. She met with the boy's caretakers, Lázaro and Marisleysis González at the home of Sister Jeanne O'Laughlin, president of Barry University and Reno's erstwhile friend, who had changed her mind and begun advocating for Elián to remain with his Miami relatives. The meeting was a disaster. Lázaro stormed out. Less than fifteen hours later, he failed to obey Reno's order to turn the boy over to federal authorities. He was backed up by Ramon Saul Sanchez, a pugnacious, in-your-face exile who led crowds chanting "Reno, you coward! Miami is on fire!" Reno again postponed the deadline. Flags were raised and the crowds chanted, "Justice! Justice! Justice!"

Reno's fathomless patience could not continue. US laws were being flaunted, making the government appear weak and ineffectual. And all because the judicial process, which Clinton had been so certain would back him up, refused to do so. The Eleventh Circuit Court of Appeals criticized the government's—and, by implication, Reno's—handling of the case. The judges complained that the INS should have considered whether six-year-old Elián, himself, could request political asylum. It seemed far-fetched that a child could make this decision. But the emotional pitch in Miami and Washington, stoked by the diaspora, Castro, and the agonizing judicial process, had turned a custody case into a heated ideological battle. Newspapers and television kept viewers apprised of Juan Míguel's every move in and around Washington, DC, even recording him giving the finger to someone who asked if he would defect.

It was becoming increasingly clear that a showdown was at hand. The US government had to enforce its writ or lose the respect of the American people. In Miami, crowds chanting, "War! War! War!" sur-

Me leaving the Cuban Foreign Ministry after discussing Elián's fate.

(Photo credit: Reuters)

The stately mansion in which I lived—once the residence of our ambassadors.
(*Courtesy of Alexandra Huddleston*)

Fidel is everywhere! (*Courtesy of Alexandra Huddleston*)

My birthday gives me a chance to make a point official.

(Photo courtesy of author)

The Million Man March protesting Cuba's three big complaints: the embargo (or "*bloqueo*"), the Cuban Adjustment Act, and Guantanamo Naval Base.
(Courtesy of Alexandra Huddleston)

A huge march protesting the "kidnapping of Elián"—the Cuban boy miraculously found floating on an inner tube in the Florida Straits.   *(Photo courtesy of author)*

Fidel leading a protest past the Interests Section.

(Courtesy of Alexandra Huddleston)

Above: Cuban national hero, José Martí, with small child pointing at the Interests Section. He is telling the child a Cuban joke: "That is where you get your visa."

Right: The amazing Peter Corsell, manager of the outreach program.

(*Both courtesy of Alexandra Huddleston*)

The prize-winning "Havana"—lovely like the city Havana, but young and well-cared-for.

(*Courtesy of Alexandra Huddleston*)

Havana and her amazing trainer, Ana Maria González.

(*Courtesy of Alexandra Huddleston*)

Northeast Gate: the only land entrance to Guantanamo Naval Base.

(Photo courtesy of author)

rounded Lázaro's home. They defiantly declared that they would fight any effort to take the child from the house. Reno warned that if the relatives would not give him up, he would have to be taken by force. Rumors began to spread that some individuals in the crowd were armed. The negotiations had again reached an impasse.

During the previous months, Reno had eschewed using force, but now it was imperative. Compromise with members of the Cuban diaspora had proven impossible. Yet they were unwilling to comply with US law and continued to flout the demands from the INS to turn over the boy. The endless saga on both sides of the Straits was an embarrassment to the Clinton administration. On April 22, an immigration task force stormed into Lázaro's house, seized Elián, wrapped him in a blanket, and took him to the airport. For Lázaro, Marisleysis, and the Cuban American community it was over. Only hours later two photographs summed up both the defeat and the victory: one shows an armed INS agent in full body-armor confronting a terrified Elián in the arms of Donato Dalrymple, one of the fishermen who found him at sea; the other shows a smiling child in the arms of his father.

On June 29, almost two months after Elián was snatched away from the Cuban American community, the US Supreme Court dismissed without a hearing an appeal from Lázaro's lawyers to allow the child to remain with his Miami relatives. The same day, Elián and his family and friends landed at Havana's José Martí airport. *Granma* headlines blared, "At Last in the Fatherland." But much to my dismay and that of many worn-out Cubans, Castro announced that the battle for Elián was just the beginning; down came the Elián billboards and up went new ones condemning the Cuban Adjustment Act, the embargo, and the US Naval Base at Guantanamo Bay.

Castro paraded Elián in rallies throughout the countryside, and his American supporters joined in. Jerry Brown, who would later become governor of California, had an aide call to ask if he could meet me at my residence. I said I would be willing to meet, but he could under no circumstances bring along Philip Agee, a disgraced former CIA operative who had arranged Brown's tour to Cuba through his Cuba Linda (Pretty Cuba) travel agency. Agee, who had fled to Cuba, was wanted in the United States for betraying his country; he had exposed CIA agents, at least one of whom was killed as a result of his disclosures. Brown didn't visit my residence, but I would have liked to have met him to ensure that he was aware of Agee's crimes.

Castro's victory was complete. His enemies had lost everything: the child they desired and their hope that this conflict might destroy the hated revolution. Castro had his ersatz son back and was celebrating his victory. The American public, annoyed by the Cuban American community's open disregard for the laws of their adopted country, supported the first weakening of the embargo since it was enacted in 1962. A Republican-controlled Congress passed—and President Clinton signed into law—regulations that permitted the sale of agricultural goods to Cuba. But the diaspora did manage to tack on a quid pro quo that banned American tourism to Cuba. Thus, unlike other embargo regulations that can be modified by the president through the secretary of the Treasury, tourism is illegal until this law is repealed or superseded.

Yet time would prove that Castro and his revolution had lost as well. The strenuous campaign marked the beginning of Castro's health problems. Shortly before Elián's return, he fainted in a poor Havana barrio on a hot and sunny June day in the middle of a speech demanding Elián's return. As aides rushed to his rescue, Felipe Pérez Roque, the foreign minister, grabbed the microphone to call out, "Viva Fidel, viva Raúl, long live the revolution." The statement had the ominous ring of, "The king is dead, long live the king." But the king was still very much alive. It would be another four years until illness drove Fidel to hand over power to his brother Raúl.

Nor did Fidel Castro succeed in using his victory to end the embargo. The passage of the law permitting agricultural sales to Cuba must have convinced him that the US Congress would end the embargo, and he could in turn disregard the Clinton administration. His attitude also might have reflected the fact that he distrusted President Clinton who, upon seeking electoral victory in 1992, had said that the H.W. Bush administration had missed a big opportunity "to put the hammer down on Fidel Castro." and then in 1996 had signed into law the draconian Cuban Liberty and Democratic Solidary Act, after Cuba shot down two unarmed civilian aircraft. Dagoberto Rodríguez Barrera, my interlocutor at the Foreign Ministry, told me that his government was confident that Castro's courting of congressional leaders and American VIPs would lead to the repeal of sanctions. I warned him that he was far too optimistic. But in his blaze of victory, Castro appeared to underestimate the power of his enemies in the diaspora who were intent on revenge.

Elián González would not have returned without the full force of the US government. Clinton had firmly backed Reno's decision to take Elián by force, pointing out that "The law has been upheld. I think it was the right things to do." But there was not a single thank you from Cuba, nor any effort to use the cooperation between our governments that had resulted in Elián's return as a foundation for talks that might lead to improved relations. Clinton was uninterested in exploring this possibility because he realized that returning Elián to Fidel, his ersatz father, had already done serious damage to Al Gore's chances of winning Florida. Politically, his best option was to close down any further possibility of better relations. He did so by declaring that there would be no further effort to improve relations "until there is a bipartisan majority that believes that there has been some effort on the part of the Cuban government to reach out to us as well."

The defeated Cuban Americans were not appeased. They wanted revenge, and they got it in less time than it took to return Elián to Cuba. In November—a little over four months after the boy went home—diaspora Cubans who were infuriated by their egregious loss voted massively against Al Gore. While Clinton had received about one-third of the Cuban American vote, Gore got slightly less than one-fifth. All that Gore would have needed to win Florida's electoral votes and the presidency was another five hundred votes. Instead, large numbers of Cuban Americans—in what they called *el voto castigo* (the punishment vote)—joined other conservatives in voting for George W. Bush and in protesting the vote recount. The US Supreme Court ultimately stepped in to quell the tension over who won Florida, deciding the presidency on a vote of 5 to 4. Had Elián remained in Miami, grateful Cuban American would have easily provided the votes needed to elect Gore, thereby avoiding the recount and the partisan decision by the Supreme Court. It is not a stretch to claim that Elián González, a Cuban child found floating in the Florida Straits, lost Al Gore the presidency.

In the summer of 2000, with Elián at his side, Castro basked in the admiration of his compatriots and the world. He had triumphed in what would be his last battle with the Cuban diaspora, winning a decisive victory and reinvigorating his revolution. It seemed to me that Fidel might rule for another decade or two. My staff and I had a bird's-eye view from the fifth-floor balcony of the US Interests Section. Seated below, in the front row of the Tribuna Abierta, were Juan Míguel with his family and beloved son, Elián, and surrounding them were Fidel, his seldom seen wife Dalia, and most of the Cuban hierarchy. No one looked up or acknowledged our presence. Yet I could have thrown a stone and hit Fidel. More realistically, I might have broadcast loud music to drown out the festivities below. Instead, we watched quietly, wondering whether and for how long the ripples from the battle for Elián would continue to rake the shores of both Havana and Miami. Below Cuba's leaders sat without ever imagining that we—such a close and trusted enemy—might pose a danger.

In truth, despite the harm we do each other, the United States and Cuba are no longer real enemies. The United States has not been engaged in a hot or even a cold war with Cuba for many years. Nevertheless, American presidents, for domestic political gain, have allowed themselves to become entangled in a family feud, in which Fidel Castro's in-laws the Díaz-Balarts and other conservative Cuban diaspora families struggle endlessly to defeat the Castro brothers and the revolution that forced them to flee the country they loved. Yet over the ensuing half century Cuba has changed beyond their recognition; it will never return to what it once was. Even if Cuba suddenly became a democracy, it would not magically become the country they left in the 1960s and 1970s. Cuba's values and vision of itself have irreparably changed, and it is today a different country from the one it might have been.

PART III

2001-2002: US INTERESTS SECTION; PRESIDENT GEORGE W. BUSH

CHAPTER 8

REGIME CHANGE: OURS

IGHTY PERCENT OF CUBAN AMERICANS VOTED FOR GEORGE W. Bush in the 2000 presidential elections, though it would be more accurate to say that they voted *against* Al Gore in revenge for the loss of Elián González. In return, they expected President Bush to punish Castro by ending the Clinton-era measures that permitted people-to-people travel to Cuba for humanitarian, cultural, and religious reasons. The first wave of Cuban migrants, many of whom translated successful lives in Cuba into prosperous and happy lives in the States, wanted to strictly isolate Cuba, ending all travel to the island. They had cut their ties to Cuba and, having become American citizens, made their desires known through active lobbying, voting, and financially supporting mostly Republican candidates who agreed with and cultivated their anger toward Castro and Cuba. Those Cubans who came to the United States after the mid-1980s were generally different from their predecessors in that they wished to retain the right to visit their families and friends in Cuba. Still, when Bush took office in 2001 most people in both groups agreed that travel to the island by non-Cubans should end.

Cuban Americans feared that American interests—and diplomats who didn't understand their losses—would come to dominant relations with Cuba, undermining the diaspora's control over US policy. Moreover, if non-Cuban Americans developed ties with the island, the opportunities for reestablishing Cuban American economic dominance would be diminished. Thus, the importance of maintaining the embargo. To this end, President of the Cuban American Foundation (CANF),Jorge Mas Canosa successfully convinced top American companies to refrain from pushing for the right to invest in Cuba after the Soviet Union and Eastern European bloc lost its sway over the Cuban economy in 1991. Mas Canosa, who some were calling *el presidente* (of the new Cuba) was the chairman of the Blue Ribbon Commission, which enlisted American companies in designing a free and open economy that would replace Cuba's communist system. The side benefit was that the companies who participated in the commission agreed not to invest in Cuba until there was a new government—which Mas Canosa hoped he might lead.

By February 2001 Mas Canosa's son had lost the battle for Elián, and Cuba was recovering from the devastation of the Special Period in Time of Peace. It should have been evident that the revolution would endure no matter how punitive America policy. Still, the conservative diaspora had sufficient influence to convince President Bush to propose far-right Cuban American Otto Reich to manage US relations with the Western Hemisphere. He likely did so to repay Cuban American voters for their overwhelming support and to satisfy his brother, Jeb, who would be seeking reelection as Florida's governor in 2002. But Reich was thwarted by Senators Richard Lugar (R-IN) and Chris Dodd (D-CT), who controlled the powerful Senate Foreign Relations Committee. They refused to hold a hearing for him, claiming he was ill qualified for the job of assistant secretary of state for the Western Hemisphere. Reich, the son of an Austrian Jewish immigrant to Cuba and a Catholic mother, had left Cuba with his parents when he was fifteen. A formidable foe of the revolution, he was admired and supported by right-wing conservatives and militant exiles, while the Cuban government both feared and loathed him. The *Granma* newspaper and Cuban media blasted Reich, accusing him of assisting Orlando Bosch, the alleged co-conspirator in the downing of Cubana Airlines flight 445 in 1976, to escape justice by illegally seeking refuge in the United States.

The Senate's rejection of Reich and the president's refusal to withdraw his candidate meant that there would be no change in Cuba policy in the short term—so long as I, the lead American in Cuba, advocated engagement and Secretary of State Colin Powell remained disinclined to dismantle the Clinton administration's liberal travel measures and cooperation with Cuba. The acting assistant secretary of state, Lino Gutierrez, a career bureaucrat and conservative Cuban American, would likely have been pleased to enact harsher policies but was unable to do so as long as Powell objected to gratuitously punishing Castro. Thus, much to the disgust of conservative Cuban Americans (including Reich, who was watching from the sidelines), the Clinton-era travel policies remained in place, allowing hundreds of thousands of Americans in addition to Cubans living in the United States to visit the island. This unforeseen combination of events meant that relations under George W. Bush—the president elected to crack down on Cuba—actually improved during his first year in office.

Castro, too, contributed to better relations though what the media dubbed his "charm offensive" to persuade visiting Americans, especially senators, congressmen, and business leaders that it was in the best interest of both countries to end the embargo. Castro considered these American visitors as his advance team who would press for a more moderate US policy toward Cuba when they returned home. Moreover, he also greatly enjoyed hosting these VIP American visitors. Those who dined with him provided him a platform on which to perform. They stroked Castro's ego and reassured him that he was respected and esteemed by famous Americans, even as our government, at the behest of the Cuban diaspora, continued to undermine his revolution.

After a late-night/early-morning dinner with Fidel Castro, Arthur Miller presciently pointed out that Castro was "A lonely old man hungry for some fresh human contact, which could only get more and more rare as he ages." Miller had come to Cuba with William Styron, author of *Sophie's Choice*, and Ambassador William Luers, the president of the United Nations Association, and their wives. Their visit in March 2000 had been one of the first and most important visits under Clinton's new people-to-people travel regulations. Castro's good friend, Nobel Laureate Gabriel García Márquez, had invited the authors to Havana. In turn they invited my husband Bob, our political officer Jeff DeLaurentis, and me to breakfast at their hotel, the lovely Santa Isabel. The hotel was located on the far side of the Plaza de Armas, across from the Palacio de los Capitanes Generales, once the headquarters for Spanish aristocrat Isabel de Bombilla, who ruled Cuba during the years her husband, governor of Cuba and conquistador Hernando de Soto, was exploring what would one day become Florida and Louisiana. (Little bronze statues of Isabel—the first woman to rule in the Western Hemisphere, even if unofficially—can be bought along Havana's streets.) I also pointed out that the building on the near side of the hotel, with a flagpole and no flag, was once the US consulate in the days when American consuls with immense powers ensured the safety of our investments and had the last word on Cuba's foreign relations.

Bill Luers's wife Wendy told us that her husband wouldn't be joining us for breakfast because he was still sleeping. Castro had wanted to reminisce about old times with Luers, who had negotiated the Interests Section agreement in 1977 on behalf of President Jimmy Carter. Wendy added that she had had an adventure the previous night. When she awoke and found that Bill wasn't in the room, she got up, threw on a robe, and opened the door to the terrace that overlooks the Plaza de Armas. As she stepped outside, she heard the ominous clicks of safety switches being turned off and saw long rifles pointed at her. She quickly retreated. Cuban security was guarding Fidel Castro and Bill Luers, who were still reminiscing in Castro's black limousine, which was parked in front of the hotel.

Miller and Styron regaled us with details about their dinner with Fidel. They said that Castro would pick a topic, expansively lay out his views, and then turn to them for comments, which he didn't allow to last long before expounding on yet another issue. Miller said that Castro seemed to expect their total agreement and approval. Thus Fidel was surprised and disappointed when Miller stopped him midsentence with a plea: "Please, Mr. President, forgive me, but when we arrived you will recall that you said I was 11 years, five months and 14 days older than you." Miller paused and then said, "It is now 15 days."

With the battle for Elián González on everyone's mind, I asked Miller what he thought about Cuba policy. He responded by paraphrasing William Shakespeare's *Macbeth*: "When the hurly-burly's done, when the battle's lost and won, I hope there might an opportunity to move toward a more normal relationship." I don't think either of us could have imagined that almost twenty years later the embargo would still remain in place.

A year later, when Bush took office in 2001, people-to-people visits—like the one Miller and Styron were on—had increased in frequency, as had the number of public figures seeking an invitation to dine with Castro or at least meet with Ricardo Alarcón, the top official responsible for Cuba's policy toward the United States. Alarcón was so convinced that Castro's charm offensive would succeed in weakening if not ending the embargo that he proudly told me, "Vicki, I'm so busy briefing Americans groups that I hardly have time to sleep." I warned him that Castro's strategy was unlikely to prove effective. Congress might pass legislation to weaken or repeal the embargo, but Bush—who had narrowly won Florida with the help of Cuban Americans—would veto it. But for Castro there were other benefits: he enjoyed meeting with the visitors and Cuba was earning hard currency from their stay.

The most high-profile visit in 2001 was that of the Council on Foreign Relations led by David Rockefeller, banker and philanthropist. I held a large dinner in his honor with ambassadors from European and

Latin American countries who offered them their candid views of Cuba and of US policy. The following evening, the Rockefeller group dined with Fidel who, as was customary, did 80 to 90 percent of the talking. They also visited with Elizardo Sánchez, the human rights activist. It seemed to me that a visit with Sánchez was well worth the price of a protracted dinner with Castro. I knew that Rockefeller wouldn't convince Fidel to become a capitalist, but so long as Castro continued to enjoy his American visitors he would be more tolerant of the dissidents, because one depended upon the other. If Castro jailed the dissidents it would provide the conservatives the excuse they needed to insist that Bush punish Castro by tightening the embargo.

I didn't expect to be invited to the dinners with Fidel; it certainly would have been uncomfortable for all present. I would have been obliged to defend US policy, and the dinner guests would have been dismayed if I interrupted or contradicted him. Neither were my staff or I invited to accompany the American groups on their visits to schools, hospitals, and museums. Visits to these institutions were not, as one might imagine, required by the Cuban government. Rather, they were a mandatory part of people-to-people visits, whose purpose was to inform Americans of Cuban culture and society. The US Treasury's Office of Foreign Assets Control (OFAC), which enforced the embargo, insisted that the tour groups that arranged the people-to-people travel include visiting Cuban educational and cultural institutions. Yet because Cuban officials organized the actual visits it gave them a chance to advocate ending the embargo; they did so by showing the very best of Cuban education and health care. The loyal Cuban tour guides inevitably helped by explaining that the lack of supplies and the decrepit state of these institutions and the island's infrastructure was the result of the US embargo.

On one occasion, I did accompany a tour. Former Texas governor Ann Richards invited me to join her group on a visit to Pinar del Rio, on the western end of the island. When I briefed her group I lamented that the Cuban government carefully orchestrated every tour, making sure that visitors leave with a good impression. Thus, I opined, they didn't see that life in rural areas was tightly restricted and the possibility of advancement almost nonexistent. Intrigued, Richards invited me to show the group a rural village. I consented and joined the group, but when I asked the tour guide to turn off the main highway, he refused. I insisted, but to no avail: neither he nor the bus driver wanted to get in trouble with their superiors, who wouldn't approve of a deviation from the planned route. I told Richards that at the next exit she would have to reinforce my request. A lesser woman might have backed down, but Richards didn't.

The village where we stopped was less than five minutes off the main road, and was typical of rural towns all over the island: isolated, poor, and depressing. On either side of an unpaved gravel lane there were tiny one-story houses with peeling paint. There was only one store, which provided goods that could be bought with the government-provided ration card and also served as a post office. There were no cars; a few bicycles and a tired horse tethered to a buggy were the only means of transportation. The people were friendly, but frightened at the appearance of a luxury bus and a gaggle of well-dressed Americans, few of whom spoke Spanish. After a brief visit, the guides herded us back to the bus. The Americans were dismayed and disturbed by the poverty and isolation in this small town only thirty minutes outside Havana. The guides explained it was all the fault of the embargo. But I had made my point, and at least one group had had a more realistic view of life in Cuba.

My all-time favorite encounter with visiting dignitaries almost persuaded me to change my political party affiliation. After meeting with Senators Daniel Akaka (D-HI), Max Baucus (D-MT), and Pat Roberts (R-KS) at the Hotel Nacional, Roberts invited me to accompany them to the airport, something that I could have done in any country other than Cuba. I regretfully declined his offer, explaining that I would be blocked from joining them in the airport VIP waiting room. Senator Roberts was outraged that the Cubans would treat the American representative this way. Wanting to show the Cubans that he disapproved of their actions—and possibly to confirm my story— he asked me to join him and his colleagues in their car. I squeezed into the back seat with Roberts and Baucus; Akaka sat in the front with the chauffeur. At the airport, as we began walking toward a small VIP guest room, a Cuban official blocked my way. The senators and I protested to no avail as I was escorted to a separate room. But less than five minutes later, I was ushered into the room where the senators were silently and stonily staring at their hosts. As I entered, everyone— Cubans included—stood and greeted me. Roberts had told the Cubans that until I joined them there would be no discussion. The Cubans gave in and I joined the group. Roberts had thrown down a challenge, forcing the Cubans to back off. I wished that more American officials would press the Cubans on their treatment of our diplomatic representatives in Cuba. I was proud of the senators—especially Roberts— and decided that like Roberts I would stand up to the Cubans for what I believed to be right.

I was very much in favor of the people-to-people visits because Americans were learning about Cuba, and Cuban officials were learning that Americans were surprised to discover the limits the government placed on the lives of Cuban citizens, including barring them from tourist hotels and the absence of media and the Internet. Still, most groups were favorably impressed with Cuba. I didn't think that Americans should hear only one side of the story, nor did I like that idea of allowing Cuban officials to dominate the narrative. Cuba's innumerable problems and deficiencies were not principally the result of hostile US policy, as they claimed. We certainly had an adversarial relationship—I was Castro's biggest annoyance, my country his avowed enemy, and our policies were designed to harm his government. But Castro's authoritarian regime bore most of the blame. In order to remain in power, Fidel restricted individual freedom, persecuted dissent, and imposed a communist orthodoxy that deprived Cubans of political and economic opportunity.

To provide the visiting groups a more balanced view of Cuba and US-Cuba relations, my staff and I offered detailed policy briefings to visiting American groups. Two officers generally gave the briefing, there was no script, and each team had its own approach. I often began with the Spanish-American War because the United States played a critical role in helping Cuba gain independence from Spain. Turning to the Cuban Revolution, I acknowledged the frustration that led Cubans to support Castro's rebels in ridding the country of Fulgencio Batista and the Mafia bosses led by Meyer Lansky. I also put the current US-Cuba relationship in context, pointing out that it was a product of our cold war with the Soviet Union, which had seized the opportunity to befriend Castro and gain an outpost, including military bases, ninety miles from our shores. I revealed that both Democratic and Republican presidents had attempted to improve relations, but their efforts ran afoul of either Castro or the Cuban diaspora. I didn't hesitate to remind our listeners that Castro was a dictator who controlled every aspect of life on the island.

I made the case that US policy was not a question of black or white but instead many shades of gray. Over the years our policy had become increasingly polarized, as Cuban Americans became a powerful voting bloc. Having suffered at Castro's hands, they could see absolutely no redeeming qualities in his regime. When it became increasingly clear that the US embargo would not topple the regime, they refused to give up, clinging to the sanctions as a way of punishing Castro more than a way of bringing freedom to the island. At the same time, anti-embargo advocates became all the more convinced that US policy was misguided, serving only to increase the poverty and reinforce that Cuban government's control over their lives.

Our briefings were popular with audiences from universities and cultural organizations, as well as foreign affairs and business groups.

Usually we gave our briefings at the US Interests Section in a room that featured the head of the eagle that had been torn off the USS *Maine* Monument by Castro's rebels or at the hotels where the visitors were staying. We made the briefings and the Q and A sessions lively and entertaining and, of course, we defended US policy. We were American diplomats, and that was our job. I made one point that always flummoxed my listeners: I told them that so long as Fidel Castro remained in power, Cuba posed no threat to the United States or the region. But if during a transition the Cuban government was unable to maintain internal security, it would likely become a haven for crime, narcotics trafficking, or even terrorism.

Castro didn't like the competition from our briefings, which countered his version of Cuba and our relationship, but he couldn't stop them. Occasionally he indulged in a bit of skullduggery. One evening as I rode home in the official car, I was astonished to find the large group that I was scheduled to brief walking along an avenue a few blocks from the residence. Their bus driver—presumably a good revolutionary—had refused to take them to the American residence. When he remained adamant, they demanded to be let off the bus and allowed to find their own way. Several who were elderly accepted a ride in my car, and I walked with the others to the residence. Omar, the head butler, was ready with mojitos, Cuba's national drink. My visitors enjoyed their rum cocktails, the beautiful house, and the briefing. Despite Castro's trick which had caused them some inconvenience, most still believed that US policy was outdated and unethical.

Of the hundreds of briefings my staff and I gave during 2001, only one didn't go well, and it was my fault. I hadn't been warned that the Semester at Sea, with its hundreds of students, had been given a license to dock in Cuba. So I was dismayed when I saw a photograph in the *Granma* newspaper of American students hugging a grandfatherly Fidel Castro. The article said that he told them, "Your presence here helps because in your willingness to exchange opinions you learn a little more about Cuba and we learn a little about your country." I agreed with the sentiment but thought that their visit with Castro was a mistake. This type of visit—cruise ship and kids—would be used by critics to try to convince Bush to terminate people-to-people travel.

The best I could do was to ensure that the students heard our side of the story.

Jeff DeLaurentis, the political officer, and Peter Corsell, my special assistant and a former intelligence officer, gave a spirited briefing, which according to my husband Bob the students enjoyed. But the following day *Granma* announced that I refused to serve the hot and tired students "ni una gota d'agua" (not a drop of water), even though the briefing had been held on the terrace with a hot sun overhead. I was embarrassed, I looked bad, and I was partially at fault. Annoyed about the visit, I had told Omar, who was in charge of the house, "I don't care what you serve them, just no mojitos." When the hot and restless students arrived, there was no food or drink. Fortunately Bob stepped in and the students were happy with the belated arrival of soft drinks and popcorn. Omar may have misunderstood me, or perhaps he intentionally misinterpreted my instructions in order to please Cuban security, to whom he regularly reported. It was a reminder to watch my temper, because the Cubans would exploit my slightest mistake for propaganda purposes.

Castro wasn't relying on the American visitors or the possibility of better relations to keep Cuba afloat, because he had found a new savior in Hugo Chávez, president of oil-rich Venezuela. The two leaders were quite similar: both were big men with larger-than-life personalities who had attempted and failed to seize power when they were young but some years later had succeeded—Castro through a popular revolt and Chávez through democratic elections. Together the duo expanded their influence throughout Latin America. Chávez established an oil facility that provided 50 percent financing for Caribbean and Central American countries, but for Cuba the terms were even more generous.

With help from its new ally, Cuba had begun to emerge from the deprivations of the Special Period in Time of Peace, when the loss of Soviet subsidies and the tightening of the embargo imposed severe hardship on every Cuban except those at the very pinnacle of the government. The economy was slowly improving thanks to Chávez's largess and the advent of some internal reforms that allowed Cuban farmers to sell a portion of their produce at open markets and families to run small restaurants and rent rooms in their homes to tourists. Infrastructure was still in bad shape, although several blocks along the Malecón had received a new coat of amazingly ugly, garish blue, pink, and orange paint—reputedly a gift from the Italian government. It covered the splintered wood and provided some protection against the damage done by the sea air and water. For other buildings, the paint was too late: they had tumbled down, shearing off from adjacent buildings. The Malecón seemed to be losing its struggle against time and neglect.

Yet there was hope for beautiful Habana Vieja (Old Havana), which was undergoing a metamorphosis due to the vision and determination of Eusebio Leal Spangler, who was informally known as the Mayor of Old Havana. Leal, by his own admission, was a "madman." When he was young he laid down in front of construction equipment that was about to pave over a historic wooden road. In time he was able to convince the government that Old Havana was worth saving. His first project was restoration of the Palacio de los Capitanes Generales in the Plaza de Armas, which he used as an office as he methodologically went about saving Habana Vieja block by block, including the Hotel Ambos Mundos (Two Worlds), where Ernest Hemingway lived for a time and where he wrote *For Whom the Bell Tolls*. Today much of the old city is beautifully preserved because, as Leal told me when I visited him, "I am in love with this city." When the visit ended, he gave me a simple blue rosebud vase, which I treasure.

Castro extended his charm to Europe with great success. The

European Union accounted for half of all foreign investment and tourism. Castro was flattered when a left-leaning member of Norway's parliament nominated him for the Nobel Peace Prize. That same month he hosted American and former Russian officials at a three-day conference on the fortieth anniversary of the Bay of Pigs invasion This meeting was followed a year later by an even larger gathering dedicated to reviewing the events surrounding the October 1962 Missile Crisis. To everyone's surprise, Castro announced at the conference that Cuba had tactical nuclear weapons in the country when President John F. Kennedy ordered a naval blockade to prevent the arrival of additional weaponry. Had Kennedy and his generals known that nuclear weapons were already in Cuba, Kennedy probably would have taken an even stronger stance, perhaps ordering air strikes. Castro, furious with having been left on the sidelines as Kennedy and Khrushchev resolved the crisis, advocated a nuclear missile strike on the United States; Khrushchev wisely ignored his erstwhile ally. The Cuban diaspora wasn't happy either, when some years later they discovered that Kennedy had secretly agreed not to invade Cuba in exchange for the Soviets withdrawing the missiles.

Castro had less success with Vladimir Putin who, much to Fidel's annoyance, shuttered the last vestiges of Russia's presence in Cuba: the Lourdes Signals Intelligence facility, which intercepted satellite communications. If there was any lingering doubt, this final dissolution of the Havana-Moscow axis should have demonstrated that Cuba was no longer a threat to our country. The Russian ambassador, who was a good colleague, explained that dire economic conditions had forced Putin to concentrate solely on securing Russia's borders. Military bases in Cuba had become a luxury his government could no longer afford.

This was 2001, and the Cold War was long over; Russia was no longer interested in continuing its strategic alliance with Cuba. Castro had survived our embargo and was staying afloat with the aid of Venezuela's Chávez. His charm offensive hadn't succeeded with Putin, but it had done so with a number of European countries. And much to everyone's surprise, US-Cuban relations were improving, which in turn resulted in somewhat more freedom for civil society and the dissidents. I believed that if this period of informal détente continued, it would benefit both countries, but many within the diaspora disagreed.

CHAPTER 9

FROM FIDEL WITH LOVE

URING MY THIRTY-FIVE-YEAR CAREER IN GOVERNMENT THE TWO most impressive figures I encountered were Colin Powell and Fidel Castro. Accustomed to wielding power, they both radiated charisma, yet their approaches to the use of power differed greatly: Powell built force through uniting his followers around a common goal, while Castro maintained power by tolerating nothing less than complete obedience. Of course, there can be no comparison between the moral character of Powell, a soldier and a man of principle, and Castro, a charismatic dictator. I would simply observe that both men carried themselves with an aura of greatness. If you met either one, you would never forget him.

I met Castro in 1991 when the Soviet Union was ending its five billion dollars in annual subsidies to Cuba. The fact that Castro managed to remain in power and eventually pull Cuba out of its depression, despite the fact that the Cuban economy had shrunk by more than one-third, is a clear measure of his abilities. By 2001, George W. Bush had been elected president, and Venezuela's Hugo Chávez had revived Cuba's economy with low-priced oil. And due to the more permissive travel rules, Castro was entertaining scores of American VIPs, congressmen, senators, and movie stars, most of whom disliked the sanctions and thought that it was time for a change in US policy.

Now, eighteen months into my three-year term as the head of the US Interests Section, I thought it was time for me to visit the new US secretary of state, Colin Powell, and Otto Reich, who was awaiting a hearing on his nomination to be assistant secretary of state for the Western Hemisphere. I especially looked forward to meeting Powell, whom I had admired for many years. Since I had been appointed by the administration of President Bill Clinton, it was appropriate for the secretary to inform me of President Bush's approach to Cuba. Moreover, I had my own agenda. I wanted to tell the secretary that I believed that engagement rather than isolation represented a much more effective way of bringing change to Cuba. I wanted to obtain his blessing for a new outreach program that I had initiated and was hoping to expand with funding from the State Department.

Powell's assistant welcomed me and led me through the secretary's enormous public office, into a small private room that was Powell's inner sanctum where he escaped from the pomp and elegance required in official meetings with the world's leaders. As I entered he took my hand, and with his other hand he waved me toward a chair.

"Vicki, I have something to show you," he said as he sorted through a pile of papers on his desk. He then extracted a single sheet of paper, laid it on the copier, pushed a button, and handed me a copy of the document while smiling broadly. It was a letter from Fidel to Powell in praise of his book *My American Journey*:

Dear Mr. Powell,
You are no longer a candidate to the Presidency of the United States. Therefore I hope this note will not be of inconvenience to you. Your book was received with great interest by all of us. In record time—five days—we had it translated into Spanish by our interpreters. We have printed

only a few copies for some of our top officials. We are not planning to have an edition printed. We will respect your copyright. We would suggest that you make a quick edition of the book in our language—something that usually takes a lot of time in the case of good books in English. If in any way this text is useful, it is at your disposal. We won't charge you anything. Now that you are a free man, I hope nothing will hinder you from coming one day to Cuba to get acquainted with our country. We promise we will not put you aboard a helicopter. Please excuse the small stationery and the minute handwriting.

Greetings.

Fidel Castro—November 11th, 1995.

The letter proved Arthur Miller's point that Fidel craved human contact. General Powell, who had written his memoir after retiring as the chairman of the Joint Chiefs of Staff, didn't accept Fidel's offer of help with the Spanish translation, nor did he visit Cuba. Instead, six years later he became the American official responsible for US policies designed to defeat his erstwhile admirer. As I read the letter I realized that Castro's admiration for Powell might lend itself to a process that would result in a normalization of relations. If President Bush were willing, Powell could craft an opening with Cuba that would be similar to Secretary of State Henry Kissinger's restoration of relations with mainland China. In fact, Kissinger had envisioned that he would move on to repair relations with Cuba, but he was unable to do so when President Richard Nixon's term was cut short by impeachment. When I walked into Powell's office I had been worried that Bush might be contemplating a punitive policy toward Cuba, but with Powell's revelation of Castro's letter, I suddenly could imagine a different outcome.

Powell wanted to know what I thought about US policy and where our relations might be headed. I told him that the best way to foster change in Cuba was though contact and communications, not hostility. Economic and even political conditions in Cuba were improving, and there was more to eat and somewhat more freedom for civil society, but the state's control over every aspect of life remained pervasive. Venezuela's largess had allowed Cuba to emerge from a decade-long depression. In addition, Castro had achieved a momentous victory in securing the return of little Elián González to his father in Cuba. Castro was enjoying a surge in American visitors that had begun with the Clinton administration's liberalization of travel regulations, and I hoped it would continue under President Bush. These people-to-people visits for religious, cultural, and humanitarian purposes were forging bonds between American groups and their counterparts. American religious organizations were helping Cuban churches organize youth clubs, feed the elderly, and provide medicines for the sick. Humanitarian outreach gave Cuban surgeons a chance to learn the latest medical procedures by operating alongside their American counterparts. Cuban artists could now display their work in major American cities, and inevitably they returned to Cuba with fresh ideas and firsthand observations of our society and culture. I said that I believed that if these visits were allowed to continue, they would help build democracy at the grassroots level.

I explained to Powell that my staff and I were also promoting change in Cuba. We had created an outreach program under which we were distributing books to private libraries around the country and encouraging independent journalists by bringing them together in our homes where they could exchange ideas and safely network. I said that I hoped that he might concur in its expansion because we could reach many more people if we had more resources. Powell asked if the Cuban government would interfere. I responded that Castro didn't appreciate our—or anyone's—support of the dissidents; Fidel didn't like opposition in any form and he severely limited the flow of information to the Cuban people. In my view it was in our interests to dilute Castro's monopoly on information and expand our support to dissidents. Addressing Powell's query, I said that I didn't think that Castro would stop our efforts because he was simultaneously engaged in a charm offensive; he and other top officials were attempting to convince American visitors to end or weaken the embargo. But if the Bush administration reverted to a hostile policy and ended the people-to-people visits, Castro would not hesitate to suppress dissent, impede cooperation between American and Cuban groups, and block our outreach program.

The secretary responded, "I will help you around the flank." I was delighted and hopeful, as it seemed to me he understood that a punitive policy would not bring about change. To me it was abundantly clear that our isolationist policy, now forty years old, had failed. The embargo only enhanced the dynamics that kept Cubans poor and impeded their access to news, information, and ideas that might lead them to press for change. With the meeting over, Powell and I took his private elevator down to the first-floor lobby, where he was meeting an important visitor. As we entered the bright, open, foyer, I admired the impressive display of flags from all the countries with which we have relations. There was no Cuban flag, even though my staff and I in Havana were American diplomats.

The fiction that we had no relations with Cuba was so deep that it extended even to the State Department. Yet enormous amounts of time, money, and attention went into managing Cuban relations. The Cuba office was among the largest in the Bureau for Western Hemisphere Affairs, rivaling those of Brazil and Mexico. The US Treasury Department's Office of Foreign Assets Control had more personnel working on Cuba than on any other sanctioned country, and even USAID had a Cuba office. The 1996 Cuban Liberty and Democratic Solidarity Act, commonly called the Helms-Burton Act, had authorized assistance to individuals and groups living in Cuba.

My next meeting was with Otto Reich, who had been provided an office at the State Department while he awaited a Senate hearing that he hoped would confirm him as the assistant secretary of state for the Western Hemisphere. Reich, a pleasant looking man with excellent manners (except when confronted with opinions favorable to the Cuban Revolution), asked whether I thought that Castro's power might be weakening. I assured him that this was not the case. In my view, the Elián González debacle had allowed Castro to reinforce his power and control. Reich frowned, his visage growing red. I knew very well that conservative Cuban Americans always believed that Castro was about to fall, either from illness, loss of an ally, or an imagined uprising. But I was unwilling to perpetuate this fiction. Doing so led to demands that we tighten the embargo in order to provide the final push that would lead to the regime's fall. I thought that if Reich were to lead our policy toward Cuba, he deserved the truth. He listened as I described the outreach program. He didn't give me his opinion, possibly because he did not yet have an official position at the State Department, but he wasn't opposed.

The office that manages our Cuba policy was more problematic. I explained to the office director and his deputy that in order to expand the program, I would need additional resources and someone to manage the program. My choice was Peter Corsell, a brilliant young officer within the intelligence community whose agency had permitted him to spend several months working with me in Havana. The deputy who disapproved of the program told me that the intelligence agency that employed Corsell had rejected my proposal that he manage the outreach program. The agency, he claimed, believed that if one of their people were running outreach, Cuban security would conclude that it was a covert intelligence operation, not a State Department program. I argued unsuccessfully that Corsell effectively had been running the program for the past several months. We were at an impasse, but the director agreed he would send the proposal forward for a decision by the secretary if I could resolve the issue of who would manage the outreach program. When I returned to Havana and explained the impasse to Peter, he settled the issue by resigning his position at the intelligence agency.

Peter was a rising star among young intelligence analysts, and Cuba was his passion. I first met him when he invited me to attend a closed-door conference he had organized for policy makers and intelligence officials about Cuba and Fidel Castro. Peter had managed to convince several prominent Cuba scholars and Castro biographers to present their views to relevant US government officials across various departments and agencies. It was an excellent conference and unusual in that it brought together so many talented minds from both government and academia.

When I congratulated Peter after the event, he asked if he could work for me in Havana. I told him that I would be delighted to have him. I liked his spirit and can-do attitude. More important, he said he would be pleased to manage my new outreach program. We decided that Peter's title would be special assistant, because it would be imprudent to announce that he was in charge of a program that the Cuban government disliked. It was better to be discreet so that, at least for a while, Cuban state security wouldn't harass him.

All that remained was for the State Department to officially approve funding for the outreach program. The memo went forward not to Secretary Powell, whom I already considered an ally, but to archconservative John Bolton, undersecretary for arms control and international security. Fortunately, Bolton had heard about the project and was an enthusiastic backer. His close ties to Cuban American conservatives meant that he, like them, viewed the outreach program as a way of undermining the Castro regime's iron grip on the flow of information to the Cuban people.

Once the program had been approved, Peter reached out to leaders within the Cuban American community and convinced them of the value of our outreach program, turning them from skeptics to supporters of the US Interests Section. Historically, many in the community wanted to see the Interests Section closed because they disapproved of relations with the Cuban government. Now, for the first time, they applauded the work of our diplomats rather than accusing us of cozying up to Castro. We had become a willing and useful tool in their long struggle against the revolution. But the conflict between their views and mine simply went underground. The conservative diaspora wanted to believe that the objective of our activities was to incite revolt, while I believed that we were promoting a process that would lead to gradual and peaceful change. I was confident that undermining the regime would not work because Cuban security would sooner or later expose our efforts and jail the dissidents. It was far more effective to operate within the boundaries established by the regime, and equally subversive to give Cubans the tools to take greater control of their lives and, over time, the manner in which they were governed.

To protect the recipients I ensured that the Interest Section's outreach activities were neither clandestine nor illegal. I wanted to ensure that we did not harm the dissident community by embracing its members too tightly. They had sufficient problems without being accused of being pro-American. Therefore we were prudent in the manner in which we expanded our outreach. We placed computers in the waiting area of the consular section so visa applicants and anyone else, including the dissidents, could access the Internet from the Interests Section. We improved and expanded our assistance to libraries that were managed by civic and religious groups, as well as by dissidents, by providing more books, magazine subscriptions, and shelving. We distributed directly to independent journalists a kit that contained a tape recorder, which delighted them and likely annoyed the Cuban government, but not sufficiently to cause retaliation. We also hosted events for dissidents in our homes, helping the independent librarians and journalists to network with each other. This type of assistance would certainly not inspire any group to resort to violence. Very likely Castro understood this and that was why Cuban state security did not interfere with our efforts. Fidel had become somewhat more tolerant of dissent, but he also allowed no activities that he could not easily extinguish. If our efforts ever became dangerous to regime survival, he would shut us down either by jailing the dissidents or throwing me out of the country—and likely both.

Conservative Cuban American organizations wanted us to provide cash funding directly to the dissidents, but Senator Chris Dodd (D-MA), chairman of the Senate Foreign Relations Committee, was adamant that we not cross that line. He feared that if we did so the Cuban government would claim that their opponents were being "paid" by our government and accuse them of treason. In addition, critics of our outreach program would claim that such funding would prove that the dissidents were simply our pawns. Prudently, we did not fund the dissidents, but we did fund a few civic projects for religious organizations, which were unlikely to be jeopardized by receiving our money.

The USAID assistance program was equally benign and managed separately from the outreach program. During the years in which I was in charge of the US Interests Section (1999–2002), the USAID program was principally carried out by small, Miami-based nongovernmental organizations that were managed by Cuban Americans. Their main activities were distributing medicines, used clothing, sports equipment, and household items to the Cuban people, many of whom had friends and families in Miami. David Mutchler, a USAID officer, looked after this Cuban American cottage industry that benefited the diaspora as much as it helped the Cuban people. If the Cuban government had considered USAID's program a threat, Mutchler would have been denied a visa, thus preventing him from visiting Cuba. I believe that the Cuban government tolerated the aid program because it lessened the poverty among recipients without challenging the government's control. The goods provided by the USAID contractors were brought into Cuba by "mules"—members of the Cuban diaspora who were paid to deliver them. The program had limited impact, and it certainly wasn't directed toward inciting internal revolt. The Cuban government simply ignored it, and even the dissidents had their complaints. Marta Beatriz Roque, a major dissident, once snapped, "We aren't beggars, we don't need your castoffs."

After the September 11, 2001, terrorist attacks on the United States, Castro unexpectedly reached out to the Bush administration. Cuba offered medical assistance, including blood and health care brigades, as well as intelligence on terrorists. While the Bush administration did not accept these offers of assistance, we appreciated the newly cooperative attitude displayed by the Cubans. Another positive sign was that the Bush administration did not retaliate against Cuba when a senior Defense Intelligence Agency official, Ana Belén Montes, was revealed to have been spying for Cuba. It was likely because they were distracted with much larger issues that followed the September 11 attacks.

The arrest of Belén Montes resolved the mystery dubbed Spidey at the US Interests Section. Every night for several months, US government temporary duty personnel—I called them night watchers—slept in one of the Interests Section's vault-like offices to ensure that our building was not penetrated by a Cuban spy. In my opinion, this was a pointless exercise. I told the intelligence agencies that it was impossible for anyone to enter the Interests Section due to the marine guards and cameras that monitored the building day and night, as well as the heavy combination safe doors guarding the entrances to rooms where classified materials were kept. When one of the night watchers suffered an emotional breakdown and was discovered curled up in the bathtub of her room at the Hotel Riviera I decided that enough was enough. I told the intelligence agencies that it was ridiculous to imagine that someone might crawl up the glass facade like Spider-Man, pry open a window, and slip into the Interests Section. My suggestion to end the night watcher program was summarily rejected. The intelligence community was clearly worried about some unknown vulnerability at the Interests Section.

Nevertheless, I suggested that the night watchers not be lodged at the Hotel Riviera, where the woman had had her breakdown. I knew from personal experience that the Riviera was heavily penetrated with all manner of Cuban security. On my first visit to Havana, ten years earlier, I had arrived at the Riviera to find state security loitering by the reception desk. It was clear to me, even though I was new to Cuba, that these men in white Guayaberas (the popular Cuban shirt) worked for the Ministry of the Interior and that their assignment was to monitor foreign guests—especially American officials. They stood alone or in pairs, most of them smoking, all keeping an eye on my every move. Matters deteriorated further as I walked off the elevator that had stopped and started at every floor. A man scurried down the darkened hall, and when I stepped into my room it reeked of cigarette smoke. Two shabby pictures were lopsided, and I suspected that behind them were listening devices. What I disliked most about this experience was the attempt to intimidate me by making it clear that I was being watched.

Ten minutes later I slipped down the back stairway where cement had been gouged out of the walls, perhaps from decay or an attempt to conceal the heavy black wires that drooped over the stairwell. I took a taxi to Old Havana, where I checked in at the newly renovated Hotel Inglaterra, located next to the Gran Teatro de la Habana and a few blocks from the Museo de la Revolución, which featured the cabin cruiser *Granma*, in which Fidel and his rebels had sailed to Cuba in 1956 to reignite their revolution. Not long after I had settled in, I got a call from a friend who warned me that the hotel had connected and reconnected his call several times. He concluded, "Vicki, I think you are being monitored." I laughed and told him that Cuban state security had undoubtedly caught up with me.

In the Spidey case it turned out that Cuban state security was not the culprit. There was no Cuban spy who climbed the Interests Section's walls in the dark of night. Rather, Belén Montes, the senior US intelligence official, was the culprit. I suspect that she betrayed her country for love of Fidel and the revolution, because she did not receive any money for her crimes.

Castro's offer of assistance and cooperation after the 9/11 tragedy must have impressed Washington because, in response to my urging, the State Department offered Cuba assistance after Hurricane Michelle, the strongest storm in nearly fifty years to strike the island. The hurricane made landfall at the Bay of Pigs on November 3, 2001, and then raged across the breadth of the island, ravaging Pinar del Rio, Havana, and Cayo Coco. Over 590,000 tourists, students, and residents were evacuated, 150,000 of them in and around Havana. The Category 4 storm severely damaged the sugarcane crop, Cuba's principal export, and destroyed property, but few were killed due to the island's extraordinary program of emergency response. The most dilapidated buildings along the Malecón came down, but Eusebio Leal Spangler's restoration saved Habana Vieja. Ultimately, Venezuela's oil subsidies saved Cuba from bankruptcy. Chávez allowed Castro to postpone payments for Venezuelan petroleum and over time almost doubled Cuba's subsidized oil from fifty-three thousand barrels to ninety thousand barrels. In return, Castro raised the number of Cuban advisers and experts serving in Venezuela from twenty thousand to forty thousand.

As the New Year approached, it seemed that 2002 might be the moment to grasp the hand that Castro was offering. Over the past year, both countries had benefited from a more positive relationship. There was no longer any chance that hard times would lead Cubans to rebel and neither would our outreach or assistance programs. The country had survived eight years on its own from 1991, when it lost Soviet subsidies, until the advent of Chávez's largess in 1999. Cuba had ceased supporting revolutions abroad and, as far as I was concerned, was only kept on the State Department's list of state sponsors of terrorism for domestic political reasons as a sop to Cuban Americans. The American people were in favor of normalizing our relationship with Cuba, and it felt like the time had come to further loosen our policy from the captive snares of the Cuban diaspora.

If President Bush continued to allow this less threatening approach, it could lead to more political freedom and space for dissent and civil society on the island. Over time the Cuban government might even become more pragmatic and open to economic, if not political, reform. (I did not imagine that the regime was then or is now in any danger of dissolution.) Thus, an opening with Cuba might be achieved, especially since there was one man in the United States who had the credibility with Castro that could lead to a new more positive relationship. That man was Secretary of State Colin Powell.

CHAPTER 10

HAVANA, MY AFGHAN HOUND

SOME YEARS AFTER I LEFT CUBA, RICARDO ALARCÓN, CASTRO'S point man for all things American, said that except for my Afghan hound and my "little radios," I had been a good envoy. It struck me as an amazing admission that a hound dog and the hundreds of small AM/FM/shortwave radios that we had distributed to the Cuban people had unsettled Fidel Castro and the Cuban government! It seemed to me proof that had Cuban Americans engaged rather than isolated Castro, they might have helped unravel the revolution. Humor can be a powerful tool in exposing the follies and foibles of a leader to his citizens, just as Hans Christian Andersen's short tale *The Emperor's New Clothes* reveals. The emperor in Andersen's story walks through the streets naked believing he is resplendent in a magnificent suit until a child exclaims, "He isn't wearing anything at all." Like the emperor, Fidel's advisers refused to criticize him for fear that they might appear stupid or lose their jobs. But I did openly criticize Fidel, becoming one of the few people who ever publicly challenged or poked fun at Cuba's emperor.

This is the story of how my Afghan hound, Havana, her Afro-Cuban trainer Ana Maria González, and I made Castro look foolish and back down. I named my hound Havana because she was beautiful, like the city for whom she was named. Fidel would later claim that I had insulted Havana, the city, by doing so, but that was just sour grapes. I don't believe Fidel cared much for either Havana, since he allowed the city to fall into such disrepair during his long reign. In any case, it wasn't an insult. Fidel would treat both Havanas—the city and the hound—badly and later make amends. He eventually pardoned my hound and belatedly began to restore the city.

Amid the national upheaval that followed the revolution, gangsters and celebrities—like actress Rita Hayworth and her husband Prince Aly Khan, vanished along with Havana's elites. But dog shows and vintage cars remained, providing proud owners and admirers with reminders of stolen pleasures. Cubans loved their show dogs, almost as much as the old American cars they tenderly coddled through the decades. Everyone who has visited Cuba has either seen or ridden in a beautifully restored or still broken-down 1950s Buick, Chevrolet, or other vintage car, which often serve as taxicabs for foreign visitors. But few have seen Havana's international dog shows, complete with judges, ribbons, and Afghan hounds. A few show dog owners come from abroad, but most participants are Cubans from Havana and a few from Camaguey and Pinar del Rio. They often proudly show their dogs on a large vacant lot alongside the Malecón, which is only partially hidden by a low wall whose blue and white paint has long-ago worn away.

My hound, thanks to her trainer, Ana Maria, was a star in Havana's dog shows until I received a letter from Amalia Castro, president of the Cuban Afghan Hound Association. (I never learned whether she was related to Fidel, but I doubt it.) It began "Distinguida Señora Vicky [sic] Huddleston," and proceeded to tell me that my membership in the Afghan Hound Association had been canceled (my best translation of darle de baja). Amalia claimed that I was unworthy of membership because of my government's and my hostility and transgressions, which were enumerated as inviting dissidents to my home, the official residence of the chief of the American diplomatic mission in Cuba, and briefing professors and students who had visited Cuba as part of the Semester at Sea program. The letter concluded, "You should understand that your government's and your actions are incompatible with the morale of the Afghan Hound Association."

I had been booted out of a dog club for incompatibility with its morale! Only in Cuba could such a bizarre incident occur. It made no sense whatsoever—that is, it made no sense if taken at face value, but politically it made all the sense in the world. Amalia, possibly Fidel, and certainly the security services thought that they could punish me without leaving fingerprints. They knew that I loved my dog and was protective of her Cuban trainer, Ana Maria. But to their dismay, I was neither angry nor intimidated. I thought the letter was hilarious and should be shared with the public. The office of Cuban affairs, contacted Al Kamen who penned the *Washington Post*'s "In the Loop" column that shares rumors about government officials. He wrote, "The Cuban Regime has gone as low as you can go in communist dogma. Huddleston got a letter yesterday—in the midst of the popular Westminster Kennel Club televised competition, no less—that she and Havana were being expelled from the Afghan hound club of Cuba. Guess if they can't kick Huddleston, they'll try to kick her dog. Hmmm, wonder if her counterpart here, Fernando Remirez, has a dog?"

This set off a minor international media frenzy riddled with canine metaphors. The *Miami Herald* reported that Charles Shapiro, the director of Cuban Affairs, told them, "We will not retaliate against the (Chief of the Cuban Interests Section) Remírez's dog, I'm not going to stoop so low as to sniff around that one." And the same day, February 13, 2001, Agence France-Presse picked up the scent: "The United States snarled Tuesday at Cuban attempts at doggie diplomacy, branding as 'Orwellian' the ouster of Washington's envoy from a Havana canine club." The State Department spokesman said, "I guess we would say that it's unfortunate that the Cuban government would even kick Ambassador Huddleston's dog." A smiling senior official—probably Secretary of State Colin Powell—pointed out, "We've always known that Castro's bark is worse than his bite." We were on a roll. The State Department was enjoying having a chance to pull Cuba's chain. NPR's *Morning Edition* host Renee Montagne wanted to know, "Why are there Afghan hounds in Cuba? I mean, they're long-haired show dogs. Isn't the very idea of a show dog rather counterrevolutionary?" I slipped my diplomatic leash, telling her, "Well, I hope so. I would welcome a little counterrevolutionary activity in Cuba."

Karen DeYoung in an article, *Message Sent Via Diplomatic Pooch*, captured perfectly my intent to tease Castro, she wrote, "Relations between Cuba and the United States have been frosty for more than forty years, but a new bilateral low is always just around the corner. First there was the Cuban revolution and all the nasty things they said about us. Then the embargo, and those Soviet nuclear missiles. Castro assassination attempts. Cuba shoot-down of civilian aircraft. Elián González. This month's nadir came when the leadership of the Cuban National Afghan Association—that the longhaired canines, not the turbaned South Asians—kicked the top American diplomat in Havana, an ardent Afghan, lover and owner, out of their club. Yesterday, the Americans retaliated with the weapon most readily at hand—ridicule.

It was a shaggy dog story that had grown legs, if not paws. Havana and I were featured on ABC and Univision, and stories about Havana (the dog) were in hundreds of local newspapers across the United States, proving that there is nothing as good as a woman-bites-dog story. Plus, it provided amusing insights into life in Cuba, giving me an opportunity to poke fun at the regime and share stories about how restricted life in Cuba is for everyone, including diplomats. But I expressed doubt that this was an intergovernmental spat, pointing out that, as far as I knew, Amalia Castro was upset because my dog Havana was beating out her hounds in the dog show competition.

Undoubtedly realizing that he had been outperformed, Fidel decided to curb the negative publicity. He did so by grandly announcing to a visiting former US military general that "I'm going to give her husband's dog a pardon." He couldn't quite bring himself to admit that he was pardoning *my* hound, not my husband's. The next morning, Dagoberto Rodríguez Barrera, Cuba's director of North American affairs, called to officially confirm the pardon. Fidel Castro, the president of Cuba and the first secretary of the Cuban Communist Party, had pardoned the American envoy's Afghan hound!

A few days later the villainous Amalia Castro and the six-person board of the Afghan Hound Association sent me a letter that read, "It has come to our attention through the international foreign media that there has been a distortion of the letter sent to you. . . . We wish to clarify that at no point in the letter did we talk about expulsion . . . rather, this was a matter of patriotism." This meant that only *I* had been expelled—not the lovely Havana! Still, Amalia conceded that Havana had been "slandered," and, "We wish to pay an homage of amends to the beautiful and exemplary daughter of Hassan [Havana's sire]." Asked for a reaction, the State Department spokesman said, "Woof, woof."

Havana's tale was also a story about her trainer, Ana Maria, whose keen intelligence and Afro-Cuban heritage had brought her to the attention of the government when she was young. Identified as a promising student and potential loyalist, she was sent to school on the Isla de Juventud (Island of Youth) where Castro built schools for foreign students. Each block-like structure housed five hundred students from foreign countries, among them Ethiopia, Namibia, South Africa, and the Soviet Union. Fidel had a special interest in the island because he and the survivors of the aborted attack on the 1953 Moncada Barracks had once been imprisoned there for nineteen months. At that time it was known as the Isla de Pinos for its large pine trees. There, among the many foreign students, Ana Maria learned to throw the javelin and qualified for a scholarship to study computers at Patrice Lumumba University outside Moscow.

Ana Maria and other Afro-Cubans had benefited from the government's efforts to improve the lives of its black population by providing educational opportunities. Nevertheless, Cuban society remains highly attuned to color. All shades of Cubans live together in the same apartment buildings and housing projects, and there is considerable intermarriage among them, but prejudice remains. Cubans describe each other by the shade of their skin and whether they have curly or straight hair. They will draw two fingers across their wrist to indicate—without having to say it—that someone is black. Habaneros generally look down on darker skinned Cubans from the east. There are only a few blacks in the top ranks of the Council of Ministers, and high-level political leaders in Cuba are mostly lighter skinned.

Blacks are generally poorer then lighter-skinned Cubans. I never met an Afro-Cuban who owned a show dog; to feed, groom, and train a purebred hound, an owner had to be sufficiently well-off. Ana Maria couldn't afford the care of a show dog on her wage of about twelve dollars (in Cuban pesos) per month. She had been raised in one of Havana's poorer barrios and would have never left the small house she shared with her mother, far from the center of the city, had she not been extremely ambitious and courageous.

Ana Maria aspired to a better life and was willing to take big risks to get it. A dog whisperer, she demonstrated her uncanny ability to train police dogs before moving on to show dogs. When I met Ana Maria, her clients included the owners of Havana's sire, Alina and Jaime, as well as a colonel at the Ministry of the Interior. Working for me initially changed Ana Maria's life for the better. I introduced her to the Swiss ambassador and another American diplomat who both paid her in dollars for training their dogs. This arrangement made Ana Maria rich by Cuban standards, leading her to quit her job as a computer technician with an Italian firm that paid her in pesos. The only downside of working for me was that Cuban state security—the Ministry of the Interior—did not approve. Within a week, state security stopped and questioned Ana Maria. This was standard practice for any Cuban who dared associate with me.

Alina and Jaime had been questioned after they were seen talking with me at the Jose Martí International Airport. I had been fascinated with their beautiful Afghan, Hassan, and I asked them to contact me if they had a litter in the future. In typical Cuban entrepreneurial fashion Alina had brought Hassan to the airport hoping to find a foreigner with dollars who wanted to buy puppies. They called the next day to offer me a puppy for two hundred dollars, which was a good deal for me but a significant sum for a Cuban. They also asked me why state security had stopped and questioned them. I told them who I was and explained that security officials not only followed me but questioned Cubans who came in contact with me. I assured them I would buy a puppy and asked if they could recommend a trainer, which was how Ana Maria and Havana became part of my life.

Ana Maria followed my advice and answered state security's questions honestly; there was nothing she could tell them that my Cuban household staff had not already divulged. A few weeks later I asked Ana Maria to stay at the residence to care for Havana while I traveled around the island with my family. A day or two after I departed, security officers picked her up in the narrow back alley between my house and Castro's fortified residence that doubles as a military barracks. I suspected the security officers were annoyed because Ana Maria's presence in the house while I was away would have prevented them from checking or installing listening and video devices. They warned her not to return to the residence. Fearing to leave Havana with no one to look after her, she disobeyed them and returned to the residence to collect Havana and take her to her own home. It was brave of Ana Maria to defy state security. I was grateful, but they were not pleased.

Ana Maria's life was changing fast. This was her chance to have a champion dog and make a decent living. She asked me to register Havana in both our names, believing that if she were a co-owner the organizers could not exclude Havana from the dog shows simply because she belonged to me, the regime's number one enemy on the island. Ana

Maria was wise to suspect that the dog show hierarchy might use the fact that I owned Havana as an excuse to rid itself of the competition. But she also had another problem: the more time she spent training Havana the unhappier state security became. What they disliked was her continual presence in the residence. The other staff was thoroughly vetted and provided to me through the state employment agency. Ministry of the Interior officials likely feared that Ana Maria, a keen observer of humans as well as dogs, would inform me of who among the staff was an informant. Moreover, Ana Maria set a bad example for the staff, because she could come and go as she wished, and it was becoming increasingly clear that she neither feared nor respected the state security agents. I worried that a confrontation was coming, but was surprised by the cleverness of the attack—I was informed by the Ministry of Foreign Affairs that I had illegally hired Ana Maria and that she would have to immediately leave the job. It was true that I had not hired her through the state employment agency, which provides Cuban workers to all foreign entities, embassies, and hotels—but had instead hired her directly. I also paid her in dollars, which was another infraction of the rules.

Ana Maria was a fighter. She liked her new life and the opportunities it offered. As co-owner of the lovely Havana, this was her big chance to have a prized show dog and perhaps one day realize her dream of becoming a renowned trainer. Determined not to lose this opportunity, Ana Maria obtained the list of jobs that the government has authority to fill, and dog trainer was not among them. She gleefully shared the news with me: I now had a good excuse to reject the government's order to fire her. I invited Dagoberto, the Cuban official with whom I usually dealt on all but the most sensitive issues, to lunch so I could argue our case. I pointed out that Ana Maria worked for the Swiss ambassador and another American diplomat, so she should be able to work for me. He remained unconvinced. Then I made Ana Maria's point that dog trainer was not included among the jobs that the government alone was authorized to fill. Dagoberto, a reasonable man who stuck closely to the rules, was impressed with this argument. He conceded that for the time being Ana Maria could continue to work for me.

As a result of working for me, Ana Maria began to see the Cuban government through my eyes. Although she was apolitical, she happily sought out opportunities to exercise her independence that would test but not actually provoke the authorities. Until she met me she had no idea that there were dissidents, learning about them only when I advised her to stay away from the house because I didn't want her to be associated with a lunch I was hosting for independent journalists. She was impressed that I would stand up to the Cuban government because no one on the island did so without suffering severe consequences. There were also consequences for me, but they weren't severe because I was a diplomat and a foreigner, a fact that Ana Maria sometimes forgot when she rebelled. Although Ana Maria was as defiant as the dissidents, she wasn't interested in publicly protesting the government. Her desire was simply to act independently, but in Cuba that often meant confronting the government, whose expectations were that every individual would behave in accordance with established norms. Ana Maria wanted to emulate my willingness to ignore the petty rules and do as she wished, but I had the power of the US government behind me, and she did not.

Ana Maria couldn't resist making sure that her competitors knew that she worked for the *jefa* (chief) of the US Interests Section. She delighted in bringing my husband Bob or me to the dog shows, if for no other reason than to introduce us to the colonel who owned Havana's sister and to Amalia Castro, the president of the Afghan Hound Association. It is hard to say to what degree our problems originated with state security, the colonel who feared even to shake hands with me, or Amalia. The colonel and Amalia were unhappy that Havana took prizes away from their Afghan hounds. And state security resented the fact that I had outmaneuvered them and continued to employ Ana Maria, who clearly had no respect for them.

Ana Maria provided me with all manner of insights into Cuban life. With her at my side, I could pass for a *Cubana* so long as I kept quiet so no one would hear my American accent. We walked all over the city with Havana, around El Laguito, the upscale prerevolutionary housing development where Elián González's family had lived for a time, and through popular barrios on the other side of Havana Bay. We struck up conversations with kids who wanted to pet Havana and with people sitting in parks. I saw how difficult life was for most Cubans, who despite having little hope for the future could always make fun of themselves and their leader—without mentioning his name, of course.

Life was tough even for the dog owners. On one occasion, dogs and their owners from Camaguey arrived wet and bedraggled for the show. They had all endured a long rainy day sitting in the back of a flatbed truck. Transportation was scarce for everyone, but especially those who were accompanied by large dogs. Even the Ministry of the Interior colonel had difficulties. His hound, a beautiful silver-gray Afghan, had become increasingly aggressive. In Ana Maria's opinion, the problem was that he kept her locked up in a windowless room. His home was small and he didn't have the resources to pay someone to walk the dog regularly, but he wasn't about to give up his prizewinning dog. Everyone, from the Afghan owners in Camaguey to the colonel, Amalia, and Ana Maria enjoyed presenting their dogs to the judges from Canada, Mexico, and Spain. It was an adventure, an escape from a life of prescribed monotony.

It seemed as if Ana Maria's dream might come true. The champion dogs, including Havana, were invited to represent Cuba at an international dog show in Mexico City. Ana Maria applied and received a passport, but then she was denied an exit visa. Ana Maria suspected that Amalia had intervened with the authorities, recommending that Ana Maria not be allowed to travel to Mexico with the others. After all, it would be embarrassing if the Cuban champion turned out to be Havana, a hound owned by the top American official in Cuba.

I was not a good role model for Ana Maria. I got away with confronting the Cuban hierarchy, ignoring various rules, and supporting the dissidents. The more Ana Maria accompanied me, the more daring she became. State security was becoming increasingly annoyed. One of her offenses occurred when I returned from the United States with a new very short haircut. Seeing someone who looked like my daughter, Alexandra, who had short hair, driving the official car, my minders, who were never far away, ran their little white Lada right up next to the official sedan, which I was driving. As they began taking photographs, which presumably they would use to blackmail me for breaking my government's rules by allowing my daughter to drive the car, I turned and looked at them. Shocked to see me, not my daughter, they quickly stowed their cameras and dropped back, but not before seeing Ana Maria, who was sitting in the passenger seat, heartily laughing at them for their mistake.

My transgressions were adding up. I had broken into a meeting of senior officials at the airport, held an alternative art exhibit during the Biennial, and was carrying out an increasingly aggressive outreach program to assist the dissidents. No Cuban, least of all one that had the audacity to laugh at them, should be allowed to associate with me. I had no doubt that my minders were fed up.

Thus, shortly after the embarrassing media spectacle during which Fidel was compelled to "pardon" Havana, Ana Maria was informed that she would have to submit to an *acto de repudio* (act of repudiation), a humiliating event that is usually only used by the regime against dissidents. Ana Maria would be forced to sit and listen while her fellow association members enumerated and criticized her presumed faults. The event was similar to a tribunal pronouncing a prison sentence for a counterrevolutionary.

Ana Maria always had an abundance of courage, but now she

feared she would never again be allowed to train dogs. If she could not follow her passion, she would be miserable and left without a source of income. Her friends would fear to support her, lest they also be subject to retaliation. I, too, was shaken. Dissidents who were subjected to an *acto de repudio* were spit on and beaten up; a poet had been made to eat her poetry and dragged down the stairs of her apartment building. The regime claimed that these were spontaneous events organized by neighbors who were disgusted with antisocial behavior. Although Ana Maria's shaming would likely not be violent, the consequences would be disastrous. She would be humiliated, intimidated, isolated, and never allowed to show dogs again. She would also never be able to work in an official job and would in several respects become a nonperson.

I was furious. I couldn't let this happen, especially because I felt responsible. I called Dagoberto, who by now was probably doing his best to forget he had anything to do with the embarrassing Afghan hound incident. I told him that if the Cuban government wanted to fight a second round, I was ready and willing. I would inform the international press corps about the proposed *acto de repudio* and would make sure they understood that Ana Maria was being targeted as a scapegoat. I reminded Dagoberto that I had made clear to the media that the original incident was not government sponsored; however, if the government was going to punish Ana Maria, I would make sure the media knew that the Cuban government treats its own people worse than dogs. Dagoberto did not have to check with his bosses; he assured me that there would be no *acto de repudio*. Ana Maria and Havana returned to the ring and won even more ribbons. But after I left Cuba, Ana Maria had no protection and state security struck again. They attempted to revoke the exit visa she had recently obtained for a visit to the United States. Without a second thought, she boarded a plane to the United States before the order went into effect.

Today Ana Maria is an American citizen, but leaving Cuba was not easy. She made a difficult choice, as do tens of thousands of Cubans each year. She left because she justifiably feared she would be marginalized, barred from her profession, and unable to find employment. Far too many Cubans face the same difficult choice. Some, like Ana Maria, flee because they fear persecution and marginalization, but most leave in search of better lives.

In order to provide a legal way to immigrate to the States as well as reunite families and protect those who are persecuted, an INS refugee processing center in Havana provided refugee visas to those who qualified. Many of those who successfully applied were internally displaced rebels and their families who had fought against the revolution until the mid-1960s. After their victory, the government forcibly relocated these rebels from Trinidad, a town in the verdant mountainous region near Cienfuegos, to encampments in flat, hot, and dry western Cuba. On a road trip to the western tip of the island, I saw the chain-link fences that surrounded these communities. Over thirty years later, these former rebels and their children were still kept segregated, though perhaps a better word would be *imprisoned*. But most Cubans are neither refugees like the displaced and abused former rebels nor part of the dissident community.

The consular section issued immigrant visas for those who were not refugees, if they were fortunate enough to either win a spot in the international or special Cuba visa lottery or have close relatives in the United States. Otherwise they must decide whether to flee or remain in Cuba. The Wet Foot–Dry Foot policy which allowed Cubans who made it to US soil remain in the States, tempted Cubans to attempt the hazardous journey across the Florida Straits in an unsafe vessel or pay a smuggler with a fast boat. Using a smuggler, who was often paid several thousand dollars by a relative in Miami, was generally safer and more likely to succeed. But there were no guarantees; some migrants are killed, abandoned by the smuggler, or never make it to the border, where then can declare themselves Cuban and freely enter the United States.

I did not agree with the United States' Wet Foot–Dry Foot policy because it encouraged Cubans to risk their lives. Those who managed to reach US soil could remain, but those who were intercepted at sea by the US Coast Guard often suffered even greater troubles once back in Cuba. Despite promising that it would not retaliate, the Cuban government always fired returned migrants from their jobs in the tourist industry, using as an excuse the fact that they had left their job without giving notice. Others were harassed and jailed; some relief was provided by the 1994 migration agreement, which allowed the US Interests Section to periodically check on those whom the Coast Guard brought back to Cuba.

I joined our consul general, Patty Murphy, on one of her visits to check on the condition of returned migrants. In the beach town of Varadero, we climbed the stairs to a second-floor apartment that by Cuban standards was quite comfortable, with large windows, a living room, a kitchen, and a bathroom. The mother of a young woman who had left in a small boat, told us that her daughter was too much of a "free spirit" to acclimate to life in Cuba—another Ana Maria. Even as a schoolgirl she had questioned the rules and rebelled against authority. Her mother had tried to persuade her to soften her outspoken views and independent ways. The neighborhood committee boss labeled her a troublemaker, removing the option of attending college or landing a job in one of the hotels reserved for foreign tourists. With little hope of a happy life, she tried to reach the United States. The attempt failed, and the US Coast Guard returned her and others picked up at sea to the Cuban port of Mariel. Home again, she found that she had become a marked woman: security personnel and government loyalists mocked and harassed her constantly. Her mother begged us to help her reach the United States because she had no future in Cuba. Just as we were leaving, we met the daughter, a tall, slender woman who was deeply unhappy. My heart went out to her. She was unconventional and outspoken, and I completely understood her inability to lead a productive life within the highly restrictive Cuban system. Having once tried and failed to escape to a new life, her only option would be to try again. If she had relatives in Miami who were willing to hire a smuggler, she would probably make it to Florida. If she tried again to leave in an unsafe boat, her odds of success would be considerably reduced. There was a good chance that she would again be intercepted and returned, or that she might lose her life. I told her that she could apply for refugee status but that she was unlikely to be approved because she did not belong to a human rights group and had never been jailed. I would have liked to have done more, but not even the principal officer could interfere in the issuance of visas.

Typical of those who found themselves without a legal way to emigrate was a bare-chested young man in cutoff jeans who was standing on the roof of a one-story house where he had built his own small shelter. He didn't come down, so I yelled to him, "Is everything all right?"

"I have tried twenty times and I will try again," he replied. "I have nothing here."

For two returnees in Matanzas, a large coastal town east of Havana, life was demonstrably better. The couple lived in a nice home with an expensive stereo system and large television, which they had purchased with money sent to them by relatives in Miami. Still, they thought life would be better in La Yuma—the United States—and were committed to trying again.

There is also the desolation of those family members left behind. In Cárdenas we visited a white-haired woman, thin and sad, in a faded gray gown. She invited us into her dilapidated living room, which must have once been lovely with a high ceiling and long windows with wooden shutters. The room had only two chairs, a small table with uneven legs, and no rugs on the worn hardwood floor. The ceiling fan had stopped working long ago. With the shutters closed to keep out the heat, the room was dark and silent. Over time the woman's entire family had deserted her for Miami. Once they left, she never heard from them again. Perhaps they forgot about her or were lost at sea. Alone, with no means of support, she sold off her furniture and personal possessions while she waited for news, or a visit, or change, or death.

Too often those who leave—especially those who left in the sixties and seventies—break contact and faith with those left behind. Some of the early migrants, the best educated and most successful, blame those who stayed behind for not deposing Castro. But I think these Cuban Americans are naive. How could those left behind confront an authoritarian regime with a world-class military and neighborhood block committees that monitor the lives of every citizen, jailing dissenters and even young men for minor infractions?

In addition to those who fled Cuba because they were persecuted, dejected, or wanted a better life, there were political defectors who worked for the government but had become disillusioned over time. Orestes Lorenzo Pérez trained as a MiG pilot in the Soviet Union, where he became disenchanted with the communist system. In March 1991 he flew his MiG-23 Flogger, the newest among Cuba's Soviet aircraft, to the US Naval Station in Key West, Florida. One of the US jet pilots that had been scrambled to intercept the intruder exclaimed, "My God, there is a Soviet MiG in the landing pattern!" A week later, we allowed a Cuban pilot to fly the MiG back to its base in San Antonio de los Banos. (The intelligence community kept the MiG's black box for another month, after which I returned it to the chief of the Cuban Interests Section.)

I got to know Orestes when he visited the State Department to ask if we would issue visas to his wife Vicky and their two children. I told him I would gladly arrange for their visas, but that the Cuban government would never allow them leave. He was stunned. He could not imagine that the government would retaliate against his family. After waiting a year, he borrowed an old Cessna and flew it to Cuba. Although he narrowly missed colliding with a truck as he landed on the coastal highway about thirty minutes outside Havana, Orestes managed to evade Cuba's air defenses. His waiting family climbed into the little Cessna, and Orestes flew them safely to the United States, evading the Cuban Air Force once again upon departure. It was a truly amazing story.

The tragedy for Cuba is that so many of its citizens want to leave so badly that they are literally willing to risk their lives to escape. Of course, it would be better if they remained on the island and attempted to change the conditions that compel them to leave, but their actions are understandable because our immigration policy at the time encouraged them to risk the journey, and they preferred to risk their lives rather than provoke the Castro government.

CHAPTER 11

THE BEST OF ENEMIES: GUANTANAMO NAVAL BASE

IDEL CASTRO ONCE DECLARED THAT "GUANTANAMO BASE IS A DAGGER plunged into the heart of Cuba." Castro never reconciled himself to what he perceived as the US occupation of Cuban territory, but he was also wise enough not to directly attempt to dislodge the United States. Since the early 1990s, so-called fence-line talks between the United States and Cuba have led to mutually cooperative military relations that have benefited both countries. Still, the Castro regime longs to regain the territory over which Cuba retains "ultimate sovereignty," yet cannot exercise that sovereignty so long as the Treaty of 1934, which superseded the Treaty of 1903, provides the United States "complete jurisdiction and control" over the land on which the base is situated. The US government agreed to pay Cuba two thousand gold coins annually for use of the base, an amount that has been determined to amount to the modest sum of $4,085. Since taking power in 1959, neither Fidel nor Raúl Castro has ever cashed the annual checks delivered by the US government. The treaty also stipulates that the territory on which the base is situated will only be returned to Cuban jurisdiction when either both governments consent to its return or the United States abandons the facility. It is this provision that has allowed the US military to occupy the territory for well over one hundred years.

Guantanamo Naval Reservation, often referred to as Guantanamo

Bay or in more recent years just Gitmo, is located along Cuba's south-eastern coast, forty-eight miles from Santiago de Cuba, where the US Navy destroyed the Spanish Fleet on July 3, 1898. Protected by the Cuzco Hills and encircled by two mountain ranges, the Sierra Maestra in the west and the Sierra del Maguey in the east, the deepwater port at Guantanamo Bay consists of forty-five miles of land and sea, shaped like a figure eight, of which the United States occupies the lower half and Cuba controls the upper half.

Guantanamo Bay exemplifies the contradictions and myths of US-Cuba relations. Despite the widespread belief—or myth—that we have sovereignty over the naval base, we do not. The US presence in Guantanamo Bay contradicts our general practice because it is the only military base in the world that we occupy over the objections of the host government. I saw this contradiction firsthand when, in the early 1990s, I watched as a freighter flying the Soviet Hammer and Sickle steamed through the waters of the base on its way to the Cuban town of Caimanera, which is situated in the upper half of Guantanamo Bay.

In the early years of the revolution Castro planted eight miles of opuntia cactus along the northeast perimeter, dubbing his creation the Cactus Curtain. He also created one of the largest minefields in the world, thereby isolating the US naval base from the rest of Cuba. During the Cold War, the Cuban Frontier Brigade yelled obscenities at US Marines, who in turn "mooned" the Cuban soldiers from a watchtower that overlooks Cuban territory. Just in case the mines and the Cactus Curtain were insufficient to keep the two enemies apart, two large gun emplacements containing ten to fifteen M198 howitzers prevented any movement into or out of the base. The current state of the bilateral relationship was reflected by the proximity of the towed artillery that would be moved closer when US-Cuban rhetoric spiked.

When the Soviet Union broke apart, ending the Cold War, the United States scaled down its military presence in Guantanamo Bay. The US Navy ceased using the offshore waters for target practice and closed the aerial bombing range on the leeward side of the base. Gitmo's principal function of overhauling naval vessels ended with the repair of the USS *Stark*, which had been severely damaged by two Exocet missiles fired by an Iraqi aircraft in 1987. At that point Gitmo might have been decommissioned with the overall realignment of US military bases, but the Cuban American community objected. Leaders of the community understood that the territory would revert to Cuba if it were no longer used as a military base and deemed it an unwarranted gift to Castro.

In 1992 the base commander, W.C. McCamy, Jr., invited me to speak at his change-of-command ceremony. He had successfully managed the refugee camps set up on the base to temporarily house thirty thousand Haitian migrants, who had fled their country after President Jean-Bertrand Aristide was deposed by a military coup d'état. With the migrant camps closed and the Haitians returned to Haiti, the captain was moving on to his next command post. This was my first visit to Gitmo, and it gave me an opportunity both to learn about the base's operations and assess its security.

As I toured the base with my escort, a navy captain from Norfolk Naval Station Virginia, I began to realize that Gitmo was vulnerable to being overrun by Cubans. Several times a year, desperate Cubans attempted to cross the minefields or even swim across the shark-infested narrow strait between the upper and lower bay, and occasionally someone would fly a small airplane onto the base. Since those who successfully gained entry to the base were few in number, they were quietly sent up to the United States. But the vulnerability that concerned us did not arise from these attempts to enter the base by swimming or flying; rather, the threat emanated from those who might walk into the base through the Northeast Gate.

Conceivably, Castro could provoke a mass migration by removing his guards from the entrance to the mile-long path that led to the Northeast Gate. Only a handful of Cuban workers, who for years had walked to work at the base, were allowed past the military post. But if the Cuban military closed the checkpoint, any Cuban who wished to flee the country could walk down the path to the Northeast Gate, the only land entrance to the base. Finding it closed they would likely gather outside rather than returning to the highlands behind the base. As more and more Cubans walked down the path, they would be stuck in an in-hospitable no-man's-land surrounded by mines and cactus plants. Blocked from entering the base, these hundreds of Cubans would be-come ill from exposure and lack of food and water. There would be no place to sleep other than the small spit of land in front of the gate where no more than fifty people could safely gather. Some would wander into the surrounding minefields and be injured or killed. Sooner or later, the US Navy would be forced to render medical assistance. In doing so it would be confronted with a humanitarian nightmare: hundreds of des-perate Cubans rushing the gate.

We concluded that the navy would have no option but to allow the would-be migrants into the base. Given the number of Cubans who wanted to leave Cuba and the ease of simply walking down the mile-long path, if unguarded—as compared with the dangerous voyage across the Florida Straits—it was possible that Cubans would eventu-ally overrun the base, which has a limited supply of potable water and food. If the Cubans flooded in, the base commander would have to evacuate US families and pull his workforce off their regular duties in order to care for the migrants. To resolve the crisis Cubans allowed into the base would be brought to the United States, where they would re-main, and more would follow as long as the Cuban military did not prevent them from taking the path leading to the base's Northeast Gate.

A few weeks later, the captain and I presented this hypothetical crisis to policy makers at the Departments of State and Defense. We ar-gued that the only way to prevent a migration crisis was to ensure good relations between the US and Cuban militaries. The departments agreed, authorizing the base commander to conduct monthly fence-line talks at the Northeast Gate with the Cuban general responsible for eastern Cuba.

Over the next two decades the fence-line talks ensured the security of the base and the surrounding countryside. They were held in a small office building that formed part of the Northeast Gate. The Cuban general and his aides would walk down—and then afterward back up—the mile-long narrow path. Over time the fence-line talks laid the foundation for more than two decades of close cooperation between US and Cuban armed forces. The Cubans removed their howitzers and the US military removed mines that lay within the base perimeter. The two militaries cooperated on health and environmental issues, developing strategies to fight wildfires and disease. A forest fire aided by the high winds would damage surrounding towns as well as the base if effective preventative actions were not taken. Over the years the talks broadened to include joint exercises on security, health, and the environment.

As I feared, Castro did set off another mass migration by telling Cubans that if they wanted to leave by sea they would not be stopped. Fortunately, he did not target the Northeast Gate at Guantanamo Bay. During the crisis, however, the US Coast Guard brought many migrants rescued at sea to Guantanamo, along with a large number of Haitian migrants. At the height of the crisis more than fifty thousand migrants were installed in camps set up for the two nationalities. The pressure for essential goods and services was so great that dependents of our military forces working at the base were evacuated to Norfolk, Virginia.

For years Cubans have lived and worked on the base. During my first visit, I told a community gathering of several hundred that they could remain in their bougainvillea-covered wooden houses when they retired. Most had been living on the base since the Cuban Revolution. Some decided to relocate with their families to the base after Castro took power; others came seeking work. And there they remained for the rest of their lives. These workers raised families, retired, and died on the base, although they were given the opportunity to either return to Cuba or relocate to the United States. By the beginning of the twenty-first century, the navy found it necessary to build a geriatric health care.

The hospital also played a role in building good relations with both the Cuban military and civilian populations. As a result of the fence-line talks, the military hospital administrators cooperated with the hospital in nearby Guantanamo City, sharing medical information on diseases and illnesses of patients on and off the base. Today the number of Cubans on the base is small; most have died and been buried in a special area set aside for them within the base cemetery. But local cooperation between Cubans and Americans at the base continues.

Like its elderly Cuban residents, Guantanamo Bay was slowly losing its relevance, coming alive only when the excitement of a mass migration resulted in tens of thousands of Cubans and Haitians living in temporary camps on the base. By the 1990s, there were few if any military operations; Gitmo's principal activities were the provision of logistical support to the US Coast Guard and the US Drug Enforcement Agency in the fight against smuggling and narcotics trafficking.

Then, on January 11, 2002, Guantanamo Bay was transformed into a military prison. Four months to the day after Al-Qaeda's terrorist attacks on American soil, twenty shackled, blindfolded "unlawful enemy combatants" were marched off a C-17 military transport aircraft and into Camp X-Ray. As the detainees shuffled into their prison and knelt down with bowed heads, I was congratulating myself on a small diplomatic coup because I had gained Castro's cooperation in the use of Gitmo for their detention. Years later I would regret that day and my role in it.

In early January 2002 the new head of Cuban affairs at the State Department, Jim Carragher, called to tell me that the Pentagon was considering several locations for incarcerating prisoners from the war in Afghanistan. Among them was Guantanamo Bay. Jim added, "Don't worry Vicki, it will likely be somewhere else." Excitedly, I exclaimed, "Jim, it will be Gitmo." I suspected that Carragher, who liked to keep the peace and pass on good news, thought that it would be better for all parties if a location other that Gitmo were chosen. He was probably right, but I was certain that Gitmo would be selected. There was no other place in the world where neither US laws nor local laws applied except Guantanamo Bay. I laid out my rationale for why Gitmo would be chosen: the prisoners would not be brought to the United States because habeas corpus laws would ensure that they were brought to trial. We would have insufficient evidence to convict, yet we would not release the prisoners because they might return to the battlefield. If we held them in an allied country, that nation's laws would apply, forcing either release or a trial. But Guantanamo Bay is unique; there the only law that applies is US military law; while Cuba retains sovereignty over the territory, its laws have no force or effect, and US laws do not apply in a foreign country. I concluded that Gitmo was the logical place to incarcerate enemy combatants, keeping them off the battlefield and out of the public eye.

It wasn't that I was prescient. I had been through this before. In 1994, when our armed forces deployed to Haiti to prepare the way for returning deposed president Jean-Bertrand Aristide, our military rounded up partisans of General Raoul Cédras, the leader of the military dictatorship that had taken power in Haiti. By doing so it prevented attacks on the multinational forces and made it possible for Aristide to begin exercising authority without being confronted by his enemies. Those detained were not held at Guantanamo Bay but rather onboard a vessel in Port-au-Prince Bay, where ostensibly neither US nor Haitian law applied—but it was a stretch. Although those detained were not in the strictest sense combatants, we feared that they would promote or carry out violence against the multinational forces and Aristide's government. Some months after Aristide was more or less firmly in power, we either released or turned these people over to the Haitian government because we had no legal justification for continuing to detain them. It wasn't an ideal situation but it was a necessary one. Not all of the detentions were justified, and I especially regretted that it took months to secure the release of one innocent Haitian detainee who had been mistaken for his brother.

Back in 2002, I had assumed that (as had been the case with Haiti) the enemy combatants who were captured on the battlefield or carrying out activities on behalf of Al-Qaeda would be tried or released when the war was over. But sixteen years later there is no end in sight for the so-called War on Terror. The fight that began on September 11, 2001, has evolved into a long and bloody struggle.

The United States is still far from defeating the many terrorist groups affiliated with radical Islamic extremists who have brutalized civilian populations across the globe. Based on this experience I did not—and still do not—oppose the detention of enemy combatants. I understand the very real difficulty of conducting a judicial process when there is little evidence other than intelligence intercepts, rumors, and past deeds that are difficult to prove. The international terrorist threat is clearly a unique circumstance, and these dangerous fighters must be kept off the battlefield. But more disturbing than the length of time the enemy combatants were held at Guantanamo Bay was the manner in which they were treated. I never imagined that my government would use "enhanced interrogation" on the detainees and, when I learned that it had, I questioned my role in bringing the enemy combatants to Guantanamo.

During my early January conversation with Jim Carragher about the possibility of imprisoning the enemy combatants at Guantanamo Bay, I said that I thought Castro might refrain from criticizing our activities on the base if we informed him in advance. If Fidel dissented publicly, many developing countries that looked to Cuba as a role model would support Cuba's protest. But if he acquiesced, Castro's silence would be perceived as silent approval, thereby giving the United

States greater credibility with leaders in the developing world. Moreover, notifying Cuba would be the right thing to do because of the US military's long-standing cooperation with the Cuban military at Guantanamo Bay. Carragher expressed some hesitation because he knew that Otto Reich, President George W. Bush's nominee for assistant secretary of state for the Western Hemisphere, adamantly opposed cooperation of any sort with Cuba. Fortunately Reich was not yet in charge of Cuba policy because the US Senate had declined to schedule a confirmation hearing.

Still, he sent forward the memo with my request. After a few days of silence from Washington on the detainee question, my special assistant, Peter Corsell, was awakened long after midnight by the incessant ringing of his home telephone. It was common practice for Cuban state security to call our diplomats at all hours of the night as a subtle form of harassment. Peter, assuming this was the case, unplugged the phone and went back to bed. Then his cell phone started ringing. He accepted the call and was surprised to hear a US military official on the other end of the line: "We cannot reach Ambassador Huddleston and need to speak with her immediately," the official barked.

"It's one o'clock in the morning, she's probably asleep!" Peter replied.

"We need you to wake her up and bring her to the Interests Section for a secure phone call right away," the officer replied.

"Understood," Peter answered. "What should I tell the Ambassador this call is about?"

"Just tell her that the secretary of defense needs to speak with her," came the reply.

Peter happened to live nearby, so he got dressed and walked over to my house within the residence compound. When he woke me up, I remember thinking, "It's the middle of the night, this better be important." When we arrived at the Interests Section, and I returned the call on the secure phone, I heard the official confirmation I had been expecting for some time—the enemy combatants from Afghanistan were going to be imprisoned at Guantanamo Bay. And our huge C-17 transport aircraft were preparing to load as we were speaking. Later that morning, after I'd returned home for a shower and breakfast, Carragher called to give me the go-ahead to inform the Cuban government.

Jeff DeLaurentis, the US Interests Section political officer (and, years later, chargé d'affaires at our reopened embassy in Havana) and I met with Ricardo Alarcón and his deputy, Miguel Alvarez, to tell them about the imminent arrival of the first contingent of enemy combatants. We knew this was a risky undertaking, especially because it was rumored that President Bush would give Reich a recess appointment. If Castro denigrated our request or made it seem as if we had coming begging his approval, Reich would be the first to cite Castro's actions as an excuse to shut down communication with the Cubans.

Alarcón's office was relatively modest considering that he was president of Cuba's highest legislative authority, the National Assembly. It was adorned with a few plastic plants and well-worn white chairs and a couch, where Jeff and I invariably sat when we visited. Jeff was a consummate diplomat, with keen intelligence, warm personality, and distinguished good looks. I trusted that he would be able to ascertain whether Alarcón would cooperate. We had met with Alarcón many times during the Elián González affair, and Jeff always had a keen sense of whether he would advocate for our side of the issue with his boss, Fidel Castro. As was customary, we waited to begin our discussion until cups of Cuban espresso along with tall glasses of water were served. Alarcón was relaxed as he waited for me to speak. I had requested the meeting, so it was up to me to begin. Our personal relationship was good, hundreds of American groups were now meeting with Alarcón and other Cuban officials on a regular basis, and the dissidents had an unusual level of freedom. But we were well aware that this fragile truce might not last once Reich assumed control of Cuba policy.

I slowly warmed up to the sensitive topic of our meeting. First I complimented Alarcón on convincing Americans that all Cuba wanted was a normal relationship with the United States. He was the primary greeter-in-chief of the numerous people-to-people groups that were visiting Cuba, and he invariably made both a good impression and a persuasive argument for lifting the embargo. I also thanked him again for Cuba's condolences and offers of medical assistance following the terrorist attacks on the United States a few months earlier. Unmoved by my sugarcoating, Alarcón leaned forward in his chair, sensing that something important was on my agenda.

There was no point in delaying my bombshell any further: "Ricardo, my government plans to use Guantanamo Bay to incarcerate prisoners from Afghanistan," I announced.

"Oh, just like that, you are sending them to Guantanamo. And, of course, you are not here to ask our permission, are you?" he shot back.

"No, Ricardo, I am not asking for your permission; the prisoners are already on the way," Then I began making my case. I told him that after visiting Cuba, many American congressmen, senators, and VIPs had become advocates for lifting the embargo. If Castro denounced our use of Guantanamo Bay, he would lose their support because it would appear that Cuba was unwilling to punish the terrorists. Moreover, our two militaries had developed excellent relations at Gitmo, and Cuba's cooperation at this critical time would further cement them. In any event, if Castro denounced us, it would do no good because, with or without Cuba's permission, we were about to establish a military prison at Guantanamo. After a bit more discussion, Alarcón closed the conversation on a relatively positive note. He said, "We will see, Vicki." This meant, "I will take the issue to Castro."

Jeff and I left the meeting feeling hopeful that Castro would at least refrain from an attack on the Bush administration. But that evening a Cuban general told the media, "I hope the prisoners escape and kill their guards." I was shocked; this comment would surely result in both governments shouting insults at each other via the media. I wondered what had gone wrong. A few minutes later Alarcón called to tell me that the general was not authorized to comment and his remarks did not reflect Castro's views. It was highly unusual for the Cuban government to contradict one of its generals, but Alarcón promised that Castro would provide a very different opinion at a press conference the next morning. I was relieved. I would wait until Castro spoke before briefing Washington on his decision.

To the amazement of the assembled journalists at the press conference, Castro said something along the lines of the Americans will do whatever they want to do at Guantanamo, no matter what Cuba thinks. His words were even better than I had hoped. Castro not only did not condemn us, but he was treating our controversial use of Guantanamo Bay as an American problem. I was delighted and secretly pleased that the media were shocked and confused. They simply could not fathom why Castro would contradict one of his own generals and give the United States a pass. But I knew that Fidel always treaded cautiously when it came to our vital interests. I assumed that in this case, he wanted to be on the right side of President Bush's War on Terror, and he certainly didn't want to be a target of America's revenge.

With only a few exceptions, Castro had long sought to ensure that we would never have a compelling excuse to invade Cuba. Two incidents in the late 1980s illustrate this point. Despite intercepting communications among our warplanes that were flying to Panama in the US invasion ordered by President George H. W. Bush, Castro did not warn strongman Manuel Noriega, most likely because he did not want to provoke us. If it eventually came to light that Castro had warned Noriega, we probably would have assumed that the Soviet Union, which operated a communications facility near Havana, had provided Castro with the intelligence. This in turn would have strained our relations with both the Cubans and the Soviets. The second example was Castro's surprise detention and execution of high-ranking Cuban officials for allegedly profiting from illicit narcotics trafficking. I suspect that Castro eliminated these officials because he was worried that American intelligence agencies may have discovered their misdeeds and that the trail would lead to his brother, Raúl Castro. If it were proven that the highest levels of the Cuban government had been involved in illicit narcotics trafficking, it might give hawks within the US government a strong argument to advocate invading Cuba—as we did in Panama—or further tighten the embargo. Another factor in this purge of top military and intelligence officers was undoubtedly Castro's desire to maintain an iron grip on Cuba's military as the Soviet Union began its downward spiral.

Castro likely hoped that acquiescing to our intended use of Guantanamo would bolster his charm offensive, which was directed at convincing the US Congress to lift the embargo. Surprisingly, Castro didn't simply refrain from criticizing our decision to imprison the enemy combatants at Gitmo but ordered his military to cooperate with our military in securing the base. The full extent of cooperation between our militaries was not made public, and developed over time as more detainees arrived and as security issues began to arise. When the first plane of detainees arrived, Cuban air traffic control permitted our huge transport aircraft to use Cuban airspace. Guantanamo Bay has its own narrow "air corridor" for US military use, but it was nearly impossible for the C-17 pilots to make the tight turn from the windward to the leeward side of the base, where the airstrip is located, to enter that corridor and still remain in US airspace. The Cuban government also cooperated with American air traffic controllers in coordinating the use of airspace in eastern Cuba, thereby working with the US military to ensure the air defense of Guantanamo base and Cuban territory.

But if Fidel Castro expected some reward or at least public acknowledgment of his government's assistance, he was severely disappointed. One day after his non-comments on our use of Guantanamo Bay as a prison, and on the same day that the first group of detainees arrived, President Bush gave Otto Reich a recess appointment as the assistant secretary of state for the Western Hemisphere. This appeared to be a slap in the face to Castro, who had long held Reich responsible for engineering the escape from justice of Orlando Bosch, an alleged co-conspirator in the bombing of Cubana Airlines in 1976. But even the appointment of Reich did not dampen the cooperation between our militaries. The fence-line talks had created a relationship of mutual trust and respect that continued to enhance the security of Guantanamo Bay when it was most needed.

During the first year of Bush's presidency, the Cuban diaspora had become increasingly nervous and upset with his moderate policy. The arrival of the unlawful enemy combatants at Gitmo put the issue into high relief, igniting a concerted effort by the Cuban diaspora to return to the policies of isolation and punishment. Galvanized by the mistaken idea that some sort of deal had been made with Cuba, they began an intense effort to convince Bush to roll back President Bill Clinton's measures allowing thousands of people-to-people travelers, including movie stars and other VIPs, who came to Cuba. In their view, it was high time that Bush stop coddling Cuba and begin to retaliate for the loss of little Elián González.

If Bush's decision to give archconservative Otto Reich an interim appointment as the chief policy maker for the Western Hemisphere was an attempt to mollify Cuban Americans, it didn't work. Florida's conservative Cuban-American congressional delegation was convinced that the United States had made a deal with Castro. Surely, they reasoned, something had been given in exchange for Castro's cooperation on Guantanamo Bay. Secretary of State Colin Powell told a hearing of the House of Representatives Foreign Affairs Committee that Cuba policy had not changed one bit. But Cuban American Republican representative Ileana Ros-Lehtinen simply couldn't believe that Castro had willingly cooperated with the US military without getting something in return. Given Powell's stature and reputation for integrity at the time, his reassurances might well have calmed the Cuban American community, but Cuba's foreign minister, Felipe Pérez Roque, undermined him. Seeking to further Fidel's charm offensive, he characterized relations between our two militaries as nothing short of détente, saying, "We hope that one day the relations on all official matters can be handled with the respect and collaboration that is happening at Guantanamo."

Worried about losing Cuban American support, Bush did not acknowledge Castro's cooperation on Guantanamo. Cuba remained on the State Department's list of state sponsors of terrorism, along with Iran, Iraq, Libya, North Korea, Sudan, and Syria, despite the fact that few governments, even allies, would have allowed us to use their territory for the incarceration of the unlawful enemy combatants. But Castro, who refused to criticize us and directed his military forces to cooperate in providing security for the base, received nothing in return. Nevertheless, Cuban military and security forces continue even today to act as an early warning system, safeguarding Gitmo from an attack that would necessarily have to cross Cuban air, land, or territorial water that surrounds the base.

Ultimately, I believe that we as Americans suffered the greatest blow during this chapter of US-Cuban relations because our government failed to observe international legal standards and procedures for the treatment of enemy combatants. While there may be solid justification for delayed justice during the ongoing conflict, there can be no excuse for subjecting fellow human beings to degrading treatment. Having violated international conventions covering the treatment of enemy combatants, the consequences for our own servicepeople in a conflict situation have been compromised. And the hard-earned image of our country as one that abides by the rule of law has been forever compromised.

CHAPTER 12

FIDEL'S CHARM OFFENSIVE

O N February 7, 2002, I invited the international press for breakfast at the residence, hoping that food and comfortable surroundings might help me reinforce Secretary of State Colin Powell's reassurance to Representative Ileana Ros-Lehtinen (R-FL) that no policy changes on Cuba were anticipated. This was an unusual event, the first media interview given by a chief of the US Interests Section. Press conferences on Cuba were generally handled by political appointees at the Department of State, like Powell or newly appointed assistant secretary Otto Reich. But Washington had made an exception because I was popular with Miami's Cuban American community, who appreciated my strong stand on human rights. I wanted to follow-up on Powell's remarks, which had been directed at reassuring the Cuban diaspora that the United States had not made a deal with Fidel Castro over the use of Guantanamo Bay to imprison Al-Qaeda enemy combatants, without resorting to the nasty rhetoric that too often accompanied our government's statements on Cuba. I doubted that Powell's or my reassurances would satisfy members of the diaspora, because they simply didn't believe that we had not cut a deal with Castro. Why else would he refrain from criticizing the United States for using Gitmo as an offshore prison?

Even if they believed our statements, the conservative Cuban American National Foundation (CANF) and the Cuban Liberty Council lobbies would not be satisfied. They would use Guantanamo Bay as a club to beat the administration of President George W. Bush into switching from the moderate policies of recent years to a hostile policy that denounced Castro and tightened the embargo. I hoped that the two events, Powell's testimony to Congress and my press conference in Havana, would obviate the need for the new assistant secretary Reich, who was fiercely anti-Castro, to add his voice to an already volatile situation. Reich's remarks, which would likely be antagonistic, would please the diaspora but could lead to a verbal confrontation with the Cuban hierarchy, which was ever vigilant for any sign of disrespect toward its government.

Filled with anticipation, the international press arrived early. I knew and liked the representatives of ABC, CNN, MSNBC, and Reuters. I trusted them to get the story right because they followed US-Cuba relations closely and understood the various nuances and intricacies. It was more challenging to deal with the media from France and Spain, which were generally dumbfounded by the influence wielded by the Cuban diaspora and the acquiescence of the US government to its demands. All the reporters were hoping to get a rare scoop within the closed Cuban environment, where it was hard to find a good story. Not knowing what to expect, they must have imagined that Castro had declared me persona non grata; if he had not, then surely I would explain what was going on with the seeming détente between the United States and Cuba. It wasn't odd that these predictions were contradictory, because our relations were not only contradictory but riddled with misunderstanding and mistrust. Now the media was attempting to figure out the latest twist in our relations. Castro had brushed aside the incarceration of enemy combatants at Gitmo almost as if the issue was too insignificant to be brought to his attention. For some inexplicable reason Fidel had failed to seize the opportunity to denounce the United States both for the war in Iraq and what Cuba viewed as our "illegal" occupation of Guantanamo Bay.

The risks were substantial for me. If CANF decided that my remarks were favorable to Castro, it would strongly suggest that the Bush administration replace me, as after all I had been appointed by Clinton. If Castro disapproved of what I said, he might demand that I leave the country. Still, I was pleased to have an opportunity to defend our current approach to Cuba, which—while certainly not friendly to the regime—was in my opinion reasonable and moderate. There had not been a crisis between the United States and Cuba during the past year, and relations were definitely improving with an increasing number of American visitors and the first- in-decades sales of American corn, chicken, and other agricultural products.

I began by telling the press that the US government wasn't fooled by Castro's charm offensive, which I explained was simply his strategy to convince American visitors and our Congress to lift the embargo. Fortunately, leading with the charm offensive provided a lead for most of the reporters' articles. It was only the Spanish government press, Agencia EFE, that led with the issue of terrorism and Guantanamo Bay. I explained that Castro's more accommodating approach was simply because he didn't want to appear to be on the side of the terrorists who had carried out the September 11, 2001, attacks on the United States. In describing the charm offensive, I explained, "You cannot say there is a change because Cuba wants to say there is one. There has to be a fundamental change here, and there has not been one." Seeing this as an opportunity to advocate on the part of the dissidents, I added, "Cuba must take steps toward becoming a more open society before the United States will consider changes in its policy."

In addition to asking about the Guantanamo Bay issue, the media wanted to know if the influx of American visitors, especially the VIPs, and the recent $34 million in sales of American agricultural products meant that the Bush administration was intentionally allowing relations to improve. I didn't have a good answer, because these activities were in and of themselves a sign of better relations. But the purpose of the press conference was to reassure the diaspora, so I pointed out that Castro had made the agricultural purchases to speed Cuba's recovery from Hurricane Michelle, a Category 4 storm that had devastated western Cuba. It took only two days for agricultural products from the United States to arrive in Havana as opposed to two weeks for products from China and Europe; moreover, the goods were 20 percent cheaper. I added that while Castro might be intent on convincing the US Congress to lift the embargo, he was unlikely to succeed. Republicans who supported the embargo held a majority in the House of Representatives, and President Bush could veto any Cuba legislation he didn't like. In any case, history illustrated that US and Cuban interests seldom intertwined. President Bill Clinton had twice attempted an opening and twice failed. Now, having won the battle for Elián González, Castro was ready to engage, but President Bush was not.

One reporter asked if the increased travel of Americans to Cuba was a sign that we were a willing partner in what seemed to be a détente. I explained that American people-to-people visits were important because they helped build grassroots democracy, providing an opportunity for dissidents to meet with our political leaders. In addition, visiting Americans brought fresh ideas and information to Cubans whose access to news was strictly limited by their government. My personal opinion, which I didn't share with the journalists, was that Fidel was more interested in enjoying the company of America's cultural and political leaders than in actually ending the embargo, which provided a convenient scapegoat for Cuba's political oppression and economic depression.

The toughest issue I had to address was the administration's decision to use Guantanamo base for the incarceration of the unlawful enemy combatants. To reassure the Cuban American community, I told the press that we appreciated Havana's stance on Guantanamo but "the problem for us is that nothing has fundamentally changed in Cuba." To be removed from the State Department's list of state sponsors of terrorism Castro would have to return Americans wanted for various crimes—such as Joanne Chesimard, who had been given refuge in Cuba—and stop harboring Basque and Puerto Rican separatists. I personally hoped that by mentioning the actual reasons why Cuba remained on the terrorist list might subtly demonstrate that Cuba did not deserve to be associated with Iran, Iraq, North Korea, Sudan, and Syria. I believed that Cuba should have been removed from the terrorist list when it ended its support for international insurgencies in the 1990s. Cuban American legislators knew as well as I did that Fidel Castro wasn't sponsoring terrorism. But they and the conservative Cuban American lobby would attack any effort to remove Cuba from the list because doing so would eliminate a powerful rationale for continuing the embargo. In any event, Cuba would remain on the list no matter what I said.

I thought the press conference had gone well. I had focused the media's attention on Castro's actions, underscoring that there had been no change in US policy. By mentioning that Cuba would remain on the terrorist list, I had preempted Florida's Cuban American congressional representatives, Republicans Ileana Ros-Lehtinen and Lincoln Díaz-Balart, who, having been shocked and concerned by the unexpected arrival of enemy combatants at Guantanamo, would now focus on ensuring that Castro would not benefit in any way from Cuba's cooperation. This meant that despite having assisted in the War on Terror, Cuba would remain on the State Department's list of state sponsors of terrorism. As the reporters filed out, the US Interest Section's public affairs officer Gonzalo Gallegos, who was a first-class diplomat, assured me that it had gone exceedingly well. But we had not counted on Spain's Agencia EFE writing an article that misquoted me.

The next day, Cuba's new head of North American affairs, Raphael Dausa, summoned me to the Foreign Ministry. This meant that I was in serious trouble, but I could think of only one remark that would have given offense, and it was off the record. Determined to defend myself, I arrived at the ministry with my deputy chief of mission, Lou Nigro, because I thought it prudent to have a witness who could confirm what was said. As usual, we were ushered into one of the small rooms reserved for meetings with diplomats. It was adorned with large plastic plants, which likely conceal cameras and listening devices. The room also had a two-way mirror, behind which would likely be additional observers. I wished that the congenial Dagoberto Rodríguez Barrera, the former head of North American affairs, had not been posted to lead the Cuban Interests Section in Washington, DC. Dausa was a harder man, more dogmatic and unlikely to give much credence to my explanation. Lou and I stood and shook hands with Dausa and two other officials, but they barely touched our hands, coolly looking us over as if we were a particularly odious species of capitalist.

There were no pleasantries. Dausa immediately asked if I was speaking for the State Department or myself. If I did not have the State Department's backing, Castro could demand that I leave the country and be done with the entire affair. I assured Dausa that I had the full support of the State Department. I had my fingers crossed. I had not submitted my remarks in advance for the department's approval because I did not want Reich to make them harsher, and I was confident that I could handle the press conference. Dausa's next salvo revealed the crux of the matter. How dare I claim that the Cubans were not cooperating with the United States on Guantanamo? I was stunned.

"I didn't say that!" I exclaimed. Then Dausa accused me of saying that Cuba "debe hacer mas" (ought to do more) in the fight against terrorism. With that I knew that my message had been misinterpreted. I replied that they should read a transcript, which they could get from any of the reporters who had attended the press conference or presumably through their own clandestine recording.

I explained that I had not denigrated Cuba's cooperation on terrorism; rather, I had said, "Cuba has reacted in a positive manner to bringing the illegal combatants to the base." I had added that to be removed from the terrorist list, Cuba would have to stop harboring Basque and Puerto Rican separatists and American criminals. But that was quite different from saying Cuba should do more to cooperate with the US against terrorism.

As we left the meeting I turned to Lou, who had also been the political officer when I was chargé d'affaires in Haiti. I trusted Lou completely and knew that he would tell me the truth. He squeezed my arm and said he thought that I had probably dodged a bullet. I agreed, but only because Castro and his staff would review the recording of the press conference. In doing so they would discover that Agencia EFE had misinterpreted my remarks. I had not denigrated Fidel's decision to cooperate with us on Guantanamo Bay. And I knew that the rest of my press conference was not sufficiently irritating to result in Castro expelling me from Cuba. But I would need the State Department to support me. At the daily press conference the department spokesman announced, "We back what Huddleston said one hundred percent." I was relieved because I knew that Reich didn't fully supported me. He appreciated and applauded my stand on behalf of the dissidents, but he opposed my advocacy of a cooperative relationship between the United States and Cuba.

The challenge for me in my job as the chief American diplomat was that no one was ever satisfied. In the case of the press conference, Castro was unhappy because I had not given him sufficient recognition for his cooperation; but if I had done so, my boss, Otto Reich, and other conservatives would reproach me for being too gracious toward Cuba. The same dynamic prevailed with those who advocated better relations with Cuba, many of whom now criticized me for too aggressively championing human rights. Most of the time I enjoyed seeing just how far I could push both sides without stepping over the boundaries. It was hard to succeed in Cuba, but it was never boring.

With the State Department firmly behind me, all I had to worry about was Castro's reaction. Fidel wouldn't like my quip that "Castro is a man of the past, not the future." It wouldn't get me thrown out of the country, but it also wouldn't further the détente I was trying to promote. At the beginning of the press conference I had told the reporters that they could quote me, but I asked that they not repeat my unflattering remark about Castro. But if Fidel reviewed the tapes he would hear what I had said and he would find a way to pay me back.

Castro pronounced his verdict by belittling me. He said, "There is not a country in the world where diplomats don't meddle," adding "Here, where [the United States] doesn't have an ambassador, there is an Interests Section and they have tried applying the same style." I was relieved, because he had attacked me before in much harsher terms. With respect to my comments regarding Cuba's inclusion on the terrorist list, he was bitter, complaining, "They cannot imagine how much we do not care one bit whether they exclude us or not." But I imagine that he cared a great deal, and with good reason. Castro's refusal to condemn our actions at Guantanamo Bay had reassured many left-leaning governments, and his cooperation with our military had improved base security. He must have expected something in return, such as Cuba's removal from the terrorism list, but such reciprocity was not forthcoming.

The Cuban Foreign Ministry spokesman, Roberto de Armas, did a good job of explaining the commotion, claiming, "In Miami, there's extraordinary confusion—a state of alarm." The diaspora suspected that "an under-the-table deal" had been made to soften the travel ban and Armas added that they were "trying to ensure that Jeb doesn't lose a single vote." He was referring to the fact the Jeb Bush, who throughout his political career had been supported by Cuban Americans, would soon be running for a second term as governor of Florida.

American domestic politics was progressively encroaching on the relatively good, or at least benign, relations between our two countries, which during the past year had allowed a Cuban Spring to emerge—the most open period on the island since the Cuban Revolution. Even the toxic issue of political prisoners, which was historically used as a cudgel by the Cuban American community to maintain a harsh policy, had lost some of its potency. According to Elizardo Sánchez, the head of the Cuban Commission on Human Rights, there were 210 political prisoners in February 2002, a drop of 15 percent from six months earlier. But these advances did not distract the Cuban American lobby from continuing to advocate for a harsher policy. More worrisome to me was that it appeared President Bush might accommodate the lobby. He had given Reich—a hard-liner's hard-liner—an interim appointment and was reported to have responded to Uruguay's president Jorge Batlle's suggestion that he lift the US embargo by defending our policy against that "tyrant" Castro. It seemed that for American presidents it was simpler to lead the diaspora in punishing their old enemy than to assume the more difficult and risky role of convincing them that a moderate policy would improve the lives of Cubans and benefit their own country.

Knowing that at some point the president would have to make a decision about whether to continue the current policy, I traveled to Washington, DC to make the case for détente—a word I never used in public because it would have sparked great indignation among the Cuban diaspora. I invited Peter Corsell, my Special Assistant, to accompany me.

We began by seeking the approval of the secretary of the Department of Housing and Human Services, Cuban American Mel Martinez, who was President Bush's principal Cuba adviser. Martinez was a thoughtful and cordial man who listened to our arguments with an open mind. Peter successfully argued, as he had done with many groups in the Cuban American community, that our outreach activities over time could undermine the Cuban government. I didn't like that argument, but it was effective. I preferred to emphasize that a more moderate approach had been critical in producing the Cuban Spring. If the president curtailed people-to-people travel, Castro would no longer have an incentive to refrain from crushing dissent because he would have lost his American audience and the possibility of convincing the

Congress to end the embargo. Martinez was impressed and commended the outreach program. He described our efforts as a quintessential carrot-and-stick approach in which we permitted American travel so long as Castro was demonstrating good behavior. The meeting ended with Secretary Martinez asking me if I would extend my tour in Havana for a fourth year. This was clearly a strong endorsement of our approach. I responded that I would be delighted, but that would ultimately depend on Secretary Powell and the State Department.

The next day I met with Deputy Secretary of State Richard Armitage, who was both my and Assistant Secretary Reich's boss. I explained to Armitage that a détente of sorts had developed between the United States and Cuba that I hoped to nurture. Armitage, an outspoken and confident diplomat, wished me luck, which to some degree was a warning that our policy could change at any moment. After that I met with Assistant Secretary Reich. I didn't mention my views on détente to Reich, who would have been appalled. I focused on the details and success of our outreach program. Reich opposed cooperation of any kind with the Cuban government, but he supported empowering the dissidents. Unfortunately, as Reich and his conservative following would eventually discover, the latter was dependent on the former. Regardless, I would not be able to convince him to moderate his desire to punish Cuba.

The more benign US policy of recent years had produced changes in Miami, just as it had in Cuba. Younger Cuban Americans and those who had arrived during the past twenty years wanted to travel to Cuba, send remittances to their families, and seek business opportunities on the island. Many young professionals would have liked to visit but were reluctant to do so over the objections of their parents. Still, they secretly yearned for reconciliation so they could explore their roots. This new tolerance in Miami, fostered by recent migrants, was creating a vibrant bond with the island. Thousands of Cubans visited relatives in Florida, returning with huge plastic-wrapped parcels containing radios, televisions, and all manner of appliances. And many in the diaspora visited their families in Cuba bearing gifts. In Miami, entrepreneurial Cuban Americans opened money transfer and mail order services, which allowed the diaspora to send remittances and gift packages, containing everything from toys to food, to their family and friends in Cuba. These activities were not entirely legal, but the Cuban American community in Miami—more than any law—determines what is and is not acceptable when it comes to Cuba. Older Cuban Americans, who generally demanded a punitive policy and disliked any contact with the island, seemed to understand that it was prudent to make exceptions for those in the diaspora who wished to maintain links with the island.

Peter and I met with the diaspora in Miami because we knew that protecting the policy gains we had made was ultimately dependent on them. We explained our approach to Joe Garcia, the executive director of CANF, who had announced in January, "We are in the ninth year of Clinton's Cuba policy." Now, a few months later, both he and CANF's president, Jorge Mas Santos, were interested in our argument that one year of Bush's moderate policy had produced more change in Cuba than decades of hostility. I gave numerous interviews to the media, on Miami talk shows, and to Cuban American groups. But I did not meet with the feisty Ninoska Pérez Castellón, a founding member of the Cuban Liberty Council, or Congressman Lincoln Díaz-Balart, whose father had been the majority leader of Cuba's senate before Castro's revolution, because I knew that they simply wanted Castro gone and the return of the old political and social order in Cuba.

As Miami debated Cuba policy and awaited the outcome of the latest policy review—this one ordered by President Bush—Castro continued to enjoy the visits of American VIPs, and in return he tolerated our efforts through the outreach program to empower civil society. Referring to the Cuban American community Castro declared, "For 43 years they've been saying the same thing, the use of cannons must be left to prehistoric times, and replaced by ideas." But in truth, even with a more tolerant Castro and a more open-minded diaspora, there were fundamental differences that would be difficult, if not impossible, to bridge. Castro wanted a fiercely independent Cuba, in which he always had the last word, while Cuban Americans desired a Cuba fashioned in the image of their new country, the United States.

In international fora, Castro always counted on his many allies to support Cuba against the United States. Since 1992, every UN member except the United States, Israel, and occasionally one other government, voted for a resolution condemning the United States embargo. Although this vote was an annual embarrassment, the US usually was able to retaliate by garnering sufficient votes to pass a resolution—by a narrow margin—that criticized human rights in Cuba. Castro fought hard to defeat the resolution, and counted on his closest allies, especially Mexico to support him at the United Nations.

In March, 2002 a month prior to the UN vote on Cuba's human rights, the new Mexican President Vicente Fox visited Cuba in the hope of repairing relations that had deteriorated under his predecessor, Ernesto Zedillo. In Havana, Richard Pascoe, the Mexican ambassador to Cuba, made every effort to keep politics out of the visit, but on his last day in Havana, Fox met with Cuba's leading dissidents Hector Palacios, Oswaldo Payá, Raúl Rivero, Marta Beatriz Roque, and Elizardo Sánchez. Castro was furious, blaming Mexican foreign minister Jorge Castañeda Gutman, whom he believed wanted to please the conservative Cuban diaspora and the US government, for betraying Cuba. Worse, from Castro's point of view, the meeting would undoubtedly encourage other world leaders to meet with the dissidents, which might well have the effect of eroding their support for Cuba at the UN.

Although both governments claimed the Fox visit had been "satisfactory," the downward spiral of Cuban-Mexican relations had begun. Perhaps to garner praise for Fox's visit with the dissidents, Mexican foreign minister Castañeda traveled to Miami to meet with Cuban Americans. During a press interview he assured the Cuban diaspora,

"The doors of the Mexican embassy are open to all Cubans, and to Latin Americans, just as Mexico is." The last part of the sentence seemed to be an attempt to diminish the impact of the first part, which could be considered as an invitation to Cubans to defect by seeking refuge in Mexico's embassy in Havana.

In a blatant attempt to create chaos in Cuba, over the next twenty-four hours Radio Martí repeatedly broadcast the first part of Castañeda's remark, implying that the Mexican embassy would offer refuge to Cubans who wished to leave. Although Radio Martí was funded by the US government, it had become a tool of the most conservative elements of the Cuban diaspora. President Bush had appointed Salvador Lew as director of Radio Martí, and that had been a mistake. Lew was a *historico* (an older conservative Cuban American) whose antiquated management style and desire to curry favor with the hardline Cuban Liberty Council led him to put on the air fiery anti-Castro talk show hosts, such as the council's Ninoska Pérez Castellón. Lew saw Castañeda's ill-advised remark as an opportunity to attack Castro and promote his standing with Ninoska and the council.

Right on cue, twenty-one young men hijacked a city bus and crashed it through the gates of the Mexican embassy in Havana. When they refused to leave, more young men gathered in front of the embassy, hoping to join those inside. Fearing that they were about to invade the embassy, Cuban police using steel bars and truncheons brutally broke up the crowd. A friend in the media told me that he had been hurt as the police waded into the fray, indiscriminately bashing anyone in their way. The following evening a Cuban state security squad entered the embassy and removed the invaders.

Shortly after the Mexican embassy incident, I invited Ambassador Pascoe, a handsome man with white hair and intense blue eyes, for lunch at La Guarida, a popular family-run restaurant. I considered Pascoe a friend and I knew we would have a candid conversation.

Once I had climbed the marble stairs to the fifth floor of the once-elegant but now run-down apartment building in which the restaurant was located, I was ready for a mojito, a delicious sugary rum drink. In the modest dining room, presided over by an ancient blue refrigerator that had appeared in one of Cuba's best movies, *Strawberries and Chocolate*, Ricardo and I looked down on the street below where old men in well-used sleeveless undershirts sat on broken chairs and empty cartons playing a never-ending game of dominos. In time, the restaurant's tremendous popularity would prompt the government to take it over, and the owners would make their way to Miami. Today a much larger version of La Guarida, with terrible food, remains a popular tourist site.

I told Ricardo that I was relieved that those who had invaded the embassy had been removed without injury or fanfare. Ricardo was aware that I, like most of his diplomatic colleagues, might not approve of his decision to permit Cuban security forces to enter his embassy, so he explained that Cuban state security had quickly and peacefully cleared the premises, leaving behind no implanted listening devices. He stressed that the invaders had not requested political asylum. Had they done so, Ricardo would have been obliged to allow them to stay, at least until the UN High Commission on Refugees interviewed them to determine whether they were fleeing for their lives. I agreed with Ricardo that these were not refugees but rather unemployed or underemployed young men who longed for better lives outside Cuba.

I had a good deal of sympathy for Ricardo's situation because I had recently experienced a similar but less dramatic event. Early one Sunday morning two young men made it over the eight-foot iron fence that surrounds the US Interests Section. They told the security officer, David Durkin, that they wanted to escape Cuba because they had no future. Like the young men who crashed through the gates of the Mexican embassy, they didn't know enough about international protocol to request political asylum. And I, like Ricardo, decided to forgo the formalities because if it became known that the US Interests Section was harboring Cubans, word would spread quickly throughout Havana, possibly inciting more incursions into our diplomatic mission and others. I called Reich and obtained his approval to remove the intruders. David, who was an exceptionally good security officer, convinced them that they had to leave. He hid them in the back of a van, drove all over Havana to ensure he wasn't being followed by Cuban security, and eventually dropped them off safely in a distant barrio.

Ricardo was convinced that the incident had been a provocation organized by Raúl Castro—who, he assumed, was worried that Fidel's newly found tolerance toward dissent would weaken regime control. He speculated that Raúl also wanted to extract a measure of revenge for President Fox's meeting with the dissidents. Ricardo doubted that Fidel had been consulted in creating the provocation. I disagreed; invading the Mexican embassy was an audacious act, the sort I associated with Fidel, not his brother. In any case, the incident delivered a reminder to young Cubans that state security was not a benign force. And it also contributed to the souring of Cuban-Mexican relations, which already were tenuous as a result of Fox's meeting with the dissidents in Havana.

When I was next in Miami I told Salvador Lew that that he should not have broadcast Castañeda's remark because it almost resulted in another mass migration. Without any embarrassment whatsoever, he responded that he was simply broadcasting news about Cuba. This was nonsense. Like every Cuban and Cuban American, Salvador knew the history of the 1980 Mariel Boatlift, in which over 125,000 Cubans came to the United States. The crisis had begun when Cubans crashed a bus through the gates of the Peruvian embassy and the Peruvian government refused to allow Cuban state security to remove the asylum seekers. As news spread across Havana, hundreds more followed suit, storming the embassy grounds and breaking into embassies throughout the city, including the US Interests Section. Unable to contain the crisis, an angry and embarrassed Fidel Castro made lemonade out of lemons by announcing that anyone who wanted to leave Cuba could do so by gathering at the Port of Mariel. When President Jimmy Carter declined to prevent Cuban Americans from sailing to Cuba to retrieve their relatives, thousands of boats left Miami and the Keys. Upon reaching Mariel, they loaded up with desperate migrants that they brought back home with them. Castro also made sure that as many "undesirables" as possible—Cubans released from the island's prisons and mental institutions—were packed into the rescue boats at gunpoint, so as to swamp Florida with a chaotic and violent mass migration.

The final indignity for Castro was to lose the vote on the UN human rights resolution. The government of Mexico joined six other Latin American countries in voting for the resolution that urged Cuba to improve its human rights practices. These Latin American countries had endorsed what they considered a mild rebuke, hoping they could appease the United States and Uruguay, the resolution's sponsor, without provoking Castro. But Fidel was not placated; he denounced the Eastern European and Latin American nations who had voted against him, and organized protests that featured large carton puppets—each about twelve feet high—depicting the leaders who had betrayed him.

Castro was particularly annoyed with Vicente Fox. The Mexican president had met with the dissidents, his foreign minister's statement had nearly caused another mass migration, and his government had voted for the UN resolution. Castro, determined on revenge, played on Cuban television a private conversation between he and Fox. On the tape Fox pleads with Fidel to leave a UN conference in Monterrey, Mexico, so that President Bush can attend. Fox's advisers had been told by Bush's staff that he would not attend the conference if Castro were present because Bush might be forced into a situation in which he had to shake hands with Castro. If the handshake occurred the conservative diaspora would never forgive him, and it might vent its anger by voting against his brother Jeb in his run for reelection as governor of Florida. Amazingly, the tape reveals that Castro peevishly agreed to accommodate Fox. The recorded conversation diminished both leaders, but especially Fox, who appeared to be, as Castro claimed, a "lapdog" of the United States.

Notwithstanding the UN vote, relations between the United States and Cuba remained relatively good during the first five months of 2002, although negative rhetoric began to escalate, principally to satisfy the Cuban American community, which was continuing to push for a harder line. At the same time, Castro was becoming wary of our outreach program and the activities of the dissidents. This was not surprising because throughout his long rule, whenever tensions with the US had increased, Castro had reduced civil liberties. Still, he refrained from taking any significant action because he did not want to lose the VIP visits. From January through July, Senators Barbara Boxer (D-CA), Maria Cantwell (D-WA), and Arlen Specter (R-PA), plus a gaggle of US representatives, visited Fidel. Cantwell led a delegation of professional women, one of whom was a creator of costume jewelry. I offered her a stay at the residence if she would return to Havana and share her skills with Cuban artisans. She agreed, returning with a beautiful collection of semiprecious stones that had been donated by jewelers around the United States. But I was unprepared for the local artisans to ask that I hold a sale so that they could sell their beautiful work. I feared that I would have to refuse because I couldn't circumvent the embargo. Then it occurred to me that I could host a jewelry sale for diplomats because they were exempt from the embargo. The Cuban artisans were delighted, and they sold every piece.

American visitors kept flowing into Cuba. The most popular with my staff and the Cubans was the actor Kevin Costner. When I announced that he was coming to visit me at the Interests Section, every woman in the building turned out to welcome him. He had planned to screen his new movie Thirteen Days—about President John F. Kennedy's handling of the Cuban Missile Crisis—in Moscow, Washington, DC, and Havana. After watching the film with Costner, Castro asked him to return the next evening to screen it for the Chinese premier, who was visiting Cuba. Costner cited a previous engagement and left for home, leaving a copy of the film with Fidel. He also left one with me to screen for my guests, who were disappointed that they wouldn't meet the famous actor.

I hoped Bush's moderate policies would continue, and I looked forward to another year in Cuba, as Martinez had suggested. I thought we were doing well. Powell and I had deflected the crisis created by the incarceration of enemy combatants at Guantanamo Bay, and Secretary Martinez had prevented attempts to curtail American travel—the unofficial détente was holding. Religious and cultural groups were working with their counterparts in Cuba, and our outreach program was distributing books and radios throughout the island and providing Internet access to Cubans in Havana. Castro continued to charm high-level American visitors, and Cubans were enjoying newfound freedoms. Fidel's charm offensive was working—for him, for us and, most of all, for the Cuban people.

CHAPTER 13

MY LITTLE RADIOS

BEGAN DISTRIBUTING MY LITTLE AM/FM/SHORTWAVE RADIOS ABOUT one year after I arrived in Havana. Initially I had used these small radios as party favors at the annual American Fourth of July celebration. As the several hundred guests departed they received a transparent plastic bag tied with red, white, and blue ribbons, containing a compact radio along with a pamphlet featuring quotations from José Martí, Cuba's national hero. The guests—which included Cuban artists and musicians as well as members of the diplomatic community—were delighted, and there was no protest from the Cuban government.

A few months later, a USAID contractor sent many more radios and pamphlets, but I had no way to distribute them. I could not include them with the books we provided to the independent libraries that were run by dissidents and the Catholic Church because the government would confiscate the radios and close the libraries. So, I began to randomly distribute radios to Cubans that I met during the course of my travels. During one such trip, my family and I were visiting Santa Clara, where Che Guevara defeated the last remnants of Fulgencio Batista's army, paving the way to Havana. After touring the massive mausoleum dedicated to Che, we returned to the city center. On one of the small backstreets in a seemingly deserted neighborhood, I spotted a boy on a bicycle and gave him a radio. Before I could close the trunk and get back in the car, I was mobbed. Twenty or more kids suddenly appeared, all demanding radios. As I did my best to fairly distribute them to the unruly crowd, my Cuban state security minders watched closely from their white Lada parked nearby.

My special assistant for the outreach program, Peter Corsell, helped me develop and execute a plan to distribute the radios. During the next two years we gave them to dissidents, to people we met while traveling around the island, and to other diplomats who wished to distribute them to their contacts. By the beginning of 2002 we were handing out several hundred radios per month. It was amazing to see how popular the radios were among ordinary Cubans, who were literally starved for accurate news and information. Of course, the dissident community also clamored for the radios. And it was their access to the subversive little devices that angered Fidel because it frustrated his efforts to keep them isolated and uninformed. The radios gave the dissidents information and connected them to one another. Radio Martí broadcast interviews with the dissidents, so the radios enabled them to keep their followers and sympathizers around the island informed of their activities as well as the government's continued repression. Castro falsely claimed that the radios only received Radio Martí transmissions, but listeners were free to listen to whatever they wanted, whether international news, popular music or Cuban state radio. What Castro really disliked was that my little radios defeated his efforts to jam Radio Martí broadcasts. The fortunate owner of the little radio could change locations, finding a place where there was little or no interference. He also could tune into a myriad of international stations as well as frequent Cuban broadcasts that denounced the radio distribution itself.

Cubans loved these little radios, which were universally seen both as a symbol of freedom and a quiet form of opposition to the Cuban government. Castro blamed the US embargo for all of the island's scarcities and to some degree he was right, the embargo reinforced Castro's efforts to restrict access to communications devices that would have given Cubans greater access to news and information. They could only purchase radios, computers, cell phones, and other communications equipment in "dollar stores," that dealt exclusively in US dollars not in Cuban pesos, even then the selection was severely limited. Most Cubans didn't have the resources to buy a new radio, and could only lament that their cheap Chinese radios had limited range and only picked up local frequencies. According to my friend Ana Maria González, when older radios that were initially capable of accessing signals from beyond Cuba's shores were taken in for repairs, they were "fixed" so that they could no longer access stations broadcasting from off the island.

Castro had become increasingly unhappy with our radio distribution program. He began by complaining to visiting American VIPs, some of whom agreed with him. Wayne Smith, a former head of the US Interests Section, said, "I think it's a terrible idea. Passing out these radios can only look like subverting Cuban internal affairs and trying to undermine the government." I replied that in Africa, US assistance programs distributed radios, and both the people and the government were delighted. When I continued to ignore Fidel's warnings he went on the offensive, condemning me for handing out the radios and claiming that the Interests Section was a "nest of spies," where American diplomats busily concocted "subversive" actions and carried out "electronic surveillance." He announced that he would hold a *tribuna abierta* (open court) on the eastern side of Havana Bay in the town of Alamar to protest my actions, specifically the radio distribution. This was a serious rebuke. Fidel had publicly criticized me soon after my arrival in Havana, but this was the first time he had rallied thousands of people to join him in denouncing me. I knew that the residents of Alamar, a large housing project initially built for athletes competing in the Pan American Games, had no choice but to attend the rally.

I could have remained home, but I decided that I would attend the *tribuna abierta*. This would break all manner of unspoken protocols and undoubtedly horrify Fidel and Foreign Minister Felipe Pérez

Roque, both of whom were expected to speak. But I decided that if I were going to be judged then I would be present. On Saturday, April 5, 2002, at about 9:00 a.m., Consul General Teddy Taylor, Human Rights Officer Victor Vockerot, and I headed to Alamar in my official car, a white sedan with diplomatic license plate "010" that identified the car as belong to the chief of the Interests Section. It could not have been more obvious: I was coming to face my accusers.

There was no place to park; bicycles, cars, and buses were lined up for miles on both sides of the road. There was only one option, which was to park in an area reserved for Castro's and other official vehicles. I couldn't imagine retreating for lack of a parking space, so I maneuvered the car into an open space among the official black sedans and white Ladas. As Teddy, Victor, and I quickly walked away we could hear the loudspeaker repeatedly addressing whomever had left a white sedan in the reserved parking area: "¡Por favor, regresen!" (Please return!). But we kept walking.

As we moved deeper into the crowd, I wondered how long we could escape Cuban state security. Victor and I might blend in, but Teddy, an African American who was well over six feet tall and looked like a former boxing champion, stood out; he was considerably bigger than most Cubans. Still, for perhaps an hour we mingled with the crowd, chatting with those around us. Then we were silently encircled and cordoned off by plainclothes police officers. Amid the crowd of some twenty to thirty thousand people, we three became an island unto ourselves. No one would have dared approach us; everyone recognized that we were in some kind of trouble. I wondered if Cuban state security would demand that we return to our car and leave the rally. But they said nothing to us or anyone else, and seldom even looked our way. Our guards were there to keep the crowd away from us and make sure we behaved.

In the midst of the crowd I could hardly see the stage, but I could hear Foreign Minister Pérez Roque telling the crowd that he was ready to punish me and the Interests Section. He complained about our push to sanction Cuba for human rights violations at the UN, our assistance to dissidents, illegal distribution of propaganda—perhaps books for libraries—and electronic espionage. If that weren't sufficient, he accused the United States of attempting to subvert the Cuban political system through our radio distribution. Although most Cubans would have loved to receive one of my little radios, Pérez Roque claimed, "In this country, we are the ones in charge," adding, "[we] won't let others conspire and subvert the order." Then he warned that he would not allow any little games of conspiracies. I, however, felt perfectly safe with Teddy and Victor at my side.

The big surprise of the day was that Fidel didn't speak. After Pérez Roque's harsh critique, I imagined that Fidel would outdo him by pointing me out to the crowd and claiming that I had attended the *tribuna abierta* in order to sabotage it. I began to worry that the three of us might become targets of a spontaneous *acto de repudio* (act of repudiation). I will never know why Fidel remained silent, but I suspect that he didn't want to give the international media a great story. Imagine the headline: "American Diplomat Openly Defies Castro," daring him to respond to her defiant distribution of portable radios. He likely calculated that it was better to ignore our presence than to provide thirty thousand Cubans with an egregious example of open defiance.

Because we were not subjected to the traditional hours-long oration from Fidel, we arrived back at the Interests Section by noon, where we found one of my favorite dissidents, Felix Bonne. He, like Teddy, was a big man, unlikely to be intimidated by Castro or anyone else. To my surprise he knew that we had been among the crowd at the *tribuna*. (Rumors travel fast in Havana.) I was delighted when he praised my courage in confronting Castro: "You reminded me of a battlefield colonel leading her troops." His flattery was a preface to what he really wanted to communicate, which was to warn me that I must be careful not to push the Cuban government too far. He said that the very existence of the human rights movement would be jeopardized if Castro forced the closure of the US Interests Section; we would no longer be able to witness and report on the suppression of dissent. Without witnesses Castro would become more aggressive in silencing the opposition. Felix said that he and his comrades would have no voice to the outside world if my challenges to the regime resulted in my departure. I knew he was right, but it would be very difficult to stop distributing my little radios.

A few days later the *Dallas Morning News* reported, "Cuban and American officials accused each other of violating international standards Monday in a fiery display of in-your-face diplomacy." I responded that Pérez Roque's assertion that distribution of the radios was a violation of Cuban sovereignty and the Vienna Convention, was false. "It is legal—and not counter to the Vienna Convention," I claimed. More importantly we are trying to bring the world to Cuba's doorstep so that Cubans can make choices about their lives and their futures. Another official at the Interests Section—I assume Gonzalo Gallegos, the head of public affairs—said, "It is ironic that the Cuban regime, which prides itself on waging a battle of ideas, is so concerned about a few radios coming into the hands of average Cuban citizens." A Cuban official immediately responded, "Our diplomats meet with your people to try to normalize relations. We are not trying to subvert internal order. But that's exactly what your people are trying to do here." I thought that if a few thousand radios could create all of this controversy, supposedly undermining the foundations of the Cuban Revolution, we should simply end the embargo and flood the country with free radios!

Pérez Roque's charge was utter nonsense, so I was surprised that some observers believed him. I explained to Mary Murray, the MSNBC bureau chief, that USAID distributed wind-up radios in isolated regions of the world that had no electricity. After Cuba, when I was ambassador to Mali, the USAID director and I started a program in which we distributed "suitcase" radio stations to villages in the northern Sahel and the Sahara Desert; everything that was needed to broadcast was packaged into two suitcases. The villagers were ecstatic because they not only had access to news but were able to announce events and even call for assistance if someone were injured or ill. To this day I know of no government that bans radios. Most authoritarian regimes stick to censoring content rather than preventing their citizens from owning a radio or other communication device.

The question was, what to do now? I didn't want to completely back down, but I knew that it would be folly to continue robustly handing out radios in the face of Castro's and Pérez Roque's threats. I told Peter Corsell, who was even more aggressive than I was in distributing the radios, to slow down. So I was startled one morning when I saw him piling cartons of radios into his car. He explained that Marta Beatriz Roque, one of Cuba's most outspoken dissidents, was planning to distribute them to members of her group. I was worried. It was clear that we were giving the dissidents a vital tool in their efforts to oppose the government. Yet, if we continued to push the envelope, the outreach program could wreck our newly minted détente and I might be asked to leave the country. Nor did I want to be responsible for Marta or other dissidents being jailed. I told Peter to make certain that Marta understood the risks, although it was clear that she, like Castro, saw the radios as a potent weapon in the dissidents' struggle to be heard. I also urged Peter to be even more discreet. After all, Cuban guards who stood watch outside his apartment had undoubtedly watched him pack his car; hopefully they didn't know that radios were in the boxes.

I ultimately couldn't bring myself to curtail support for the dissidents. My not-so-subtle solution was only to provide dissidents with radios when I invited them to the residence. Yet since there were many dissidents outside Havana, I decided to bring the radios to them personally. Elizardo Sánchez, who ran a human rights group, provided me with a list of names and locations of dissidents who lived throughout

the island. I began by meeting with allies of Oswaldo Payá in a small
town outside Matanzas, a port city to the east. They were collecting
signatures for Payá's Project Varela, a petition they hoped would trigger
a referendum on the Cuban Constitution. Knowing that the Ministry
of Foreign Affairs wouldn't approve my travel if I indicated that I would
be visiting dissidents, I sought and obtained permission for the human
rights officer Victor Vockerodt and I to visit Communist Party officials
in Matanzas. (All our travel outside of Havana had to be approved sev-
enty-two hours in advance, in the form of a detailed travel plan, so state
security could prepare to monitor our activities.)

After meeting with the regional party hierarchy, we did not return
on the main highway as I had indicated in the approved plan. Rather,
we set out to find the small rural town where Payá's partisans lived.
Arriving late, having lost our way on the backcountry dirt roads, we
found six men patiently waiting for us and the radios. They told us that
none of their members had been arrested for circulating the petition,
but one member had narrowly escaped having the signatures he had
collected from towns around the area confiscated. In their small town,
some citizens who had signed the petition had been threatened with jail
or losing their jobs if they didn't remove their names. But they bravely
refused to back down.

It was a strange town, almost a hotbed of resistance. It attracted
dissidents and those who had been blacklisted from jobs in tourism
after attempting to flee to the United States. It made sense that those
who had been cast out by the system might choose to live in close proximity to one another. The Cuban government built towns in the countryside that were exclusively for retired military, security, and police
forces. I was amused to imagine that scattered throughout the countryside were a few towns that catered to dissidents as well as the many
that were home to loyal military retirees. It also made me realize that
we knew very little about rural Cuba.

Castro hoped to derail Payá's Project Varela without attracting

Me and one of my little radios that so annoyed Fidel. (*Photo credit: Associated Press*)

Not even the pouring rain could dampen Fidel's wrath. (*Photo credit: Reuters*)

Alexandra's painting that I feared Fidel might covet. (*Photo courtesy of author*)

The eagle that flew off the USS *Maine* Monument and was given to the US ambassador as a symbol of friendship—how long before those bonds between our countries will be restored? (*Photo courtesy of author*)

Revolución is Independence! Not all Cubans believe that. *(Photo courtesy of author)*

Long Live the Revolución! *(Photo courtesy of author)*

Victory at the Bay of Pigs—Fidel claimed it was the first military victory against
US imperialism in the hemisphere. *(Photo courtesy of author)*

Country or Death! Some take it literally and lose their lives attempting to cross
the Florida Straits in flimsy crafts and without provisions. *(Photo courtesy of author)*

The cardboard Fidel who was both loved and feared.　(*Photo courtesy of author*)

Granma, the overloaded yacht that broughi Fidel and his rebels back to Cuba.
(*Photo courtesy of author*)

Havana and me—my only absolutely clear victory in my ongoing competition with Fidel.

(*Photo credit: Reuters*)

attention from the media or international human rights groups. If successful, his cat and mouse game would defeat the initiative by making it impossible to collect signatures and deliver the petitions to Cuba's National Assembly. Castro could have quickly ended Project Varela by jailing the organizers, but he evidently did not want to risk curtailing American travel, which would be the most obvious form of retaliation. Even more worrisome was the possibility that negative publicity would lead former president Jimmy Carter to cancel his upcoming visit to Cuba.

We wished the men good luck, left our radios and books, and started back to Havana. It wasn't long before I saw a woman trudging along the side of a dirt road. I stopped and offered her a ride. Once she was settled in the car, I handed her a radio. When I glanced back, tears were running down her cheeks. When I asked why she was crying, she replied, "Now, I have a birthday present for my son." After dropping her off and finding our way onto a paved road, we picked up two young women to whom I also gave a couple of radios. One asked, "Can I have two more?" The girls explained that they wanted radios for their brothers were imprisoned in the large gray building we had passed a mile back. They had been sentenced to twenty years for killing a neighbor's pig.

I had now been in Cuba almost three years. The longer I stayed, the more I liked the country and the people, and the sorrier I felt for those who were forced to live under the omnipresent and pervasive control of the Castro regime. There was no doubt in my mind that Cubans were deprived of essential freedoms, but I didn't think that our policy of isolation was an effective way to bring about change. I believed that the best way to promote change in Cuba was by empowering the Cuban people. Helping to keep them poor and isolated only helped Castro to maintain control. Yet everything we did to enable the Cuban people to seek change depended on the regime's forbearance. If we were too aggressive, Castro would smash our endeavors by throwing me or my officers out of the country or by jailing the dissidents. But I was finding it increasingly difficult to assess the costs and benefits of my actions, like the radio distribution program. Sometimes I wanted to aggressively confront the oppressive power of the Cuban state, yet I knew that this was dangerous, and I was already treading near the edge of Castro's patience.

Having successfully delivered radios to supporters of Project Varela, I decided to take a six-day tour of the island, which is shaped like a shark jumping out of the sea. I planned that Victor and I would drive from Havana, at the base of the shark's head, down its spine to the second-largest city, Santiago de Cuba, located on the shark's tail. During our travels, we met with government officials, average citizens, and dissidents, leaving behind radios and books with everyone but the officials. Our first stop was the large city of Camaguey in central Cuba, where we visited three Protestant churches. I left several cartons of radios with a young, dynamic pastor of a large Baptist church. He was delighted, until the next morning when he showed up sheepishly at our hotel to ask that we take the radios back. He apologized profusely, but did not explain his decision. It was clear he had been warned not to keep them.

The next day we reached the small village of El Cobre where Cuba's patron saint, the Virgin of Charity, is enshrined in a basilica that overlooks the bay surrounding Santiago de Cuba. She is known as the Mambisa Virgin because she was venerated by Cuba's independence fighters—called *Mambises*—who fought alongside Teddy Roosevelt and his Rough Riders. Jewels and small favors left by the humble and the mighty were displayed in a glass container. Ernest Hemingway gave his Nobel Prize for the story of a Cuban fisherman, *The Old Man and the Sea*, to the virgin. Hemingway loved Cuba, where he lived until shortly before his death in a beautiful home called Finca Vigía (Lookout House) on a hill outside Havana. We didn't leave any radios with the virgin but we did drop off a few in El Cobre.

When we reached Santiago de Cuba, dissidents were waiting for us in a wooden three-story house, likely built in the early twentieth century. We were escorted up a few flights of rickety stairs and ushered into room that seemed to have been set up solely to receive us. There were a few chairs, but no tables, rugs, or pictures. Before we could exchange pleasantries, one of the dissidents took the carton of radios from Victor, thanked him, and disappeared. The dissidents explained that they knew that state security was watching us and, fearing that the radios would be confiscated, planned to immediately give them to their members. I was troubled because it seemed as if we had inadvertently become involved in subversive activities. I suggested that I might stop the distribution to prevent them from being harassed or jailed. "Oh, no," they exclaimed, "the radios are well worth the risk. They connect us, so we aren't alone."

It wasn't simply the loss of a job or Communist Party position that made life difficult for those Cubans who defied authority; rather, it was unkind neighbors who would ostracize their entire family. It was not unusual for those with independent views, whether or not they were labeled dissidents, to be expelled from their jobs and the party. We visited a former party official who had lost her job as a schoolteacher and been expelled from the party for a perceived failure to conform strictly to party orthodoxy. To make her life even more miserable, local officials moved another family into her home. The male head of the new family harassed her and her daughters, calling them *putas* (whores). She had no way to stop the abusive new occupant of her home. To maintain a modicum of peace, she drew a chalk line down the middle of the living room, over which no member of either family could pass. We dropped off books for her library and left a few radios. We also visited a small library established by a physical education teacher who had lost his job and now instructed neighborhood children in basketball and other sports.

One safe harbor was Father Conrado's church, located a few blocks from the Moncada Barracks, where Castro's failed attack on

July 26, 1953, ignited the revolution. The wooden church had a high ceiling, windows with wooden shutters, and hand-hewn pews. It was peaceful, clean, and simple, a place where those who were shunned found sanctuary. Behind the nave, Father Conrado had built a kitchen and a library so that he could offer substance for body and soul. Our books supplied the library and our radios helped connect those who had been cut off from friends, jobs, and social lives.

I was relieved to leave Santiago de Cuba; we had met too many wretched people who had little hope of creating better lives. We were scheduled to make one last stop, just off the principal highway. I parked the car on a steep incline, a few feet from the door of a house that looked as if it would tumble off its perch in a strong wind. Our host had been the leader of an independent farmers' union that had called a nationwide strike. He and the other strike leaders were jailed and the strike squelched. After serving their prison terms, the farmers were released, but still harassed, and often denied the right to purchase seeds or fertilizer for their small plots of land. Although his wife had divorced him and his neighbors avoided him, the farmer did not regret his opposition to the government.

As we wound down the hill, a small white Lada waited to bid us farewell. Undoubtedly its occupants were relieved that no more radios would be given out in their region. An hour or so later, we arrived at Guantanamo City, which is relatively prosperous because of the pensions paid to those Cubans who once worked at the US naval base. We didn't find our contact at home, so we continued into the Sierra Maestra just as a tropical storm struck. Torrents of rain pushed dirt and rocks down the steep and winding highway known as La Farola (The Lamppost or The Streetlamp) because the new road, built through the mountains by Castro's revolutionary government, lighted the way to Baracoa on the east coast. We pressed ahead into the rain and mist, at times waiting for passing truckers to clear the debris with shovels and rakes. Christopher Columbus wrote in his log that Baracoa was the "most beautiful place in the world," but it didn't seem so to me. As we descended toward the coast, the evening was still gray and drizzling rain, making the countryside appear dreary, decaying, and uncomfortably cold.

We went directly to the Catedral Nuestra Señora de la Asunción, a massive structure with a rich interior of stained-glass windows and carved saints. Parishioners were praying, cleaning, and admiring a replica of a cross that Columbus planted when he sailed into the sheltered Bahía del Miel (Bay of Honey). The next day we chatted with the Spanish priest responsible for the region, who told us that he often traveled because there were too few priests to minister to the faithful in the countryside. He lamented that the government strictly limited the number of foreign priests, and there were few local seminaries to train Cubans. We left behind several boxes of books with radios hidden beneath them. Before we left town, I gave a woman and her child several comic-book style children's books. She was delighted. Unlike in other Caribbean countries, there weren't many children in the towns we visited, or in Cuba generally. The widespread access to birth control combined with a housing shortage and a well-educated population contribute to a very low birth rate. Although there is little political liberty, the Cuban government since the 1990s has seldom interfered in personal issues such as religious belief and social norms. Just across the Windward Passage, Haitians have considerably more individual liberty but are much poorer, and have less access to education and health care. Consequently, Haiti's ten to eleven million people barely survive on one-third of an island, whereas Cubans with the same population numbers as Haiti live on the largest island in the Caribbean. Overpopulated Haiti had been denuded of trees, soil, and potential for a better future. Cuba's low birth rate had contributed to preserving its lush environment, but the absence of personal liberty dims the promise of a better life for most Cubans.

We departed Baracoa on a gravel road that snaked along the coast into one of the most isolated regions in the entire Caribbean, the Alejandro de Humboldt National Park, named for a German scientist, Alexander von Humboldt, who in the 1800s documented its profuse biodiversity and endemic species. Less than an hour later we reached a paved road where brownish liquid spurted from the large gray pipes that carried polluted water from the huge nickel mines nearby. Every few miles, signs sitting in stale, red puddles and ponds warned us not to trespass and not to take photos. As we entered the mining town of Moa—which was formerly property of the US government—heavy dark clouds billowed over rows of dung-colored dormitories, housing for mine workers. On the other side of Moa we headed up an incline passed the headquarters of Sherritt International, the Canadian company that runs the mines. The checkpoint gate was open, so I went sailing through onto a packed-dirt road that led straight into an enormous red-earth, open-pit mine. Winding our way upward, we could see the sluggish mud-colored river far below the scarred landscape, denuded of all vegetation. Although it was midday the sky was dark and the air heavy, as huge yellow dump trucks loaded with nickel ore lumbered toward the processing plant. It was otherworldly, something akin to Dante's inferno, as each level became yet a wider expanse of barren, red earth.

As we reached the top of the open-pit mine, a white pickup truck with two security guards frantically waved us down. As they closed in on us, I shoved Victor's camera under the seat. The guard yelled in Spanish, "What are you doing here? You are trespassing. Do you have a camera?"

"No," I lied. Attempting to pretend that we were naïve tourists who'd lost their way, I asked "Where are we?" Ordering us to follow him, the guard stomped away. We proceeded down the hill, with the pickup in front and a very large yellow dump truck—the tire of which could have easily obliterated our car—tailing us. Approaching the Sherritt offices, the guard waved us to a stop. I didn't hesitate; I just kept driving. I had no doubt that even I, the head of the American mission, would suffer a good deal of abuse for entering the mine without permission. I wasn't going to risk being detained in Moa. These guards weren't like the local Havana police who had orders to never to confront diplomats.

Back on the main highway, I stepped on the gas but could see the white pickup behind us. I sped up, then slowed down, to confirm that they were tailing us. They were. Several miles up the road, the pickup pulled up next to us as the guard shouted that we must pull over. I shook my head, not a chance. Then, the driver swerved, attempting to force us off the road. I stepped on the gas pedal, narrowly escaping our pursuers. After another ten minutes, as we outdistanced them, they finally gave up the chase.

Back home in Havana, I was relieved that I didn't receive an official complaint for entering private property without permission. Perhaps Sherritt was too embarrassed to protest our intrusion, having negligently left the gates to the mine open and then having failed to prevent our escape. I complained to the Canadian ambassador about the environmental disaster in Moa and showed him the photos that Victor had taken of the open-pit mine. We also sent them to the US State Department, but nothing could be done because Sherritt executives were already under US sanctions for operating in Cuba on expropriated property. I have visited mines in Ethiopia, Madagascar, Peru, and Sierra Leone, but never have I seen anything approaching the dreadful conditions in Moa. No care was taken to repair pipes, to prevent erosion into the river, or to control the spewing fumes that completely blocked the sun. Castro's government had forfeited its sovereignty over this wrecked place without protest. Sherritt had created an environmental disaster that no Cuban could protest and no international environmental organization could visit. Yet, less than one hundred miles to the south, the US military operated the Guantanamo Bay Naval Base with scrupulous regard for the environment and the health of its workers.

It was becoming evident to the Cuban government that neither my staff nor I were cowed by Castro's threats. Distributing the radios was like an addiction that once started was hard to stop, and it was contagious. I gave Lynda Hare, the spouse of the British ambassador, cartons of radios to give to children in Havana's principal cancer facility, where she arranged regular outings for the patients. Ryan Dooley, who replaced Victor while he was on vacation, was as brazen as Peter and me. One Saturday, Ryan and I set out to locate the former residence of our ambassadors and the counsels before them. Ryan assured me he had found the house, which had been used prior to the completion in 1942 of the American residence where I lived. We pulled up in front of a desolate shell, open to the weather, and completely uninhabitable. We were greeted at the entrance by a nine-foot-tall statue of Venus out of whose breasts water once flowed. "Ryan," I exclaimed, "There is no way this could have been an American envoy's house."

Laughing, we took a last look around and headed back to the road, where a few youngsters were admiring our sedan. I opened the trunk and, as Ryan was getting out the radios, a white Lada came around the block. I yelled at him to forget the radios and get in the car. As we drove away I looked back, only to discover that state security officers had gotten out to inspect a cardboard box sitting in the middle of the road. Ryan had tossed the box of radios onto the road, hoping the kids would take them. A few years later, after a speech I made in California, a young Cuban woman told me that her father who worked for Cuba's Ministry of the Interior had obtained one of my radios, which she said he loved. I suspect that box of radios Ryan had left for the kids instead went to the men in the white Lada.

My confrontational attitude toward the Cuban government earned me many critics, including several congresspeople and former State Department colleagues like Wayne Smith, a chief of the Interests Section from 1979 to 1982, whose memoir, *The Closest of Enemies: A Personal and Diplomatic Account of U.S. – Cuban Relations Since 1957*, revealed his disillusionment with our policy. I agreed with Wayne that our policy was too often ineffective and even harmful, but I thought that the embargo should not be used to excuse Castro's oppressive rule. It seemed to me that if we were going to appease Castro, we would have to stop defending the dissidents, which was something I was unwilling to do. I also felt strongly that too often those who advocate on either side of our Cuba policy become polarized, perceiving every issue and incident in black and white rather than shades of gray.

Being an outspoken diplomat who tested the limits of Castro's patience meant there was no middle ground. To those who opposed US policy toward Cuba I was a troublemaker and antagonist, and to those who hated Castro I was a conquering heroine. This binary distinction bothered me because I was not a fervent anti-Castro crusader. I rejected and lamented Fidel's absolute control over Cuba, but I very much wanted to foster better relations between our countries. In February 2002, I briefed a delegation of Democratic congressional representatives from California. This was well before Castro condemned my radio distribution in April, but after he had bitterly criticized my press conference about Guantanamo Bay. We met the delegation at the grand old Hotel Nacional, which overlooks Havana's seafront as well as the Interests Section. My husband Bob and I entered a small room that had been reserved for the meeting. Three men and a woman sat around a large, polished wooden table in the center of the room. Having been appointed by President Bill Clinton, I was unconsciously expecting a warm welcome, but the congresspersons did not seem friendly; they merely nodded, not bothering to stand or shake hands. I smiled, welcomed them to Cuba, and began to deliver my standard briefing. Only a few minutes passed before a large red-faced congressman interrupted. "Who do you think you are representing here in Cuba?" he snarled. I replied that I had been sent by President Clinton but now represented the Bush administration. Then another member of the delegation, a large woman with very red lipstick averred, "You are not fit to represent our country," adding haughtily, "I am a former ambassador, and I am ashamed of you." One of the men chimed in, "I'll get you fired." I told them that I was doing my best and then left. I had been summoned not to give a briefing but to receive a scolding.

Just like the anti-Castro Cuban Americans, the California delegation saw Cuba only in terms of black and white. Castro had publicly complained about me, so I was a poor representative. To Cuban Americans, for the same reason, I was terrific. It didn't matter to either side whether I was right or wrong on any given issue or generally doing an objectively good job in representing our country. All that mattered was what Castro thought about me. Some of the criticism stung, but I had long ago become accustomed to doing what I believed was right. In truth, both sides had good reason to dislike me. The Cuban Americans opposed my efforts to keep in place the Clinton administration's liberal travel measures but appreciated my confrontations with Castro. The California delegation, which was ironically taking advantage of the travel measures for which I had advocated, was disgusted with me because I refused to appease Fidel.

I wished that those who were supportive of and opposed to the revolution could see Cuba as it was, not as they wished it to be. The embargo was an unfair and ineffective punishment, but opposing the embargo didn't make Fidel Castro any less of a dictator. Both US policy and the Cuban government deserved criticism. Perhaps I did as well. I was walking a tightrope, persuading Bush to continue the Clinton policies while simultaneously frustrating the regime through various acts of confrontation.

I couldn't help but think that if the pro-Castro California congressional representatives had been as dedicated as their Cuban American counterparts, they might have served as an effective counterweight against them. But the Californians were much more interested in dinner and a photo op with Fidel than in doing the actual work required to modify US policy toward Cuba. Thus the policy remained under the influence of the conservative Cuban Americans who were absolutely dedicated to undermining Castro and his revolution.

CHAPTER 14

THE PRESIDENT AND THE DISSIDENT

THE INTERNATIONAL PRESS HAD SWARMED INTO HAVANA IN ANTICI-
pation of former president Jimmy Carter's visit, the first presidential trip to Cuba since Calvin Coolidge visited the island in
1928. With a few days to spare before Carter's arrival, the media was
looking for stories. Gonzalo Gallegos, the US Interests Sections' public
affairs officer, pointed them toward the dissidents. The *Washington
Post* wrote, "Victor Rolando Arroyo has a brand-new shortwave radio,
a powerful little thing that allows him to pick up programs from all
over the world, including his favorite: Radio Martí." Prior to Carter's
arrival I had met with Arroyo and other dissidents in the western town
of Pinar del Rio, leaving behind the little radios that Fidel so detested.

The presence of hundreds of reporters in Havana for the former
president's visit created a feeling of excitement and anticipation. ABC's
George Stephanopoulos, who had once been a senior adviser to Bill
Clinton, was broadcasting live from the Havana Hilton, which was
christened the Habana Libre when it was completed in 1958, only a
year before Castro set up his temporary headquarters there after defeating Fulgencio Batista. Before our on-air interview I took the opportunity to tell Stephanopoulos that Oswaldo Payá's Project Varela was
close to having gathered the ten thousand signatures needed to request
a vote on the Cuban Constitution. Demonstrating his political acumen,
Stephanopoulos predicted that Payá would present the petition to the

National Assembly a few days before Carter arrived, thereby giving the project maximum exposure. Proving that he was an equally impressive political strategist, Payá did exactly that. The media immediately broadcast the news that dissidents were challenging Castro's government, demanding freedom of speech, private enterprise, and the release of political prisoners.

Payá had put the former president in a difficult position even before he arrived in Havana. If Carter endorsed Project Varela it would deeply antagonize his host, Fidel Castro. But if he failed to do so, it could undermine his standing as a strong advocate for human rights. No matter which way Carter decided, the press would have a great story.

Project Varela wasn't the only difficulty that Carter would confront during his Cuba visit. Only days before his arrival, on May 7, John Bolton, the undersecretary of state for arms control, gave a speech at the Heritage Foundation accusing the Cuban government of having "a limited offensive biological warfare research and development effort" and "provided dual-use biotechnology to other rogue states." The spokesman for the Cuban Interests Section in Washington, DC, sharply responded, "What he said is a big lie and a big slander."

In 1991 Jorge Mas Canosa of the Cuban American National Foundation (CANF) had done the same thing, but his concern was somewhat more valid. He claimed that shoddy construction of the Juraguá Nuclear Power Plant by the Soviet Union was threatening Florida and the East Coast. The Cuban government responded by allowing an inspection of the facility by the International Atomic Energy Commission, which indeed found shoddy work on the connections among cooling pipes. The need for extensive repairs, combined with a lack of financing and pressure from the United States, halted construction and the power plant was never completed. The large dome can still be seen from the town of Cienfuegos on Cuba's western coast. Bolton's claim, like Mas Canosa's, was designed to energize the diaspora. It was, however, untrue. Cuba was not manufacturing biological weapons.

Carter and his team felt that they had been blindsided. They had specifically asked the intelligence agencies and the State Department if Cuba was involved in any terrorist activities. The response was negative. It seemed to Carter's staff that Bolton was deliberately trying to sabotage his visit. Three years earlier, prior to my taking the post in Havana, the intelligence community had briefed me on Cuba's manufacture, research, and development of medicines. Their conclusion was that Cuba was not involved in producing bioweapons. I doubted that much had changed and suspected that Bolton was attempting both to undermine Carter's visit and to provide conservatives with justification for returning to a hardline policy toward Cuba.

On May 12, 2002, President and Mrs. Carter arrived in Havana with Bolton's accusation hanging over them and the press waiting to see how Carter would respond to Project Varela. Standing alongside other diplomats and the Cuban hierarchy, I watched as Carter's private jet circled and landed at the José Martí International airport. The plane rolled to a stop, a ramp was pushed to the door, and Jimmy and Rosalynn Carter stepped onto Cuban soil. Fidel, dressed in a handsome double-breasted pinstriped suit and a patterned red tie, shook their hands and walked them down the line of official greeters. The media had been waiting for the handshake between Fidel and me. If I shook his hand, some in the Cuban diaspora would feel that I—their champion who was defying Castro—had betrayed them. To me the handshake meant little; it was standard protocol, and I was prepared for some bad publicity. But Fidel grabbed and released my hand so quickly that the media missed the photo opportunity. I later told them that Fidel was afraid that I was going to slip him one of my little radios.

I couldn't help but be hopeful for our two estranged countries as we stood at attention for the playing of the American and Cuban national anthems and the US and Cuban flags waved side by side in the tropical breeze. Castro welcomed Carter by commending his courage in visiting Cuba amid the recent controversy. He denounced Bolton's "sinister lies," telling Carter that he could visit any facility he wished along with experts of his choice. Avoiding the controversy, Carter replied that he was indeed courageous because he was going to give his remarks in Spanish, adding only that he was looking forward to meeting the Cuban people. After the ceremony Rosalynn, President Carter, and Castro drove to the Hotel Santa Isabel in Fidel's Soviet-era, armored ZiL limousine, trailed by a caravan of white Ladas and Mercedes-Benzes. Eusebio Leal Spangler, the historian of the city of Havana who had done so much to restore the city, guided them on a walking tour through Cathedral Square and to the Hotel Ambos Mundos (Two Worlds), where Ernest Hemingway lived when he first arrived in Cuba.

In the afternoon the Carters came to my residence for a Country Team briefing and to meet with the families of our diplomatic staff. I was nervous because I had to convince Carter that he must meet with Payá prior to his speech at the University of Havana, which would be broadcast live across the island on Tuesday afternoon. The problem was that Carter didn't plan to meet with the dissidents until after his speech, once the official part of his visit was completed. But if he didn't meet with Payá before the speech, it was unlikely that he would mention Project Varela. Carter had been told by Cuban officials like Ricardo Alarcón that it was a "North American" project, and critics of my outreach program had reinforced the idea that the dissidents, including Payá, were financially supported by the US Interests Section. I had tried to overcome this incorrect impression by sending Carter a letter describing Project Varela and the Cuban Spring it was helping to create. I also attempted to sway Carter and his advisers by telling the host of a popular television show in Miami that I was certain the former president would address democracy and human rights in his speech.

Carter's speech was the only way that Cubans would learn that some of their compatriots were demanding a change in the way they were governed. Most had negligible access to international newspapers, TV, or radio broadcasts (except for the radios we were handing out), so they were unaware of the discussion surrounding Project Varela. But if Carter didn't endorse the initiative, Cuban Americans would criticize him for missing an opportunity to promote freedom in Cuba. I knew I couldn't change Carter's view that the dissidents were creatures of President George W. Bush's administration, but if I could persuade him to meet Payá before the speech he would at least have a chance to hear him out and make up his own mind; once Carter had spoken with Payá firsthand, he could decide whether or not to include Project Varela in his remarks. I was confident that if Payá explained Project Varela to the former president, he would support it. And if he did not meet with Payá, he would certainly regret the lost opportunity to endorse publicly the dissidents' work to bring greater freedom to the Cuban people.

I was in a tough spot. In advance of Carter's visit, his staff had negotiated with the Cubans exactly how the visit would unfold. If Carter met with Payá, as I wished, it would contravene the agreement between his staff and the Cuban government, in which he would only meet with the dissidents after the official portion of his visited had ended. Moreover, Carter's staff wanted the former president to avoid taking sides in what they mistakenly believed was a political battle between Washington and Havana. Carter was coming as a peacemaker, not to roil the waters. But before Carter had even set foot on Cuban soil his visit had been politicized by Bolton and by Payá. He and his team were undoubtedly learning what I had discovered many times before: nothing is above politics when it comes to Cuba, especially if a former US president is involved.

President Carter was relaxed, friendly, and interested in hearing our opinions. The Country Team, which consisted of the political, economic, and consular sections as well as other agencies represented at the Interests Section, answered his questions about Cuba and our bilateral relations. Carter then gave me an opening by asking about Project Varela. I told him it was an entirely homegrown effort that had been named for an eighteenth-century Cuban priest who was a fierce antislavery advocate. I explained that I had initially doubted that Payá would succeed in collecting the required ten thousand signatures to file a referendum, that it would be next to impossible for him to travel throughout the country, which required permission from authorities who would be unwilling to help. Not to mention that travel was expensive and transport limited. But with the help of Elizardo Sánchez, who kept track of all the dissidents, Payá didn't have to travel; rather, he recruited dissidents across the island to collect signatures. The project had begun quietly, and it wasn't until the final months of the campaign that my staff and I realized that Payá would succeed. I suspect that Castro also had misjudged the attraction of Project Varela because state security and the local police had been slow to disrupt it. By the time they realized that the project was likely to succeed it was too late to stop it without using force. By then Castro's choices were limited; if he crushed the project Carter would cancel his visit.

I told Carter that Oswaldo Payá was a devout Catholic who in the early years of the revolution had been sent to a reeducation camp because of his beliefs. His group was aligned philosophically with Europe's Christian Democrats, who sought peaceful and legal means of initiating change. Most critically, Project Varela represented the Cuban people's profound longing for greater freedom. Carter then asked a final question that would determine whether he met with Payá in advance of his speech. "Have you given Payá any money?" His staff suspected that we had used US government funds to reinforce the dissidents. We had the funds in the outreach program that could have been used to fund the dissidents, but I decided that doing so would compromise them. I had once almost broken my self-imposed rule not to give them money when a Cuban American supporter of Marta Beatriz Roque asked me to deliver five hundred dollars to her. I took the check back to Havana with the intention of giving it to her, but decided it was too risky and returned the money. This was a fortuitous decision—a few months later Marta's trusted assistant gave Cuban state security all her records, including those that listed donors.

"No, Mr. President," I declared, "We have given them radios and books, but no money." Had we given Payá money from any American source, public or private, Carter would have considered the project tainted. I did not agree; if we had provided financial assistance, it would not have lessened the validity of Project Varela. But Payá had never asked for financial support, and we didn't provide any. With the briefing now over, President and Mrs. Carter walked to the terrace, where they greeted the families of our diplomats and the Cuban staff employed at my residence, two of whom had been hired when Carter approved the Interests Section agreement in 1977. They posed for photos on the large terrace and under the outstretched wings of the bronze eagle given to a previous American ambassador as a symbol of everlasting US-Cuban friendship.

Carter made his speech on late Tuesday afternoon in the Aula Magna (Great Classroom) at the University of Havana. My husband Bob and I were among Carter's guests. Since my arrival over two years earlier, this was the first time I had been invited to attend an official event at which Fidel was present. (The Old Timers Baseball game that some of my staff and I attended when I first arrived might be considered an invitation to an event at which Fidel was present, but it had been a mistake.) We took our seats in a small section reserved for Carter's team. It was a few feet to the right of the podium, facing Fidel and the Cuban hierarchy who were seated in the front rows. Carter opened his speech by thanking his hosts. He briefly reviewed our tangled history, concluding, "The hard truth is that neither the United States or Cuba has managed to define a positive or beneficial relationship." He suggested that the United States could take steps to improve the relationship by allowing unrestricted travel, repealing the embargo, and setting up a commission to resolve expropriated property. As for Cuba, he lamented the fact that it denies freedoms to those who oppose its socialist government.

Carter was approaching the end of his remarks and had not mentioned Project Varela. I knew that he had met with Oswaldo Payá and Elizardo Sánchez, head of the Cuban Human Rights Commission, on Monday morning, after his meeting with us at the residence. I had been hopeful, but I was beginning to despair, when Carter gently brought up the issues. He noted that, "Articles 63 and 88 of your constitution allows citizens to petition the National Assembly to permit a referendum to change laws if 10,000 or more citizens sign it. I am informed that such an effort, called the Varela Project, has gathered sufficient signatures and has presented such a petition to the National Assembly. When Cubans exercise this freedom to change laws peacefully by direct vote, the world will see that Cubans, and not foreigners, will determine the future of this country." Done! I was thankful and relieved but that didn't stop me from intently watching for Fidel's reaction. Throughout the speech, he had remained stone-faced, even as Carter called for ending the embargo. Now in the face of Carter's challenge not a flicker of emotion crossed his face. A minute or so later there was polite applause as Carter finished his speech and asked for questions. Instead of questions there were comments, as the rector of the University of Havana and several colleagues spiritedly denounced Project Varela. They claimed that there was no need to change the constitution because Cubans had all the freedoms they required. Carter responded by defending Payá's initiative. I thought their attack was a strategic mistake. Most Cubans had never heard of Project Varela until Carter mentioned it. Many might have ignored or missed the reference to it had the rector not forced Carter to defend it.

As soon as the questions were over, Fidel stood up and headed over to Carter with arms outstretched. I had started toward Carter to congratulate him, but had to quickly duck out of Fidel's path in order to avoid being caught in an embrace between the two leaders. Together Carter and Fidel made their way outside to cheering students and a media anxious to discover more about Project Varela. Fidel waved everyone away. There would be no more questions; the two leaders were going to a baseball game. Afterward Carter would go about the rest of his visit. In the meantime, Fidel would plan his response, which would come several weeks later.

The crowds and security were so heavy that my official car couldn't get through to retrieve Bob and me, so we began walking. As we were turning a corner, a small white Lada drove by, turned around, and made an abrupt stop across the street from us. Foreign Minister Felipe Pérez Roque jumped out of the Lada, greeting me with "¿Como estas, Vicki? Did you like the speech? How is everything?" I was astonished. Usually he ignored me, and now he was offering us a ride. Seeing my car and driver turning the corner, I had a good excuse to refuse. And I couldn't imagine the three of us stuffed into the back seat of his little Lada. It turned out that Pérez Roque's friendliness was for a reason—he wanted me to issue a visa to Mariela Castro, Raúl Castro's daughter, who hoped to attend an upcoming gender rights conference in California. I assured him that I would do my best. When Mariela received the visa and later traveled to California, there were no objections from Cuban American legislators. Ten years later, when the administration of President Barack Obama issued Mariela another visa to attend a Latin American Studies conference in San Francisco, Cuban American senators Bob Menendez (D-NJ) and Marco Rubio (R-FL) vehemently protested. Someone with some insight into US-Cuba relations once said, "The US never remembers and Cuba never forgets."

Carter's speech was the high point of his visit. He had bravely confronted Castro in public by telling him that he ought to respect the petition and allow a referendum on the Cuban Constitution. He had also been true to his principles by calling for an end to the US embargo. He didn't mention Bolton's accusation. There was no need to, because prior to his speech Carter had visited the Cuban Center for Genetic Engineering, the facility that Bolton alleged was manufacturing bioweapons. After touring the center, Carter told the press that the Cuban government was not engaged in manufacturing biological weapons.

Cuban scientists assured him that they strictly followed international protocols when sharing technology used in manufacturing medicines and vaccines. Carter added that the Cuban government had recently signed an agreement to share technology with Iran, but had not yet done so. Several weeks later, a congressional hearing concluded that while Cuba had the capacity to create biological weapons, there was no evidence to indicate that it was doing so. Bolton's accusation had served only to detract from Carter's visit and from Project Varela and to reveal that Assistant Secretary Reich had gained an important ally in his crusade for a harsher policy.

At his farewell press conference, President Carter reiterated that he had not come to Cuba to interfere in internal matters. Convinced that Project Varela was a homegrown initiative, and a good one, Carter again urged Castro to permit a referendum on the constitution. As Carter well understood, he had intervened in Cuba's internal politics, but in the best possible way. He had reinforced peaceful dissent. He had also narrowly escaped calling his reputation as a defender of democracy and human rights into question. Had Carter not endorsed Project Varela, critics would have claimed that he was too timid and too willing to allow Castro to control his visit. But once he met with Payá and Sánchez, he didn't hesitate to defy Castro.

Carter's visit gave the Cuban people hope, but it came at a high price. Many of the leaders associated with Project Varela were jailed a year later during the Black Spring of 2003. Payá's new found fame would protect him for the next decade, but not forever as, on July 22, 2012—a little over a decade later—he died in a suspicious car crash while traveling in eastern Cuba. It has not been proven, but it is possible that Cuban state security forced Payá's car off the road. Before his tragic death he would continue collecting signatures, bringing the total to over thirty thousand. Although Project Varela was ultimately unsuccessful, it did briefly challenge the Cuban government.

The Carters' departure was far different from the pomp and ceremony that accompanied their arrival. Neither diplomats nor the press, other than local media, were present. An unsmiling Castro was dressed in his customary fatigues, the tailored suit and tie a faint memory. Castro was making it clear that nothing had changed. He would soon take measures to correct any misimpressions that Carter's visit might have left behind.

A few weeks after Carter's departure, the Cuban Constitution was declared "irrevocable," thereby ensuring that Project Varela could never obtain its objective of making Cuba's communist system more democratic. Neighborhood block committees went door-to-door collecting signatures on a petition that declared the constitution "irrevocable." Ninety-eight percent of Cuban adults signed. One of the few who did not was my friend Ana Maria González, who managed to be away from home each time someone brought the petition to her house. The fact that so few Cubans had the courage not to sign was a strong indication that they were not about to rise up against their government, no matter how bad the conditions.

In late June, Cuba's National Assembly of 559 members unanimously voted to sanctify its "irrevocable" constitution, adding, "Capitalism will never return again." When challenged, Castro always has a handy scapegoat. In his speech to the gathered officials, Fidel once again tied the US Interests Section to the dissidents, complaining, "American diplomats go around the country as they like, organizing networks and conspiracies" and adding, "We are not willing to permit violations of our sovereignty, nor the humiliating disregard of norms ruling the conduct of diplomats." Finally, he warned that further "violation of our sovereignty" would put the migration accords and the Interests Section at risk.

CANF's Executive Director, Joe Garcia, was delighted, exclaiming, "For the first time in his life Castro is on the defensive." Castro was genuinely upset—Project Varela had disrupted Carter's visit, and he feared the consequences of shutting down our outreach program.

But I didn't agree with Joe that Castro was "creating a bubble because he has nowhere else to go." Castro was still very much in charge. I had no doubt that if he felt truly threatened, he would not hesitate to take whatever action was needed to preserve his rule, whether it was jailing the dissidents, aborting the migration accords, or closing the Interests Section.

Only days after Carter's departure I received a moving letter from Payá. He wrote that he wanted to express his appreciation for my public insistence that Cubans must determine Cuba's future. He also made clear that he hoped that the United States would neither revert to a harsh policy nor seek to impose our will on Cuba. I certainly agreed with him. President Carter's visit had given Payá hope that there might be a dialogue between our governments, and thus his letter also suggested that the dissidents participate in any discussions or negotiations we might undertake with the Cuban government. Unfortunately, that was a nonstarter—Castro would never permit the dissidents to be present. The question of the appropriate role and treatment of Cuba's dissident community remains unanswered even today, continuing to obstruct relations between the United States and Cuba.

CHAPTER 15

MR. W. VERSUS MR. CASTRO

THREE AND A HALF YEARS OF COOPERATIVE RELATIONS—TWO UNDER President Bill Clinton and eighteen months under President George W. Bush—had created the Cuban Spring of 2002, the most open period since the Cuban Revolution. Secretary of Housing and Urban Development Mel Martinez and Emilio Gonzalez, senior director for Western Hemisphere affairs at the National Security Council (NSC)—both of whom advised the president on Cuba—had expressed that they wished to continue Bush's moderate approach to Cuba, which had resulted in benefits for both governments. Fidel Castro had cooperated in the incarceration of unlawful enemy combatants from the war in Afghanistan at Guantanamo Bay, American farmers were enjoying millions of dollars in sales of agricultural products, and civil society in Cuba had more freedom to flourish. In return, Castro expected the Bush administration to continue the liberal people-to-people travel policies and the nonthreatening posture initially adopted by the Clinton administration.

President Bush was slated to give a speech in Miami on the occasion of the one hundredth anniversary of Cuban independence, May 20, 2002. Initially I had been enthusiastic about attending. I had been invited because, as head of the US Interests Section in Havana, I had become well known among the Cuban diaspora, which applauded my championing of Cuba's dissidents. Being popular with exiles in Miami had given me additional credibility within the Bush administration, but I was well aware that it might not last because I was in the midst of a struggle for control of Cuba policy. In my view, Secretary Martinez and the NSC's Gonzalez represented those in the diaspora who recognized that cooperation, or at least engagement, between our two governments was beneficial to both countries. They were reluctant to revert to a hostile policy, which would snuff out greater tolerance for dissent, diminish agricultural sales, and reduce cooperation on antinarcotics initiatives and the environment. But that was exactly what the State Department's assistant secretary for the Western Hemisphere, Otto Reich, wanted. He and Undersecretary John Bolton spoke for Cuban Americans who believed that US relations with the Cuban government lent legitimacy to the Castro regime. To them, and to many conservatives in the Cuban diaspora, engagement with Cuba—even if beneficial to both countries—was unacceptable. So far Martinez and Gonzalez had retained Bush's confidence. Emilio had assured me that I wouldn't be disappointed by the President's speech. Nevertheless, I couldn't ignore my misgivings because Reich and Bolton were gaining ground. And I knew that even if the speech didn't reverse the moderate travel measures that were allowing Americans to visit Cuba, the rhetoric would be designed to appease the diaspora.

On the day before the speech I decided that I would rather stay in Havana. I called the director of the Cuba office at the State Department and asked to be excused from attending. I didn't want to be present if Bush was going to announce a punitive policy. Nor did I want to return to Cuba draped in hostile rhetoric designed for the consumption of the Cuban diaspora. The response was immediate, Reich called me back and ordered me to attend. He said that the president was expecting me.

On the morning of May 20, before he flew down to Florida for the speech, President Bush tried out his remarks on a friendly gathering at the White House. The *New York Times* reported that he denigrated Castro but also offered some carrots to encourage reforms in Cuba.

Notably, Bush said, "Freedom sometimes grows step by step. We'll encourage those steps." I thought that was about as good as I could expect. Perhaps Cuba policy wasn't about to be taken over by the hard-liners. It seemed Bush would continue the carrot-and-stick approach. Castro would get the carrot of American visitors, so long as he showed restraint toward the dissidents. When I arrived in Miami, my spirits were further buoyed by the taxi driver who drove me from the airport to the James L. Knight Center, a huge auditorium where the president was scheduled to speak. He said it was an "honor" to give me a ride, and even refused to accept payment for the fare.

I arrived at the Knight Center early. I had left Havana that morning and come directly from the airport. People were just beginning to arrive. But those I recognized were opposed to links between the United States and Cuba. I took my chair in a section reserved for various notables and waited for the stadium to fill up. I recognized Marisleysis González, Elián's cousin and ersatz Miami mother, who was an icon to the diaspora. Also present was Elsa Morejon, who had come from Havana to campaign for the release of her husband, the prominent dissident Oscar Elías Biscet, who had again been jailed for aggressively confronting the Cuban hierarchy. We three were among the momentary heroes of the unpredictable Cuban diaspora, and no fame would be more fleeting than my own. The fact that Marisleysis and I were both popular figures in Miami made me question my own actions. Privately, I had been disdainful—like many Americans—of the feverish antics of the González family, and especially Marisleysis, whom the media had transformed into an emotionally fragile heroine. I thought that my radio distribution program in Cuba was a far more useful activity than the failed and fraught battle with Castro over a child who by all rights belonged with his father. But the Cuban diaspora's recognition wasn't based on merit; what mattered to Cuban Americans was that we had all defied Fidel Castro.

By the time the president arrived with his brother Jeb Bush, the governor of Florida, the overflow crowd was ready for a rousing speech in which President Bush denigrated Castro and promised to restore freedom to Cuba. Members of the far right Cuban Liberty Council, who were enthusiastic backers of Governor Bush's campaign for a second term, were given the honor of being seated onstage. The president's speech and a campaign event later that day were intended to provide Jeb Bush's reelection campaign additional momentum and financing. I imagined that if the diaspora had listened to the president's remarks at the White House earlier in the day, they hoped he would be more aggressive by the time he reached Miami. They knew that Bush, like his many predecessors, wouldn't invade Cuba, but he could punish Castro by tightening the embargo, eliminating travel by non-Cuban Americans, and downgrading diplomatic relations. This was not a happy crowd. They had not come to hear about the possibility of mending relations with Castro. They had lost their country, their homes, and—more recently—little Elián González. They didn't want better relations with Cuba; they wanted the Castro brothers out of power.

President Bush began by thanking his staff and noting others like myself who were present. He said he appreciated my presence; I was glad I had come. His first words about Cuba did not disappoint: "One hundred years ago, Cuba declared her independence. And nearly 50 years ago, nearly a half century, Cuba's independence and the hopes for democracy were hijacked by a brutal dictator who cares everything for his own power and *nada* [nothing] for the Cuban people." Those onstage and in the audience stood and cheered. To my relief, he added, "This country has no designs on Cuba's sovereignty. We have no designs on Cuba's sovereignty. But we'll continue to be a strong and consistent supporter of the Cuban people's aspirations for freedom." This sounded right to me, but it wasn't what his audience wanted to hear. They would have liked the United States to destroy Castro and his revolution by any means possible.

Bush praised Project Varela, telling the crowd that, "More than

11,000 brave citizens have petitioned their Government for a referendum on basic freedoms," which he said could serve as "a prelude to real change in Cuba." That was exactly what I had hoped to hear because it meant that the Bush administration accepted internal reform carried out by Cubans as a means of bringing about change. But those onstage with the president didn't want to hear about an incremental process of reform—they wanted regime change. Rafael Díaz-Balart—the father of Congressman Lincoln Díaz-Balart and former father-in-law of Fidel Castro—scowled and remained seated. In his mind, this was still a family fight with Castro, the rebel upstart who had forced him and most of Cuba's educated professionals out of power and out of Cuba. Project Varela was a socialist endeavor created by a Christian Democrat who would collaborate with the despised regime. The Díaz-Balarts and the Cuban Liberty Council didn't like the idea of homegrown reforms. In their view, Cubans who remained in Cuba were collaborators.

President Bush moved on to the heart of his speech by launching his Initiative for a New Cuba, which, in his words, "offers Cuba's government a way forward toward democracy and hope, and better relations with the United States." He said that if Cuba allowed free and fair elections to the National Assembly and released political prisoners, he would "explore ways with the United States Congress to ease sanctions," including restrictions on assistance for humanitarian and entrepreneurial activities and by negotiating direct mail service. The audience members did not want better relations; they wanted to do away with Castro, and they began to chant, "¡Cuba si, Castro no!"

Still, Bush continued to press his point: "The goal of United States policy toward Cuba is not a permanent embargo on the Cuban economy. The goal is freedom for the Cuban people." Summing up, he added, "The initiative I've outlined today offers the Cuban Government a way forward, a way towards democracy, a way towards prosperity, a way towards respect. The choice now rests with Mr. Castro." The audience wasn't interested in giving Castro a choice, and it made its displeasure known with boos. This was astonishing; supposedly friendly supporters were jeering the president.

Many Cuba scholars who focused principally on Bush's fiery delivery and tone (he had called Castro a "brutal dictator") considered the speech a return to an isolationist policy. But they were mistaken. Bush was not advocating isolating the regime or tightening the embargo; rather, he was proposing a carrot-and-stick policy. Harvard University professor and Cuba scholar Jorge Dominguez thought that the speech broke new ground. He concluded, "On May 20 President Bush delivered the most conciliatory pair of speeches of his presidency regarding Cuba." In an essay, *Debating U.S.-Cuban Relations: Shall we Play Ball?*, Dominguez, a Cuban American, argued that for the first time a Republican president proposed changing the ground rules. Rather than forcing Castro from power, Bush had suggested that his administration was ready to deal with Cuba, and this in turn would confer a degree of legitimacy on Castro and his government.

The Knight Center cleared out quickly. I was uneasy; there was no residue of excitement or enthusiasm. I had seen representatives of the Cuban Liberty Council in the auditorium, but Cuban American National Foundation (CANF) president Jorge Mas Santos and executive director Joe Garcia were nowhere to be found. CANF, not the Cuban Liberty Council, was more likely to champion Bush's Cuba initiative. CANF tolerated contact with Cuba and seemed to recognize that reform in Cuba would have to come from the Cuban people rather than being imposed by the United States. This was not the case for the Cuban Liberty Council, which recently had broken away from CANF because the council was unwilling to settle for anything less than regime change.

I suspected relations with Cuba had even caused a rift between the Bush brothers. Those in the audience who had booed the president's Cuba initiative and chanted "Cuba si, Castro no!" had likely been primed to do so by the new Cuban Liberty Council. And it must have been Jeb Bush who had determined that the council, not the more moderate CANF, would be the guests of honor. CANF would have accepted the middle ground laid out by the president in the speech that Martinez and Gonzalez had crafted, but the Cuban Liberty Council would not, and Governor Bush was catering to them. When President Bush gave a similar speech earlier that day at the White House, Jeb Bush must have protested, and this in turn might have led to a discussion between the brothers. Perhaps that explained why the president had begun his speech by saying, "I love you, Jeb."

The speech, having been poorly received by some in the audience, would force the president to resolve the divisions among his advisers as well as between himself and his brother. He could continue the current policy advocated by Martinez and Gonzalez, and to a certain extent by CANF, or revert to an isolationist and punitive policy advocated by Governor Bush, Bolton, Reich, and the Cuban Liberty Council. I knew the decision would be made that day, because as I was walking back to my hotel from the Knight Center, I encountered Otto Reich rushing to an emergency meeting with the president and his Cuba advisers.

The president decided to support a hardline approach. After May 20, there was an abrupt shift in US policy away from cooperating with Cuba. I heard no more about Bush's New Initiative for Cuba, and the administration's rhetoric became more strident. CANF, which for years had been the monolithic and unchallenged voice of Cuban Americans, lost much of its influence when the Bush administration elected to back the Cuban Liberty Council, which had cultivated a fortuitous alliance with Governor Jeb Bush. The result was that a small minority of conservative Cuban Americans captured Cuba policy and—for the remainder of the Bush administration—sought to oust the revolution by increasingly punitive measures.

Within a month's time Reich was pressing Bush to adopt a tactic best described as the Big Bang, centered on the idea that if too much air were put into a balloon it would burst loudly. The same would happen if the president increased economic and political pressure on Cuba. Desperate Cubans, no longer willing to endure poverty and lack of opportunity, would at some critical point rise up and topple the government—creating said Big Bang. Although successive American administrations had tried variations on this tactic and failed, its proponents rationalized its failure by claiming that no administration had squeezed Cuba to the bursting point. Now that Bush had sided with the hard-liners, they could once again attempt to ignite chaos in Cuba.

The first causality of the policy change was respectful dialogue. In keeping with Reich's desire to reduce relations to a minimum, I was informed that the semiannual migration talks scheduled for mid-June would be canceled. When I vehemently opposed this suggestion, Reich backed down, allowing the talks to go forward as planned. The talks were held in New York at the US Mission to the United Nations. Rafael Dausa, the director for North American affairs, led the Cuban delegation. Deputy Assistant Secretary for the Western Hemisphere Dan Fisk, who had previously worked at the Heritage Foundation and today is the chief operating officer of the International Republican Institute, was head of our delegation. In the past, these talks had been friendly and respectful; over informal lunches and dinners, we had accomplished as much as we did in the formal talks. This time the talks ended at noon. Nothing was accomplished other than sending a very clear message that the Bush administration was no longer interested in dialogue.

The next punishment was to restrict the travel of Cuban diplomats, thereby preventing the gregarious chief of the Cuban Interests Section, Dagoberto Rodríguez, from speaking at forums and events around the United States. Again, I protested. If we restricted Cuban diplomats, the Cuban government would confine US diplomats to Havana, thereby preventing our team from doing its job. We would be unable to determine if migrants returned by the US Coast Guard were being abused or jailed, and our highly successful outreach program would be severely reduced, as we would be unable to distribute radios and books or visit with dissidents around the country. I explained that if we were confined to Havana, we would be prevented from gathering firsthand information about what was going on across the island.

Again, I won the argument, but once again, only temporarily. To avoid a public showdown with me, Reich waited a few months until I left Cuba and then proceeded with his plan. Castro, as I anticipated, responded by confining American diplomats to Havana. The result was that President Bush and the State Department were informed more by rumor and wishful thinking than by solid, fact-based reporting. In retrospect, blinding the US Interests Section may have been exactly what Reich and conservatives had desired for years. If they couldn't close the building, they could at least avoid dealing with the facts as America's diplomats saw them. Instead, they could listen to their friends within the diaspora and interpret the "facts" as they wished. Perhaps this was an early harbinger of the "alternative facts" promoted by the administration of president Donald Trump?

Fidel Castro waited until June 1 to respond to President Bush's May 20 speech. In the eastern town of Holguin (not far from Birán, his birthplace), Castro warned, "Don't be foolish, Mr. W; respect the intelligence of people capable of thinking. Don't insult Martí! Show respect." Castro might have been even more caustic had he known that as he was speaking Bush was giving a speech at the West Point Military Academy outlining his new doctrine of preemptive strikes. Certainly, Castro would have been worried that Bush might have Cuba in mind.

By July 26 Castro's tone had grown as harsh as Bush's. In the small town of Ciego de Avila where he was celebrating the forty-ninth anniversary of the failed attack on the Moncada Barracks—the Cuban Revolution's most important date—Castro claimed, "The smallest municipality in Cuba is stronger than all the scum that met Bush in the James L. Knight Center in Miami." Still, he left open a small window, promising, "On this historical date for Cubans, I can assure you that we wish for a sincere, respectful, and fraternal friendship between the people of Cuba and the United States. *Viva socialismo! Patria o muerte! Vencermos!"* (Long live socialism! Country or death! We will be victorious!).

I disliked Bush's Big Bang policy. I was convinced that no matter how tough the rhetoric and how tight the embargo, it would not succeed in overturning the regime. I had little doubt that as relations deteriorated Castro would respond by curtailing the greater freedoms dissidents had gained during the past several years—most notably during the first eighteen months of Bush's presidency. Inevitably, Castro would retaliate by cracking down on the dissidents and destroying the Cuban Spring. Everything my team and I had done to empower the Cuban people would be wrecked, and Cubans would again have to await another opportunity for change, which might not arise for decades.

I decided to try one final time to convince Reich and my colleagues working on Cuba that a hostile approach would not succeed. I met with them in a conference room on the sixth floor of the State Department. They listened quietly as I reminded them that the dissidents were now stronger and more influential within Cuba than ever before, but that would undoubtedly end if we adopted a hostile policy. Project Varela had flourished because Castro believed the United States would continue its more liberal travel policy. But if the administration adopted a punitive policy, Castro would retaliate. He had already threatened to throw me out of the country, close down the US Interests Section, and end cooperation on migration if we didn't stop distributing the AM/FM/shortwave radios. In response, I had modulated the distribution because—like it or not—Cuban state security could shut down our activities in a heartbeat if Fidel was willing to pay the price. The more hostile approach that we were taking would risk the outreach program and reduce the limited newfound freedoms available to ordinary Cubans. There was little discussion. Reich had won the policy battle, and it was time for me to admit defeat and leave the field. At the end of the meeting, a smiling Reich wished me good luck in my new assignment—as US ambassador to Mali. I was discouraged because I knew

Reich was delighted that I would soon leave both Cuba and Latin America. My scheduled departure in September would remove a major obstacle in his fruitless campaign to squeeze Cuba to the point of internal collapse.

Fortunes change rapidly when dealing with Cuba. Although Secretary Martinez had earlier asked me to stay in Cuba for another year, the domestic political winds had shifted. I would either be locked in a continuous battle with Reich and my peers, or I would have to acquiesce to the new hardline policy. I did not enjoy being continually at odds with the Bush administration, which had become the norm over the last few months, nor could I could carry out a policy with which I so deeply disagreed. I would leave Havana in September when I had completed my three-year tour. Now, my choice was either to accept the assignment to Mali or resign from the Foreign Service. Fortunately, I had always loved Africa, where I hoped I would avoid any major policy disputes.

But policy differences were impossible to escape. In Africa and the Middle East, the Bush administration was engaged in its War on Terror, the rules of which had not yet been well defined. All too soon I had serious differences with Chuck Wald, the four-star general responsible for Africa, over how to confront terrorists operating in the Sahara. While we both wanted to defeat them, he preferred unilateral, long-range bombing attacks on the terrorists and insurgents in the region. I believed that the best way to defeat them was to coordinate US military operations with the Malian and regional armed forces. Blocked from bombing the terrorists, Wald focused on providing training and intelligence to regional allies, enabling them to carry out a military campaign, which destroyed the first Al-Qaeda group in the Sahara, the Salafist Group for Preaching and Combat. Unfortunately, similar groups would emerge and terrorism would spread throughout the region. Much more on this subject can be found in Joshua Hammer's excellent book *The Bad-Ass Librarians of Timbuktu.*

My daughter Alexandra, who had been staying with us in Cuba for the summer, was the first to leave. She had just completed a project consisting of ten photographs and ten paintings for Stanford University, where she was an undergraduate. Prior to leaving the island with her artwork, she took the precaution of obtaining permission from the Cuban authorities, who require that all art created or acquired in Cuba be approved for export. At the airport, Alexandra and I encountered an unpleasant customs official. She slowly unrolled each of the ten canvases, studied them, then silently rolled them back up and laid them on the table. Finally, she announced solemnly that she was confiscating a large painting of Fidel Castro and his rebels. It was Alexandra's version of the iconic photograph, which appears on the banner of *Granma*, the Cuban government's official daily newspaper, and is known to every Cuban. She had painted the figures of Fidel and his rebels holding aloft their guns in a victory salute in gray and black on a yellow background. Around the edge of her three-by-four-foot canvas, the word "Allure" was repeated as a border motif and, in the center of the canvas were the words, "Warning: Keep Out of Reach of Children. For Adult Use Only."

I quickly gathered up the paintings and walked away. I could imagine Fidel telling a visitor that the painting, which perhaps he would mount behind his desk, was made by the American ambassador's daughter. Placing the paintings on a chair some distance away, I walked back to the official and announced, "Either these paintings will go with my daughter to California or remain with me in Cuba." I wasn't about to give in. After about an hour appealing to higher authorities, Alexandra departed with all her paintings.

I received a farewell letter, "Bon Voyage, Mrs. Huddleston," which was published on the front page of *Granma*. Fidel certainly approved the missive and he might even have written it. The author, Jean-Guy Allard, could have been a pseudonym for Fidel. The article was illustrated with a photo of me on the fifth-floor balcony of the US Interests Section. It began, "She is accompanied by a purebred Afghan hound, which she named Havana, and a cat, very disrespectfully called Martí, in great irreverence toward the nation in which she represented her country for three years." I thought that Fidel had a sense of humor, but apparently not when it came to my pets. It seemed he was still annoyed that my prize hound Havana and I had embarrassed him. The *Granma* article continued, "She came in September 1999, the first year of her presence was marked by the kidnapping of Elián González in Florida, she was seen observing mass demonstrations through her binoculars from the Interests Section balcony." But when Bush came to power, according to Fidel (or Allard), "Vicky Huddleston the career diplomat suddenly abandoned all protocol to devote herself to the recruitment of agents from among the assiduous and remunerated dissidents and candidates for emigration." In other words, I had been a good diplomat when I was carrying out Clinton's instruction to manage the return of Elián, and a bad one when I supported Cuba's dissidents, in accordance with Bush's Cuba policy.

An even worse offense was that I "handed out hundreds of small radios for the purpose of listening to the sermons of Radio Martí, the official US anti-Cuban radio station." Fidel never seemed to understand that I didn't care what Cubans listened to; what I cared about was giving them access to information. And then a final dig: "Mrs. Huddleston will be taking a break before embarking on her next adventure. The State Department has assigned the outgoing head [of the Interests Section] to the US Embassy in Mali, in faraway Africa. Far away from Otto Reich and her obsession with Cuba that in itself constitutes a recompense. Bon Voyage, Mrs. Huddleston." My staff, knowing how much I would miss Cuba, if not Castro, signed the article, had it framed, and presented it to me as a farewell gift.

My best gift was a letter from Secretary of State Colin Powell, which read in part, "In particular, I would like to commend you for your actions in helping the Cuban opposition move forward. Your realization that they had reached a new stage in their development and the help you gave them was an important early step in Cuba's inevitable transition to democracy. Your radio giveaway program was particularly helpful; I believe it highlighted the importance of freedom of information. Your observation that we need to look past Fidel Castro and towards a transition was right on the mark, as were your thoughts on support for the opposition and civil society."

Thank you very much, Secretary Powell. Alas, President Bush's decision to reject the moderate policies of his first years and return to a punitive policy meant that the greater freedoms that dissidents and civil society had enjoyed during the Cuban Spring of 2002 would not return until under another American president a decade later would reach out to the island.

PART IV
2OO2 AND BEYOND

CHAPTER 16

MYTHS, CONTRADICTIONS, AND LIES: BUSH, OBAMA, AND TRUMP

O N JULY 4, 2002, I HOSTED AN INDEPENDENCE DAY CELEBRATION at the American residence in Havana, which had been my home for the last three years. The celebration appropriately doubled as my going-away party. Sadly, it was already clear that US policy toward Cuba was changing from engagement to hostility and isolation. Still, it was a glorious summer afternoon, and I was dressed in a long, sleeveless, white linen dress. My husband Bob and I welcomed five hundred musicians, artists, diplomats, and dissidents. Cuban officials would not attend because I had included the dissidents. A long line of guests snaked from outside the main gates, across the front lawn to the wide-open double doors of my residence. Notwithstanding warnings by the Cuban government not to attend, and video cameras recording everyone who showed up, no one was going to miss this party.

The musicians were the first to arrive and the first to leave. They couldn't stay because they were expected to perform at Fidel Castro's own Fourth of July party! To everyone's surprise, Fidel had recently announced that he, too, intended to celebrate our Independence Day, and had invited Havana's best musicians to play at the Karl Marx Theater with the world-famous Buena Vista Social Club. Still, we had a few attractions of our own. The great Cuban trumpeter José "El Greco" Crego played a few pieces before he joined the musicians' exodus to

Fidel's party; the US Marine Corps detachment, elegant in their dress uniforms, presented the colors; and the "Star-Spangled Banner" was performed by John Easton, a popular American pianist. I kept my remarks brief, citing Cuba's favorite American president, Abraham Lincoln, and my own, Franklin Delano Roosevelt. During the party a reporter asked if I was upset that Fidel Castro was hosting a Fourth of July party to compete with my own. I replied that I thought it was a good sign that Fidel was celebrating our Independence Day.

With the formalities over, the men in coats and ties or *Guayaberas* (the traditional Cuban dress shirts) and the women in cocktail dresses circulated throughout the gardens, taking photographs beneath the great bronze eagle that once nested atop the USS *Maine* Monument. Our chef had prepared pizza, pigs in blankets, grilled shrimp, and chicken on skewers. Cold beer and rum for the mojitos—for which the American residence was rightly famous—were provided courtesy of the Bacardi rum company. It was both a grand party and a poignant farewell as my time in Havana drew to a close. Even the *New York Times* covered the event in their July 4 issue, under the headline "Lighting Matches on the Fourth of July."

As the last guests departed I was feeling nostalgic. I had spent three great years in this wonderful house. On the walls, the paintings I had exhibited by Cuban exile artists were still hanging. I smiled as I remembered how Cuban officials had angrily claimed that my exhibit was an act of defiance designed to ruin Havana's Biennial Art Festival. In a few days, the State Department would have the works carefully packed and returned to galleries in the United States and Mexico. As I walked around the gardens, I knew that I would miss it all—especially the job. Representing the United States in Cuba was both a unique and uniquely challenging assignment. While I looked forward to the future, I also knew that I would never again find myself in similar circumstances. I wondered how long it would be before we would have normal relations with Cuba. I would not have been shocked by the idea that it might take another twelve years before a US president would open relations with Cuba, but I never would have guessed that his successor would return to the old failed policies of the past.

In the *Granma* article wishing me good riddance, Fidel Castro had claimed, "The representative of the Miami camarilla—the female general of those on the CIA payroll . . . chose the date of her country's national holiday to end her diplomatic activities." I still had two months left in Havana, but Fidel couldn't wait for me to leave. Pretty soon he would wish me back. Even though I sometimes bested Castro in our diplomatic battles, I was always reasonable and respectful. A few years later, Ricardo Alarcón, president of Cuba's National Assembly, confirmed this while attending a conference in Canada. He told the media that, except for my little radios and Havana the hound, I had been very professional.

What Castro didn't anticipate was that my replacement, Jim Cason, would make me look good by comparison. Cason was considerably more aggressive than I had ever been, mocking the regime and publicly criticizing Fidel Castro. In the view of his Cuban interlocutors, Cason was blatantly disrespectful—the one thing Castro and the Cuban government are unwilling to abide. Cuban officials uniformly refused to meet with Cason, who consequently lost any influence he might have had with the government. Neither could he meet with dissidents who lived outside Havana. After Otto Reich restricted the travel of Cuban diplomats to Washington, DC, Fidel Castro reciprocated by confining American diplomats within the city limits of Havana. Although President Bush did not renew Reich's interim appointment as assistant secretary, the damage was done. Once the Cuban government realized that American diplomats were much more disadvantaged than their Cuban counterparts in Washington—who had open access to the US Congress, several trade and foreign policy interest groups, and a vibrant US media—the Cuban government refused to rescind the restrictive travel rules.

Reich's replacement was Roger Noriega, a former staffer to North Carolina's Republican senator Jesse Helms (R-NC) and author of the draconian Cuban Liberty and Democratic Solidarity Act. Noriega's views were similar to Reich's; he believed that closing the US Interests Section in Havana would further isolate Cuba, and he hoped that Cason might make that a reality. He once proudly explained, "We told our friend James Cason that if only he could provoke the Cuban regime to expel him from the country, we could respond by closing the Interests Section." Cason did his very best to oblige Noriega, but Castro had a much smarter way of retaliating than by throwing Cason out of the country or closing our Interests Section: he targeted the dissidents.

With a hostile United States on his doorstep—Cason at the US Interests Section and Noriega at the State Department—Castro wasn't taking any chances. On the eve of the US invasion of Iraq and one year after the Cuban Spring, Castro ordered a crackdown on dissidents. The media aptly labeled it the Black Spring of 2003. There simply could not have been a more glaring example of the absolute failure of the Bush administration's hardline policy. One year earlier, the Cuban Spring of 2002 had flourished because of Bush's moderate approach, but less than a year after the administration adopted a hostile policy, Castro purged the human rights movement—which, upon this writing in 2017, still has not recovered.

In March and April 2003, six months after Cason's arrival, Castro arrested, summarily tried, and incarcerated seventy-five dissidents. The charges against them were acting against the "integrity and sovereignty of the state," collaborating with foreign media, and destabilizing the country. Their worst crime was meeting with American diplomats and writing media articles critical of Cuba. Marta Beatriz Roque, who was especially close to Cason, was the only woman arrested; she was sentenced to twenty years. Another leading dissident arrested in the purge was independent journalist and poet Raúl Rivero. About a third of those given long sentences were independent journalists and librarians who had collaborated with Osvaldo Payá's Project Varela. All of the jailed dissidents were engaged in promoting peaceful change—none incited violence—but that did not protect them from being jailed; in some cases, their loved ones were punished as well, by being fired from their jobs.

After Castro jailed the dissidents, Bush had the excuse he needed to impose his Big Bang policy. He tightened the embargo and attempted to undermine the regime by funding projects designed to promote internal unrest and foster an uprising. On October 10, 2003, the administration established the Commission for Assistance to a Free Cuba, whose objective was "to plan for Cuba's transition from Stalinist rule to a free and fair society and to identify ways to hasten the arrival of that day." USAID, which was dedicated to providing humanitarian relief and development assistance around the globe, was given the task of hastening the "transition from Stalinist rule." Castro, believing that USAID was a new weapon in an arsenal designed to bring down his government, declared its activities in Cuba illegal.

To some degree I blame myself for the use of USAID as a weapon against Castro. I had never liked the argument that our outreach program would hasten the downfall of the regime, despite having occasionally used it to gain support for our efforts. When Peter Corsell and I left Cuba in September 2002, the combination of rapidly escalating tensions and the curtailment of American diplomatic travel outside Havana crippled our very successful outreach program. The following year, the Bush administration tried to replicate and amplify our success by establishing the Commission for Assistance to a Free Cuba, which was loosely based on Peter's and my philosophy of empowering the Cuban people through the provision of communications equipment and information. But there were two major differences: the USAID budget was far beyond what could be effectively deployed in Cuba, in the tens of millions of dollars per year; and Castro had explicitly declared that receiving assistance from USAID was illegal.

In May 2004, six months before his reelection bid, President Bush announced $59 million in additional funding for TV Martí and Radio Martí, as well as for public diplomacy and USAID projects in Cuba. This level of funding meant there was now an organized and concerted campaign to denounce and destroy the Castro regime. And, Castro, by declaring USAID activities illegal, forced the agency to carry out its activities covertly in order to avoid the recipients or contractors being imprisoned. Not surprisingly, the USAID personnel were not well versed in spycraft and were naive to believe they could operate in Cuba without the government finding out. Alan Gross, who was not a spy but simply a USAID contractor working to set up a communications network for Havana's Jewish community, was arrested, imprisoned, and charged with "acts against the independence and territorial integrity of the state."

In 2005, at the beginning of his second term, Bush appointed a new Cuba policy point man. Secretary of Commerce Carlos Gutierrez replaced Mel Martinez, who had recently been elected to the US Senate. Secretary Gutierrez was born in Havana and came to the United States with his family during the first exodus, just after the Cuban Revolution. An intelligent and dedicated man, he worked his way through the ranks of the Kellogg Company to become its youngest president and CEO. When I interviewed him for this book, he described his role as continuing the policy enacted by President Bush and Congress, of which Congressman Lincoln Díaz-Balart was the principal author and advocate. By the time Gutierrez took the reins of Cuba policy, most of the administration's punitive policies were in place. In addition to the USAID initiative to create a transition in Cuba, the American people-to-people travel had been virtually eliminated and, to the considerable consternation of the diaspora, even Cuban American visits and remittances were severely restricted.

I asked Gutierrez if it was fair to label the Bush administration's Cuba policy as pursuing regime change. He conceded that the label was not false, pointing to the Commission for Assistance to a Free Cuba, whose goal was a "transition," not a "succession." Gutierrez discovered—like Bush did after his May 2002 speech to the diaspora—that for conservative Cuban Americans, free and fair elections in Cuba were not a viable option. He recounted that Congressman Lincoln Díaz-Balart became furious with him for suggesting democratic elections as a means of change. Díaz-Balart and the Cuban Liberty Council wanted nothing to do with elections—no matter how free and fair—if there was any possibility those elections would result in the Castro brothers retaining power.

Secretary Gutierrez acknowledged that the notion of regime change contained inherent contradictions. The embargo had not succeeded in ousting the Castro brothers, but a military invasion was not an option either. In context of resolving the 1962 Cuban Missile Crisis, President John F. Kennedy had pledged not to invade Cuba; and since then both Democratic and Republican presidents have found it prudent to uphold that pledge. The United States would obviously win a military contest, but Cuba's professional military would extract a high cost in American lives. Consequently, US presidents, vainly hoping that they could bring down Castro with economic sanctions, have discovered again and again that the regime is too entrenched to be removed without the use of military force, which if deployed would likely result in chaos in Cuba and universal condemnation of the United States.

According to Gutierrez the tragedy is that "the policy had likely made sense thirty or forty years ago. But if the chaos scenario were successful now, it would result in radical change, creating the conditions for another revolution in twenty-five years." The one thing that the Bush administration's harsh policies toward Cuba should have accomplished was to disprove the myth that a hostile policy could oust the Castro regime. Bush tightened the embargo to its maximum extent, funded an assistance program whose objective was to sow chaos, and indulged in a continuous stream of rhetoric designed to denigrate

Cuba's rulers. Yet even when Castro ceded power temporarily in 2006, and then permanently in 2008, there was no indication that the Cuban regime was weakened by the transfer of power from one Castro brother to another. And Bush wisely did not consider the use of force. Gutierrez confirmed, "I never heard anyone mention invasion."

The importance of the Cuban American voting bloc on Florida's electoral votes dictated that—until President Barack Obama's second term—every American president pandered to the diaspora's demands for a repressive Cuba policy. As Secretary Gutierrez put it, "The conservative diaspora doesn't like stability in our relationship. To them it means we accept the regime." They also had begun to imagine that the dissidents would become the agents of insurrection. But even at the height of their influence, when former President Carter recognized Project Varela during the Cuban Spring of 2002, the dissidents never posed a serious threat to the regime. They were merely a nuisance to Castro, bravely but ineffectively demanding reform. Theirs was a quixotic effort because the dissidents had no means of mobilizing the population, most of which didn't even know they existed. I asked Gutierrez why Castro was so paranoid about the dissidents when they posed no real threat. He gave me the best answer I have heard: "La calle es de Fidel" (The street belongs to Fidel). Once immensely popular with the people, Fidel couldn't imagine that some might willingly turn against him, even as he grew grayer and less admired. And this stubbornness is not unique to Fidel; Cuban Americans are equally tenacious. "They learn their talking points at the dinner table and stick to them," Gutierrez said.

By 2007, I was again working on Cuba, now as a private citizen, after having retired from the Foreign Service. I had joined former ambassador Carlos Pascual to colead a project on Cuba at the Brookings Institution in Washington, DC. Our objective was to define a US policy toward Cuba that would promote positive change and democracy on the island. The group of nineteen leading Cuba experts—half of which were Cuban American—included scholars, diplomats, journalists, and Francisco "Pepe" Hernandez, president of the Cuban American National Foundation (CANF). All were open to participating in simulations designed to determine what policy would best promote peaceful change in Cuba. For example, in order to determine the impact of a leadership crisis in Cuba, we developed scenarios to illustrate how the regime might react to a hostile or a moderate approach by the United States.

Conservative Cuban Americans and, initially, the Cuban government did not approve of the project. Despite my reassurances, the head of the Cuban Interests Section, Ambassador Jorge Bolaños—"Ambassador" being an honorary title from his previous positions abroad—told me that he objected. He assumed our efforts were intended to perpetuate an isolationist US policy toward Cuba, but we proved him wrong. The result of numerous discussions, simulations, and talks by leading experts was that all participants agreed that the president should adopt a policy of engagement, not isolation.

Carlos Pascual and I hoped that President Barack Obama, who had been elected just as we were finishing the project, would use our findings as a blueprint for an opening of relations with Cuba. We provided a summary of our findings to Congress as well as to the State Department. *Learning to Salsa: New Steps in U.S.–Cuba Relations* provided a step-by-step plan for normalizing relations. But interest in adopting a new Cuba policy was limited. Obama attended the April 2009 Summit of the Americas, where he briefly met and shook hands with Raúl Castro, but nothing more ensued. There was little momentum, because Cuban American senator Robert Menendez (D-NJ) successfully blocked Obama's effort to modify embargo rules other than fulfilling his promise to reinstate Cuban American travel and remittances. Realizing that change was unlikely in the short term, neither Carlos Pascual nor I remained at Brookings to press for a change in Cuba policy. Instead we both became political appointees in the Obama administration, Carlos as the ambassador to Mexico, and I as the deputy assistant secretary of defense for Africa.

The normalization of diplomatic relations has taken much too long. It should have begun in the early 1990s with the end of the Cold War and the demise of the Soviet Union and its alliance with Cuba. Three presidents failed to seize the opportunity: George H. W. Bush was goaded by Bill Clinton, his rival for the presidency, into tightening the embargo; Clinton's attempted openings were quashed by Castro; and George W. Bush tried everything short of an invasion. Fidel Castro, who clearly understood the power of Cuban Americans in the formulation of US policy, allegedly quipped in 1973, "The United States will come to talk to us when they have a black president and the world has a Latin American pope." Well, in November 2008 Americans elected a black president, and in March 2013, early in Obama's second term, the Roman Catholic papal conclave elected a humble Argentine cardinal, Jorge Mario Bergoglio, as Pope Francis.

Finally, well into his second term, President Obama decided to make a concerted effort to normalize relations between the United States and Cuba. The first public indication that Obama was contemplating a change of policy occurred on December 10, 2013. Obama and Raúl Castro shook hands at a memorial service for Nelson Mandela in South Africa, which was significant because it foreshadowed Obama's commitment to engage with Cuba; yet very little was heard from the administration other than a series of editorials and articles in the *New York Times* advocating better relations.

Nevertheless, on December 17, 2014, Obama surprised the American public by announcing that full diplomatic relations had been reestablished with Cuba. Eight months later, on August 14, 2015, Secretary of State John Kerry raised the American flag in front of the US Interests Section in Havana, making it once again the American embassy. It had been fifty-four years since our flag in Cuba was lowered by the order of President Dwight D. Eisenhower, only days before John F. Kennedy assumed the presidency.

Although these events seemed to develop almost effortlessly, a series of complex negotiations had privately taken place between the two long-term adversaries. Obama entrusted the responsibility for his Cuba opening to two close allies: Deputy National Security Adviser Ben Rhodes and Senior Director for Western Hemisphere Affairs Ricardo Zuniga. Rhodes, once an aspiring writer pursuing an MFA at New York University, had moved from writing fiction to speech writing for former Congressman Lee Hamilton (D-IN), and then joined Obama's campaign for president. Observers said that Rhodes was the critical link to Obama because he could anticipate the president's political inclinations and concerns. Zuniga, a career diplomat, provided the substantive knowledge, language skills, and patience that were essential to keeping the discussions moving forward, even when it seemed they might never reach a successful conclusion. A scion of a prominent political family in Honduras that had immigrated to the US, Zuniga had a ready smile and a good sense of humor. When Obama asked him to join the National Security Council as senior adviser for the Western Hemisphere, he was political counselor at our embassy in Brazil. Prior to that Ricardo was acting director of the Office of Cuban Affairs and had served as the human rights officer at the US Interests Section in Havana—invaluable background for dealing with the prickly Cubans.

The fact that the United States no longer had national security concerns about Cuba made negotiations between Obama and Castro both easier and harder; easier because an opening to Cuba did not endanger the United States, but harder because Cuba's relative lack of importance pushed it to the background as Obama and his senior advisers dealt with crises in Asia and the Middle East. But according to Ben Rhodes, the president was personally committed because he believed that for too long the Cuban people had been forced to live behind a wall constructed in the 1960s by American fears, enhanced in the 1990s by a diaspora intent on payback, and maintained since then by hardliners on both sides of the Florida Straits.

Before there could be any hope of improved relations, the negotiators had to arrange for the exchange of spies imprisoned in Cuba
and the United States. Former New Mexico governor Bill Richardson,
who had a reputation for negotiating the release of Americans imprisoned abroad, had been unable to obtain the release of Alan Gross, who
had been imprisoned in Cuba for attempting to set up a communications network for the Jewish community in Havana. The Cuban government considered Gross as leverage for getting back the Cuban Five,
who had been imprisoned in the US for spying. The Cuban Five formed
La Red Avispa (the Wasp Network), which was responsible for reporting on the activities of Cuban American groups in Florida that might
carry out attacks against Cuba or Fidel Castro. They were arrested in
1998, shortly after the Clinton administration and Castro agreed to an
exchange of information between the FBI and Cuban state security.
Castro believed that the information Cuba had shared with the FBI led
to their discovery and incarceration. He thought Clinton had misled
him, which only heightened his desire to gain their release. The arrest
of the Cuban Five came two years after Cuban MiGs shot down two
civilian aircraft belonging to Brothers to the Rescue. Predictably, a
Miami court convicted them of conspiracy to commit espionage and
murder, and sentenced all five of them to long prison sentences.

There were divisions in both the US and Cuban governments over
the wisdom of an opening, and Raúl Castro had the greatest challenge
because he had to overcome Fidel's concerns. The imperative of bringing home the five spies—or "heroes," as the Cubans called them—gave
Raúl the excuse he needed to engage, but Fidel still hesitated. The American negotiators had a problem as well. They knew that there would
be no deal unless they released the Cuban spies, but in the espionage
world spies are exchanged for spies. Gross was a USAID contractor,
not a spy, and neither Obama nor the intelligence community wanted
to make the exchange because it would validate Cuba's claim that
Gross was a spy. This conundrum was unexpectedly resolved when the

intelligence community admitted that they, too, had a spy they would like to bring home. He was a Cuban American intelligence agent who had been wasting away in Cuban jails for the past twenty years. By including this agent in the trade, Rhodes and Zuniga had a deal that the intelligence community could get behind—the administration would release the Cuban spies in exchange for the American spy, while Alan Gross would be released on "humanitarian" grounds.

As talks moved into the critical stage, an impartial third party was found in Pope Francis who made it difficult for either side to lie or back away from commitments made to him. A July 2014 meeting at the Vatican sealed the deal. On December 17, 2014, all the logistics were in place and the prisoner swap was confirmed. An American aircraft carrying Alan and Judy Gross, along with Senators Jeff Flake (R-AZ), Patrick Leahy (D-VT), and Chris Van Hollen (D-MD)—who had all lobbied hard for Gross's release—headed from Havana to Washington, DC. At about the same time, an aircraft carrying three of the Cuban Five headed to Havana; the other two had already completed their prison terms and were back in Cuba. The American agent's return was not recorded. He was later identified as Rolando Sarraff, and was said to have been instrumental in warning the United States about the Cuban Five (for whom he was exchanged) and the US intelligence officer Ana Belén Montes, who had been spying for Cuba until she was exposed and arrested in 2001.

While arranging the exchange, Rhodes and Zuniga had to come up with a strategy to improve relations. It included upgrading the Interests Section to an embassy; proposing an ambassador; and modifying the sanctions to permit more travel, trade, and communications. Zuniga led an interagency review to determine which sanctions could be modified and which could not be touched because they were law. For years, Cuban Americans have claimed that since the embargo was codified by the Cuban Liberty and Democratic Solidarity Act, it could not be changed by the executive branch. But this claim was misleading, as

Carlos Pascual and I pointed out in *Learning to Salsa*. Although the embargo had become law, so too had the provision that allowed the secretary of the Treasury to change sanctions regulations. Both Presidents Clinton and Bush had already modified the sanctions without congressional approval. This meant that Obama could propose a series of measures that would allow more travel—but not tourism, which was embedded in the 2000 law that allowed agricultural sales to Cuba—as well as permit licensing for trade and investment. However, full normalization would only come when the US Congress repealed the several laws that mandate the embargo.

On December 17, 2014, due largely to the hard work of Rhodes and Zuniga, Obama was ready to inform the world that he was normalizing diplomatic relations with Cuba and expanding travel, commerce, and information flows, as well as delivering the safe return of Alan Gross. Five months later, President Obama, with the support of the intelligence community, removed Cuba from the list of state sponsors of terrorism. Over the next two years, American travel to Cuba increased exponentially and American companies began establishing business links to Cuba, especially in the tourist sector. The Obama administration increased bilateral cooperation on public health, the environment, law enforcement, and counterterrorism efforts and opened talks on settlement of official claims for expropriated property. Obama's final action before leaving office was to end the Wet Foot–Dry Foot policy. Cubans migrating to the United States would now be treated like every other nationality. If they arrived undocumented and could not prove that they were suffering persecution, they would be sent back to Cuba.

The final celebration of this remarkable opening was President Obama's visit to Havana on March 22, 2016. He was the first sitting president to visit Cuba in eighty-eight years. President and Mrs. Obama and their children spent two days on the island, staying overnight at the American residence. They probably took photos beside the great bronze eagle, which might once again become a symbol of friendship between the United States and Cuba at the dawn of this new era.

According to the media, the presidential visit began with a walking tour led by Eusebio Leal Spangler, the historian of the city of Havana, followed by a meeting with Cuba's Cardinal Jaime Ortega, who had played a key role in negotiating the opening. Obama and Raúl Castro watched a baseball game between American and Cuban teams in the same ballpark where years ago I had watched Fidel's old-timers defeat Venezuela's national team with President Hugo Chávez pitching. Michelle, Malia, and Sasha Obama visited Finca Vigía (Lookout House), where Ernest Hemingway lived and worked for twenty years, and where Americans and Cubans have been working together for over a decade to preserve the writer's home and manuscripts.

Obama's speech to the Cuban people was given at the Gran Teatro Nacional. It was just as courageous as former president Jimmy Carter's speech, given some fourteen years earlier in the Aula Magna at the University of Havana. Predictably, Fidel Castro didn't like Obama's speech any better than Carter's. Obama met with dissidents at the American residence, even though some of them were unhappy because they felt that Obama should have extracted more concessions from the Cuban government. Although Obama and his team had succeeded in gaining the release of fifty-three political prisoners, following the reestablishment of full diplomatic relations in December 2015, dissent remains perilous in Cuba. Those with whom Obama met included Elizardo Sánchez; Dagoberto Valdes, an activist for the Roman Catholic Church; and Jose Daniel Ferrer, an independent journalist who, along with the late Oscar Espinosa Chepe, had been arrested in the Black Spring of 2003. Mariana Leiva, a founder of Ladies in White, and Berta Solzar, its current leader, were also present, as were a younger generation of dissidents, including a gay rights activist, a rapper, and an independent blogger.

President Obama's visit was intended to make his opening "irreversible," to give Cuba and its people greater opportunity and a chance to build better lives. As Obama acknowledged, it was the beginning of a process: "I do not expect the changes that I am announcing today to bring about the transformation of Cuban society overnight. But I am convinced that through a policy of engagement, we can more effectively stand up for our values and help the Cuban people help themselves as they move into the 21st century." And it seemed likely to succeed. Cubans were joyful and Americans were seizing opportunities to travel to Cuba afforded by better relations.

Ben Rhodes told me that President Obama's visit was designed to bring about a generational change both in Cuba and among Cuban Americans. He said that Obama perceived his role as putting a period on a chapter in history in order to open space for young people—both those who were reaching out from the Cuban diaspora and those on the island. Rhodes said that Obama purposefully brought along his daughters so that they could experience history in the making; he also hoped that bringing his family would help him connect with Cubans. Rhodes told me that with more time Obama might have led a concerted effort to lift the sanctions, by working to convince Congress "to break the legislative wall—the embargo." He also would have included Raúl Castro, who has considerable influence with Venezuelan president Nicolás Maduro, in negotiations to resolve the political and economic crisis in that country.

But Obama's dreams were shattered—as were those of Americans and Cubans alike—when on June 16, 2017 in a speech in Miami, President Donald Trump announced that he was canceling Obama's opening to Cuba and strictly enforcing the embargo. His speech was vintage hardline rhetoric, including listing Cuba's past and present crimes and misdemeanors: "killed tens of thousands . . . tried to host nuclear weapons . . . fueled chaos in Venezuela, and . . . harbor[ed] a cop killer." Like his predecessors, Trump promised the demise of the Cuban regime: Yet, as the failure of President Bush's punitive policy has proven, there is little chance that Trump will succeed. Given that Cuba is now facing a succession to a non-Castro—the first in over a half century—it is more likely that Trump's threats will result in Castro tightening his control and slowing economic reforms.

By abandoning engagement, Trump has returned to the failed policy of punishment and isolation. In Miami he signed a national security presidential memorandum that replaced Obama's presidential directive, which had directed executive branch agencies to work toward the normalization of relations. Additionally, the new policy strictly enforces and restricts travel and remittances, and bans "direct" transactions with entities that would benefit the Cuban military "disproportionately." Trump retained some of Obama's positive initiatives by leaving in place people-to-people travel, which permits group visits for educational, religious, cultural, and humanitarian purposes. He continued Cuban American travel, the possibility of obtaining licenses for trade and investment, and bilateral agreements to safeguard the environment, improve health, and cooperate to reduce crime and narcotics trafficking. Importantly, he did not downgrade the status of the American embassy, he endorsed Obama's change in migration policy that treats Cubans the same as other foreign nations, and said nothing about putting Cuba back on the list of state sponsors of terrorism.

The tragedy of Trump's Cuba policy is that it is a lie. Trump's reasons for blocking further momentum toward normalization are purely political. The deep-rooted divisions in age, wealth, and citizenship among the Cuban diaspora provided Trump with an opportunity to undo Obama's opening, which he has undertaken despite having once sought personally to do business in Cuba. Older, wealthier, Republican Cuban Americans who arrived in Florida in the 1980s and 1990s used their money and influence to convince candidate Trump to curtail Obama's opening, which most Cuban Americans had desired. According to a 2016 Florida International University poll of Cuban Americans in Miami-Dade County, 69 percent approved of Obama's policy shift and 63 percent opposed continuing the embargo. Those sentiments notwithstanding, Florida's conservative Republican Cuban American congressional delegation, consisting of Senator Marco Rubio and Representatives Ileana Ros-Lehtinen and Mario Díaz-Balart, had demanded and expected President Trump to return to a punitive policy. A recent remark by Senator Rubio made it clear that he would be on the front lines in pressing Trump to impose a stricter and crueler approach to Cuba. He said, "It's absurd and it's part of a long record of coddling dictators and tyrants that this [the Obama] administration has established." For Rubio, as it had been in the past for Fidel Castro, the other side must change first.

CHAPTER 17

THE FUTURE IS HAVANA, NOT MIAMI

N THE LATE SUMMER OF 2002, DURING THE WANING DAYS OF MY TENURE in Cuba, I was driving my official, black armored sedan down tree-lined Quinta Avenida (Fifth Avenue), sometimes called Avenida de las Americas. Seeing a group of teenagers looking for a ride, I stopped the car. Five or six youngsters happily squeezed into the back seat. Suddenly, realizing that this ride was something special, one of them asked what type of car it was. I replied, "It's a Ford Crown Victoria." In Havana, there were generally three types of cars: clunky 1950s American cars, which are mostly used as private taxis; little white Ladas used by government officials, and a fleet of black Mercedes-Benz sedans for use by Fidel Castro's inner circle and foreign VIPs. This meant that no one except foreign diplomats drove new American vehicles, which prompted one young lady to ask, "Who are you?"

I replied, "Soy la jefa de la SINA" (I am the chief of the North American Interests Section). For a minute, there was silence. I wondered if my passengers would ask that I stop and let them out. Then the young woman said, "Be our mother, take us to Miami!" We all laughed. After a few miles, I dropped them off near Coppelia Park, where they would likely join a long line queuing to buy Cuba's famous ice cream.

The point of this anecdote can be found in the words, "Take us to Miami." Those words left me with the realization—which has never really left me—that Cuba's youth deserve a future in *Havana*, not

Miami. I believed that the opening crafted by Presidents Barack Obama and Raúl Castro would offer that possibility. Obama was clearly looking toward a different and brighter future when he said during his speech at Havana's Grand Teatro Nacional, "I believe that our grandchildren will look back on this period of isolation as an aberration, as just one chapter in a longer story of family and of friendship." After over a half century of isolation and bitterness, there was finally a chance that these teens and their peers might enjoy better and fuller lives in Cuba. But those hopes were dashed by President Donald Trump's decision to roll back Obama's opening of relations with Cuba.

For almost sixty years, the overarching trajectory of US policy toward Cuba has been, with only brief exceptions, to increasingly isolate and punish the island. In 1960 President Dwight D. Eisenhower had hoped to force Fidel Castro to return expropriated American property by banning the export of American products to the island. From that point forward, bilateral relations continued to deteriorate. In October 1962, eighteen months after the aborted CIA-organized invasion at the Bay of Pigs, the Cuban Missile Crisis brought the world to the verge of nuclear Armageddon. The US-Cuba relationship did not improve until 1977, when President Jimmy Carter briefly lifted the travel ban and approved partial diplomatic relations via the US and Cuban Interests Sections in Havana and Washington, DC.

After the fall of the Soviet Union in 1991, there was no longer any plausible justification for continuing the embargo and a hostile policy toward Cuba. But Presidents George H. W. Bush, Bill Clinton, George W. Bush, and Barack Obama—during his first term—dared not lift the embargo for fear of losing the support of Florida's powerful Cuban American community. In 1992, at the behest of the Cuban National Foundation, George H. W. Bush signed a law that prohibited trade with Cuba in American products produced abroad. Only four years later, Bill Clinton signed yet another law tightening the embargo. But then Clinton slowly began easing the embargo by permitting limited people-to-people travel and family remittances to Cuba. George W. Bush continued these moderate Clinton policies, until eighteen months into his administration when—at the behest of conservative Cuban Americans and the Cuban Liberty Council, who supported his brother Jeb Bush's reelection campaign for governor of Florida—he reverted to a hostile policy. Nine months later, in the spring of 2003, Fidel Castro jailed seventy-five prominent dissidents, and bilateral relations deteriorated to their lowest point since the Cuban Missile Crisis.

President Obama optimistically stated that the years of alienation between our countries would be viewed in hindsight as an aberration, but his attempt to restore normal relations only lasted two years. President Trump's reversion to a hostile policy may have set back hopes for a normal relationship between our countries by at least a generation. By the time we have a new American president who might again engage with Cuba, the island's revolutionary-era leaders will have been replaced by a new generation of leaders, one that has been raised with and accepts that the United States is their enemy. Thus, it will be even harder to overcome the historical mistrust and begin a process of reconciliation that is acceptable to both governments. The sad truth is that unless Trump reverses course, Obama's opening may be viewed as the aberration amid our long history of antagonistic relations with Cuba.

Unfortunately, Obama did not have sufficient time to make his new Cuba policy "irrevocable," as he had wished. He likely hoped that since a slight majority of Cuban Americans supported the opening, conservative Cuban Americans would be unable to force our government to revert to a punitive policy. But he didn't count on them finding in Donald Trump a champion willing to defy the majority of Americans, including Republicans, who support normal relations with Cuba. Trump apparently believes that a punitive, isolationist policy toward Cuba will supply him with money and votes from the older, wealthier Republican Cuban Americans who would likely support his reelection should he run again in 2020. And so, once again, domestic politics trump foreign policy.

If there is to be, as Obama indicated, "a longer story of family and friendship," the American people will have to make Cuba policy a priority issue, something they have never done in the past. They will have to lobby Congress to repeal sanctions and elect a president who at the beginning of his first term will reinstate the Obama regulations and press Congress to end the embargo. Although there are currently two bipartisan bills in the Senate that would end the travel ban and allow American companies to do business in Cuba, they are unlikely to pass. And if they did, President Trump would likely veto them.

Economic embargos hurt people more than they hurt governments. Nowhere is this more evident than in Cuba, where those who suffer are ordinary citizens, not the Cuban government elite. A case in point: in chapter 1, I described the sumptuous banquet offered by Castro to delegates celebrating the conclusion of the Tripartite Accords in 1991, while hungry Cubans were unable to buy shellfish because it was reserved for the government and for export. Another example: ordinary Cubans' access to food and medicines was drastically reduced after our Congress, to please the Cuban American community, passed the Cuban Democracy Act, which tightened the embargo just as Cuba lost five billion dollars in annual Soviet subsidies. Fidel Castro labeled the ensuing seven years of poverty, 1991–98, as the Special Period in Time of Peace. Cubans lacked essentials like milk, meat, and oil, and the elderly were left in the streets to be picked up by Cuban social service agencies, which took them to asylums often run by the Catholic Church. Yet Fidel Castro and the government elite did not suffer. When Cubans began to protest, Castro unleashed the 1994 mass migration, proving that even if our Big Bang strategy of pushing desperate Cubans to the breaking point succeeded, it would not topple the Cuban hierarchy but would rather lead to another mass exodus. Cubans have always preferred flight to fight. Throughout the Special Period, the Cuban government told its citizens that the United States was responsible for their suffering. Every night, state television and radio announcers blamed the US embargo for the island's misery. We were partially responsible, but so was the fall of the Soviet Union and—most of all—the Cuban government itself, for its absolute, centralized control of the Cuban economy.

Even during hard times, Cubans have had benefits that most people in other poor countries do not enjoy. They have access to free education, decent health care, shelter, and a ration book that provides at least a bare minimum of food. What Cubans lack is any meaningful personal freedom, either political or economic, and the opportunity to improve the conditions of their own lives. My friend Ana Maria González was sent to Moscow to receive advanced training in computers. But she, like most Cubans, was unable to progress in her field. There were very few employment opportunities and, even as a supervisor, she earned the equivalent of less than twenty dollars per month. This meant she could never buy a better house (she still lived with her mother in one of Havana's poorest barrios) or purchase nice clothes, a car, or any of the consumer goods that most people aspire to own and enjoy. Ana Maria had no possibility of buying any of these things as long as she was paid in nonconvertible Cuban pesos by the Cuban government. When she began working as a dog trainer for foreigners, she earned US dollars but was harassed for working outside the official system. Eventually Ana Maria became a target of state security and, like so many other Cubans, fled to the United States. Yet, like most Cubans who have emigrated during the past fifty years, Ana Maria would tell you that she would have remained on the island if she could have found economic opportunity there.

Cuba has never been truly independent. And this to some degree accounts for the long-standing difficulties between our countries. The United States still wants to be the preeminent foreign power in Cuba. After winning the war with Spain we assumed control of its "ever faithful isle," becoming the dominant political and economic force until the Cuban Revolution triumphed in 1959. Fidel Castro quickly consolidated power and managed to steer the revolution into the orbit of the Soviet Union, ending the American era in Cuba and replacing our people and investments with Soviet patronage. Once the Soviets withdrew, Cuba was on its own until Fidel persuaded Hugo Chávez to support Cuba with Venezuela's oil largess. After the death of Chávez, Obama's policy shift, though late in coming, provided the United States with an opportunity to reestablish its dominance in the Caribbean by bringing Cuba into our sphere of interest. A seemingly logically outcome due to our geographic proximity, the large Cuban diaspora in the United States, and our former influence over the island. But a minority of aging, conservative Cuban Americans—shortsighted and rooted in the distant past—have shattered that possibility and, in so doing, may now push Cuba into the arms of our competitors and rivals like China and Russia.

How many generations will it take to reconcile the Cuban people in the diaspora and in Cuba? Almost sixty years has now passed since the revolution, yet animosity on both sides still drives the relationship. Even President Obama's opening failed to make lasting inroads into the polarized elite groups in both countries that refuse compromise and reconciliation. Although ordinary Cubans love the United States, and over 1.7 million Cubans now live here, the Cuban government, especially military and intelligence officers, deeply mistrust Cuban Americans. For their part, Cuban Americans who were once part of the island's elite loath not only Raúl Castro and the Cuban government but everyone associated with it. Cuban American senators Ted Cruz (R-TX) and Marco Rubio (R-FL) persist in urging regime change, even when all evidence indicates that a US invasion would result in chaos on the island and condemnation by the world community—especially within Latin America. These conservative politicians' obsession with Cuba, like those of hardline Cuban Americans, is not in the best interests of our country, which would profit by a stable and friendly Cuba. But by rejecting engagement with the Cuban government, this influential minority discards the best—and the only peaceful—way of bringing about change in Cuba. After so many decades of revolution, hostility, and estrangement, only a policy of constructive engagement will lead to the resolution of old scores and true reconciliation. Obama put it this way: "So the reconciliation of the Cuban people—the children and grandchildren of revolution, and the children and grandchildren of exile—that is fundamental to Cuba's future." Yet our country seems prepared to deny that future.

It seems strange that Cuban Americans who have already lost the most are so adamantly opposed to normalizing relations, because they stand to gain the most in the future. The story of the secret treasure hidden in the depths of our embassy in Havana best illustrates this conundrum. Hidden within the building's dark recesses are gold, pearls, rubies, and diamonds left behind in the 1960s by fleeing Cubans. Impulsively, and probably in a spirit of compassion, the Swiss diplomats who maintained a skeleton staff within the closed American embassy provided a service about which the US State Department appears to have been unaware: they allowed departing Cubans to take with them their most valuable possessions.

On one of my first visits to the embassy building in 1990", twelve years after President Carter had reestablished limited diplomatic relations and reopened the building by giving it a new name, the US Interests Section. One look at the building showed the significant extent to which it had been neglected. The former embassy was in a state of disrepair—the green glass that lined the facade was a patchwork of shades varying from murky brown to grayish green, each section distinct from the other; the beautiful ivory-colored travertine stone imported from Italy appeared as if it had molted, with large chunks flaking off the facade; and the lone balcony that hung off the fifth floor was clearly unsafe. Facing the Interests Section, an enormous Cuban revolutionary billboard proclaimed, "Señores Imperialistas ¡No les Tenemos Absolutemente Ningún Miedo!" (Imperialists We Have Absolutely No Fear of You!). One could understand why, by simply taking a look at the decrepit building.

Both the ravages of time and men had ruined parts of the interior. US security personnel wielding large pickaxes had conducted what they accurately termed a destructive search in their effort to locate listening devices, gouging enormous holes in the walls. The US Marines manned two checkpoints that guarded the entrances, but several cameras that monitored the building were not functional. In the basement I found all manner of items jumbled together in total disorder; they had been tossed about and damaged by floodwaters from one of Havana's frequent hurricanes. In one area there was a 1950s television set, a large safe that had been broken open, many paintings, and several tables scattered with coins, paper currency, and manila envelopes with papers sticking out. I was astonished to learn that this disarray was personal property left behind by departing Cubans.

When I returned to Washington, DC, from my visit to Havana, I informed the State Department that I had discovered these goods and shared my concern that they were not being properly secured. Initially the State Department considered transporting these items back to the United States in the diplomatic pouch, but decided against doing so because the Cuban government might seize the pouches, claiming they contained Cuban government property. If we had asked permission to ship them to the United States, our request would likely have been denied. The State Department's solution was to inventory and better secure the property.

In 1999, when I returned to Cuba as chief of the US Interests Section, the building had been renovated and a special vault-like room secured by a combination safe door had been built to secure the valuables. What at the time had appeared to be a disorderly jumble turned out to be a treasure of significant value. No one could enter the vault without signing a register. Inside, metal shelving units five to six feet long and six to seven feet high completely filled the cave-like room, which was illuminated by a single light bulb at the ceiling. Carefully placed on the shelves were bankers' boxes of corrugated cardboard; tied to each box was a tag that indicated its contents and the owner. On one shelf, a pearl necklace and other jewels spilled out of a velvet bag, but everything else appeared to be in perfect order.

Those who left their valuables with the Swiss diplomats could still recover them, yet it seems that even after Fidel Castro's death they prefer to continue a nearly six-decades long standoff with Raúl Castro. If US-Cuba relations were better, it might also be possible for Cubans to be compensated for the loss of their homes, businesses, and land. Negotiations had begun on settling the official claims of American citizens (at the time of the taking) during the Obama opening. If these negotiations were to continue and succeed, then there would be precedent for resolving the claims of Cuban citizens who lost their property as well.

Cubans who fled—with the exception of those who turned their valuables over to the Swiss—will never recuperate their personal property. In the early 1990s the Cuban government managed stores where they sold jewelry, silverware, furniture, and art confiscated from the wealthy elite. In many cases, the Cubans who fled faced a stark choice: either leave behind their material goods or stay behind and lose their liberty and possibly even their lives. East Germans, English, French, Spanish, and Soviets—and even Americans—were tempted by diamond rings, beautiful brooches of gold and silver, and necklaces of ruby or pearl; all of which could be bought for a small fraction of their real value. I once visited a government store where these goods were sold; there were many beautiful things on display, but I didn't buy anything. It simply didn't feel right.

While I was chief of the Interests Section, from 1999 to 2002, Cuban officials never mentioned the cache of valuables, although I cannot imagine that they were unaware of it. Neither do Cuban Americans usually talk about the fortune they left behind, although they lament the loss of homes, ranches, and businesses. Only once did a Cuban American raise with me the issue of his family's valuables. Sitting beside me at a luncheon in Miami, the wealthy businessman whispered that his family had left their jewelry with the Swiss diplomats. Then sadly, he said, "Ambassador, all I really care about are five gold rings; they are a family heirloom passed down from one generation to the next." I could only sympathize. No one can touch the treasure until it is conclusively determined to whom it belongs today, and that will only occur when relations improve.

Carlos Gutierrez, President Bush's former adviser on Cuba, told me that he, like many prominent Cuban Americans, had come to realize that engagement, not hostility, would bring about change in Cuba. He had moved from advocating an isolationist policy to joining Obama on his visit to Havana and attending his speech at the Gran Teatro Nacional. He told me that the audience was optimistic, hopeful, and pleased that Obama acknowledged their yearning for change. As the president wound up his stirring speech he declared, "It is time now for us to leave the past behind. It is time for us to look forward to the future together." Some of his listeners feared that this might mean we would forget that Cubans had suffered greatly during the Special Period in Time of Peace, which the United States in part had imposed on Cuba by tightening the embargo when the Soviets withdrew their financial support. Many Cubans do not want Americans to forget that we contributed to their suffering. Still, Cubans must at least forgive, if not forget, if we are to achieve Obama's dream for reconciliation between "the children and grandchildren of the revolution and the children and the grandchildren of exile."

Raúl responded to President Trump's taunts in a measured way, saying that "Cuba and the United States can cooperate and live side by side, respecting their differences. But no one should expect that for this, one should have to make concessions inherent to one's sovereignty and independence." Were Fidel Castro still alive he would have immediately and harshly denounced Trump, the Cuban diaspora, and the United States. Still, both Castro brothers share the unbreakable conviction that Cuba's independence will not be compromised. Raúl put it like this,

"But it should not be hoped that to achieve this [cooperation with the US] Cuba will make concessions inherent to its independence and sovereignty." If only we believed them, perhaps we would stop making the mistake of attempting to "get a better deal," as Trump has promised.

Fidel never caved in when threatened, and he retaliated by taking actions that were more painful for the United States than for Cuba. For example, when the Bush administration restricted the travel of Cuban diplomats in 2002, as it began to revert to a hostile policy, Cuba did the same to our diplomats. A few years later, when the State Department realized that the restriction damaged our interests more than Cuba's, we suggested mutually rescinding the rule, but Castro was unwilling to do so, and it remained in place for over a decade until the Obama opening. Similarly, in 2001 the FBI refused to approve a visa for the new deputy of the Cuban Interests Section in Washington, DC. The Cuban government retaliated by refusing visas for my deputy at our Interests Section in Havana, as well as for our public diplomacy officer. This two-for-one reprisal strategy made the situation considerably more difficult for me than for my Cuban counterpart. It seems that the Trump administration will have to learn for itself that negative actions against Cuba seldom produce the desired results and often generate reactions that are detrimental to US interests.

For a few months following President Trump's Miami speech, there was hope that the US-Cuban diplomatic relationship would survive, if not prosper. But that expectation was crushed by the strange case of injuries suffered by American and Canadian diplomats. In August 2017, the media revealed that American diplomats had suffered hearing loss, nausea, and traumatic brain injuries from some sort of sonic attack. A number of the incidents occurred in the homes of diplomats responsible for security and intelligence between November of 2016 and January of 2017. However, a few took place subsequent to February, including the one that became public in August. According to the State Department, injuries also occurred at the Hotel Nacional and the Hotel Capri. None of the attacks, which now number twenty-four against American diplomats and five against Canadian diplomats, were directed at the American embassy.

When the injuries first occurred the American and Cuban governments attempted to deal with them in a responsible manner. Raúl Castro sought out the embassy's Charge d'Affairs, Jeffrey DeLaurentis, to assure him that Cuba was not responsible, and he invited the FBI to visit Havana; which it did several times to investigate. The State Department expelled two diplomats from the Cuban embassy in Washington D.C., presumably to balance staffing as American diplomats had been forced to leave their post in Havana as a result of their ailments.

When the diplomats' injuries became public in August 2017, conservative Cuban Americans led by Senator Marco Rubio used the incidents to demand that the United States retaliate against Cuba. Ignoring the American Foreign Service Association's public statement that the diplomats were prepared to remain in Cuba and continue their work, the Trump administration cut the American embassy staff by more than half and sent all dependents home. Bowing to Rubio's demands, the administration ordered the Cuban embassy to reduce its staff by an equivalent number of diplomats. In addition, the State Department issued an aggressive travel warning, advising American visitors to avoid the island, despite that fact that only diplomats had been affected by the sonic incidents.

On October 16, 2017 President Trump added his voice to the growing tensions. At a Rose Garden new conference, he said, "I do believe Cuba's responsible. I do believe that." He did not cite any evidence for his belief. The State Department continues to assert that it neither knows who is responsible for the attacks or the type of device that caused the ailments. Cuban Foreign Minister Bruno Rodriguez Padilla rejected Trump's accusation, saying that "There is no evidence, there is no evidence whatsoever, of the occurrence of the alleged incidents or the cause or origin of these ailments reported by US diplomats." He then added, "Neither is there any suggestion that these health problems have been caused by an attack of any sort during their stay in Cuba." Castro's daughter Mariela chimed in by claiming that "Even Star Wars didn't contain such fantasies."

To restore relations to at least a modicum of civility, the US and Cuba must discover what's happened and who was behind the attacks, but it has become more difficult as rhetoric from each side has become increasingly uncivil. Nevertheless, we can assume that each govern-ment— together or separately—is seeking the culprit or culprits by ex-amining who had motive, means, and opportunity. The possible perpetrators are: the Cuban government, a rogue faction within the government, a foreign power such as Russia or China—with North Korea an outside possibility—conservatives and/or militants in the Cuban diaspora, the America government, or malfunctioning listening devices. The possible explanations, such as our own government and malfunctioning listening devices, may seem farfetched, but this is what the Cuban government now seems to believe.

Raúl Castro's government had means and opportunity, but they do not appear to have motive. The attacks began shortly after Trump won the election and continued until February, while only a few took place subsequently. Given that Castro was the coarchitect of Obama's opening, it seems unlikely that he would deliberately destroy the détente with the United States. Moreover, Castro cooperated with the United States in the aftermath of the sonic attacks, reinforcing the idea that his government wanted to amicably resolve the puzzling incidents.

As Cuba approaches its first transition in over a half century, it is possible that factions within the government are jockeying for position. A hardline faction associated with Fidel Castro, who denigrated the opening before his death in November 2016, would have motive, means, and opportunity. And, if Raúl Castro discovered that an element within his own government was responsible, he might seek to cover it up in order to demonstrate that the country is united as it prepares for a new president.

As to foreign powers, it seems likely that only Russia and China—an outside possibility is North Korea—would have had means and opportunity, and even then, they might well have required some cooperation from someone within the Cuban government. Russian military and civilian leaders continue to urge reopening the Lourdes Signals Intelligence base, which until it was closed by the Russians in 2002 intercepted US satellite communications. For its part, China might seek to use Cuba as a pawn in its discussions with the Trump administration about North Korean. Still, I am not convinced that Russia or China would consider an alliance with Cuba worth the risks inherent in attacking American diplomats.

Conservatives and/or militants within the Cuban diaspora may have motive, given their extreme opposition to improved relations. And, in the past Cuban militants have carried out attacks against Cuba and Fidel Castro. In addition, conservative Cuban Americans have used the diplomats' injuries to criticize US–Cuban relations. But they do not appear to have had the means and opportunity, unless we can imagine them cooperating with hardliners in Cuba who also oppose better relations.

Another possibility is that this was not a deliberate attack against the American and Canadian diplomats, but listening devices that malfunctioned. The *Guardian* newspaper suggested "mass hysteria" based on the opinion of senior neurologists who claimed that they know of no sonic device that could cause the range of injuries suffered by the diplomats, but Dr. Charles Rosenfarb, the State Department's medical director, debunked the idea of "mass hysteria" by pointing out that "exact findings" on medical tests couldn't be easily faked. Perhaps then the headaches, nausea, and temporary loss of hearing were caused by the sounds that were described as "high-pitched," and causing "baffling sensations." Conceivably, the more serious injuries might have been caused by complications from an illness not discovered until following exposure to the unusual sound. For example, a diplomat who suffered minor symptoms from what seemed to have been a "sonic attack" might later have contracted a virus that led to more serious ailments, including what the State Department is now labeling "mild traumatic brain injury. Still, this explanation is not entirely satisfactory as it does not explain why so many devices would malfunction or why the malfunction would occur only in those devices aimed at American and Canadian diplomats."

Even without knowing who or what caused the ailments, it is hard to escape the conclusion that those in the United States and Cuba who opposed engagement have gotten exactly what they wanted. The embassy is barely functioning with the drawdown of half of its American staff, and Secretary of State Rex Tillerson says that he is unconvinced that the alleged attacks are over. Josefina Vidal, a high-level Cuban official, who negotiated the details of the Obama opening with American diplomats, says that the Trump administration is simply engaged in an irresponsible effort to advance anti-Cuban politics. Unhappily, for Cubans who were hoping for more economic freedom, the Cuban government is circling the wagons, clamping down on critics and reversing reforms. This should come as no surprise because as has been shown throughout this book, when the United States threatens Cuba, Cuba's leaders become more repressive. This was the case in 2003 when Fidel Castro jailed seventy-five dissidents in response to George W. Bush's return to a punitive policy. The bottom line is that given the current state of relations, we are unlikely to discover the perpetrator or the cause of the injuries.

The January 9 Senate hearing chaired by Marco Rubio further politicized the issue. Acting Secretary of State Francisco Palmieri intensified Rubio's demonization of Cuba by testifying that "Cuba is a security state. The Cuban government in general has a very tight lid on everything and anything that happens in that country." His boss, Undersecretary of State Steve Goldstein was more circumspect pointing out that "we are not much further ahead than we were in finding out what occurred." Still, he insisted that Raúl Castro "knows what happened." These statements by US government officials reinforce the idea that the Cuban government must come clean about what happened before semi-normal relations are restored. This assumes they even know why the injuries occurred. Given the current impasse, and the control Rubio and hardliners are exercising over US policy toward Cuba, it is unlikely that either side will admit any fault. And, just to complicate matters, Senator Jeff Flake—long an advocate for engagement—confirmed an AP story that an FBI report concluded that evidence is insufficient to support a sonic attack theory. Adding more muddle to the mystery, Todd Brown from State's Diplomatic security posed the possibility that someone deliberately infected the diplomats with a virus.

The unfortunate fact is that even if a culprit is identified and Cuba takes action to rectify and compensate for the injuries, conservative Cuban Americans who now have gained the upper hand in US–Cuba relations, will not willingly cede control over policy. Rather, they will use their power to demand that the embassies continue with skeleton staffs and that the US government tighten the embargo. As former Secretary Gutierrez put it, "The conservative diaspora doesn't like stability in our relationship. To them it means we accept the regime."

Senator Rubio and Representative Mario Díaz-Balart (R-FL) already have complained that the new embargo regulations which were published on November 8, 2018 are insufficient. As Trump promised in his Miami speech, the regulations further restrict travel by individual Americans, but visits by people-to-people groups engaged in cultural, religious, or humanitarian activities are still permitted. The Treasury Department now prohibits Americans from engaging in financial transactions with 180 Cuban government entities that are substantially run by Cuban military or intelligence agencies. Among the business placed on a "restricted list" are hotels, such as Ambos Mundos (Two Worlds) where Ernest Hemingway lived when he arrived in Havana and businesses that serve the tourist industry by selling jewelry, flowers, and photographic services.

We can expect that Rubio, Díaz-Balart, and Senator Ted Cruz

(R-TX) will continue to press their advantage, insisting the Treasury Department issue additional sanctions, further limiting contact with Cuba. Once again—as during George W. Bush's administration—conservative Cuban American legislators will attempt to force regime change by reducing US contact with the island to an absolute minimum. Their next target most likely will be people-to-people visits and educational travel. As in the past they may also attempt to reduce travel and money transfers by the Cuban diaspora—many of whom are US citizens—whose visit family and friends and provide over one billion dollars in remittance. Even the two dozen bilateral agreements will not be immune from the efforts to constrain cooperation between the US and Cuban governments.

As has been the case in the past, the Cuban people will suffer most from these new measures. The travel warning has already reduced the number of American visitors, harming the small family businesses that sprung up as a result of Castro's privatization reforms and the influx of American visitors. The closure of the Consular section of the American embassy means that Cubans can no longer obtain visas for travel to the United States, whether to visit friends, for medical care, for business, or for cultural, religious, and sports exchanges. Although the State Department has said that it will provide a means for family reunification, as of January 16, 2018 the US embassy in Havana is not issuing visas of any type, neither for those hoping to join family in the US or escape persecution, nor for those who simply wish to visit or participate in cultural exchanges.

The poor state of US-Cuban relations may have contributed to Raúl Castro's decision to delay stepping down as the President of Cuba. The February 24, 2018 date was scrapped, according to the Cuban government because of devastation wrought by Hurricane Irma that delayed local and regional elections. The new date for handing over power, is on or shortly after the National Assembly is constituted on April 19, 2018. Castro has confirmed his intention to serve his "second and last mandate" and that Cuba "will have a new president." Whatever the reason, the additional seven weeks in office will allow Castro more time to stabilize relations with the United States and assess his successor's ability to ensure the country's internal stability.

Another less well-known reason for the delay is that it gives Castro the opportunity to confirm Russia as Cuba's closest patron and ally, a critical realignment away from impoverished Venezuela. On December 16, 2017 Russia, Venezuela, and Cuba struck a deal in which Rosneft, the Russian state-owned oil company, will take over Venezuela's stake in the Cienfuegos oil refinery. By delaying his departure until April, Castro will have time to sign the agreement, thereby confirming Russia as Cuba's newest benefactor before his successor assumes the presidency.

The succession from a Castro to a non-Castro will be facilitated by the fact that Raúl has been Cuba's leader for a relatively brief reign of ten years, and Fidel, who ruled for forty-nine years, will have been dead for more than a year. In any case, it is unlikely that we will see overt division among the government elite. Raúl will retain his role as the first secretary of the Communist Party, which means that he will continue to determine the ideological direction of the revolution. He also will retain considerable influence within the two powerful institutions he once headed, Cuba's Revolutionary Armed Forces and its Interior Ministry, which together provide for the country's external and internal defense. Should he have any concerns, Raúl has wide latitude to shape the succession by limiting the power he confers upon his successor. He could remain as chief of the armed forces. All he has to do is submit a referendum to the voters to change the constitution, just as Fidel did in 2002 when he made the constitution "irrevocable."

Still, nothing can be taken for granted. If there is indeed a hardline element—as I speculate—that carried out the sonic attacks on American diplomats, the transition may be postponed or result in an internal coup. In either of these scenarios, the probable outcome would be that the new government would reinforce the status quo by pausing, if not stopping internal reforms. Although Cuban leaders must reform the economy if the country is to prosper, many are hesitant because they fear disruptive change.

There has been some speculation that someone other than Díaz-Canel, a 57-year old party stalwart born after the Cuban revolution, might be chosen to lead Cuba, but whoever leads the government will be completely loyal to Raúl and the revolution. All of the potential candidates would broaden the Castro family's hold on power. Three of the four are family members: Raúl's son Alejandro Castro Espín, a colonel in the Ministry of the Interior who participated in negotiations with the United States; Raúl's daughter Mariela Castro Espín, a less likely candidate, but well known for establishing the Cuban National Center for Sex Education, which advocates on behalf of LGBTQ persons; and General Luis Alberto Rodríguez, and General Luis Albert Rodrìguez, Raúl's son-in-law and head of a business conglomerate managed by Cuba's armed forces.. Another possibility sometimes mentioned is Cuba's foreign minister, Bruno Rodríguez. But if Raúl were to pass over Díaz-Canel, he would most likely choose a family member.

Cuba being Cuba, there is no guarantee that Castro will give up the presidency. He can change his mind at any time and, like Fidel, remain in power until he dies or becomes too ill to rule. It would be prudent, however, to provide a transitional period, as Fidel unintentionally did by surviving several life-threatening operations. Without question, Raúl would be ready to resume power or replace his successor should he perceive any serious threat to the power of the Castro family, the military, or the party.

One sure prediction is that no matter who is president, Cubans will be poorer and have less opportunity so long as the Trump administration continues to tighten the embargo. Fewer American visitors will harm those entrepreneurial Cubans—many of whom are dissidents or disaffected—who make their living through independent activities. But the ban on Americans engaging in financial transactions with the Cuban intelligence and military services will not damage these powerful institutions. Investors from other countries will continue to patronize and invest in their tourist facilities and holding companies. The Spanish companies that have built most of Cuba's luxury hotels, will continue to do so, and China will move ahead with plans to build 108,000 new hotel rooms. American tour groups, unable to stay in military-run hotels, will be replaced by Canadian, European, and Latin American visitors.

The degree to which the Cuban government can diminish the impact of our sanctions will depend on its success in seeking political and economic alliances. Raúl Castro has done a good job of reaching out to Latin America, linking Cuba with regional organizations that have expanded his influence beyond the leftist governments of Bolivia, Ecuador, Nicaragua, and Venezuela. Brazil provided financing for extensive renovations of the Port of Mariel and participates in a variety of joint ventures with the Cuban government. Since 2008 Raúl has instituted economic reforms, which are popular at home as well as with the European Union, which is Cuba's second-largest trading partner and foreign investor after China. But Cuba's most important relations are with Russia and China.

By derailing the Obama-Castro opening, President Trump has given Vladimir Putin the opportunity to become the predominant foreign power in Cuba by replacing Venezuela as the island's major source of oil. The deal Castro struck, which he is expected to sign before leaving the presidency, puts Russian oil giant Rosneft in charge of the Cienfuegos oil refinery and awards it two gas-exploration contracts. Russia has waived $29 billion in Soviet-era debt, will invest $4 billion in Cuban infrastructure, and recently sent a tanker carrying 250,000 barrels of much-needed oil. In December 2016 Russia signed a military cooperation arrangement under which it will modernize Cuba's armed forces until 2020. President Vladimir Putin closed the Lourdes Signals Intelligence facility in 2002, hoping to improve relations with the United States. Fifteen years later, Russian officials are talking about reopening the facility, which intercepts US satellite communications.

China, too, has considerable influence in Cuba. Following the Chinese prime minister's visit to Cuba in September 2016, Raúl Castro made a state visit to China in March 2017, during which China and Cuba announced that they would deepen military ties. China is Cuba's principal trading partner; in 2016 this trade amounted to $1.8 billion, principally in communications, transportation, and machinery. Nevertheless, given the long history of Cuban-Soviet relations, it seems likely that Russia's political influence will over-shadow China's.

Cuba's growing ties with China and Russia diminish the opportunity for a strategic alliance between the United States and Cuba and reduce potential US political and economic influence. By the time the United States again attempts to improve relations, China and Russia will likely have consolidated their military partnerships with Cuba. In addition, as US sanctions are enhanced, Cuba will look to other countries for investment and trade. This will result in substantial missed opportunities for US industry, which could amount to losses of billions of dollars in revenue and thousands of American jobs. Ben Rhodes, one of the architects of Obama's opening, laid out the case for good relations: "Engagement helps empower the Cuban people and the private sector, people-to-people travel brings new ideas. Good relations with Cuba advances our relations with Latin America and prevents Russia and China from exploiting their relations with Cuba to our disadvantage. And it would be costly in trade, investment and services to reverse the Obama-Castro opening. Squeezing Cuba is not constructive to opening space. A collapse would be negative—possibly the right wing (in Cuba) would win."

Raúl Castro and Cuba's government elite will do only what is in their interests. If they feel threatened or fear that their power is being undermined, they will allow fewer freedoms. Maintaining the US embargo will not change the Cuban government, improve human rights, or promote democracy in Cuba. In fact, it will continue to delay positive change on the island by making Cubans poorer and less inclined to confront the repressive powers of their government. Our concerns about the lack of freedom in the country will be ignored, and we will have little economic or political leverage as Russia and China consolidate their positions on the island. Trump's Cuba policy will have satisfied his political base at the expense of our national interests.

Given President Trump's apparent preference for authoritarian rulers in Egypt, the Philippines, and Saudi Arabia, he would likely welcome Raúl Castro to the White House were it not for his conservative supporters within the Cuban American community. Perhaps that wouldn't be such a bad idea, if the invitation were issued after Castro steps down as president of Cuba. Then we can engage with Cuba's new leaders, seek reconciliation between our nations and regain the influence that we lost as a result of the Cuban revolution.

EPILOGUE

I N OCTOBER 2017, I VISITED CUBA AS A LECTURER FOR THE PHILADELPHIA World Affairs Council, on a tour that visited Havana, Pinar del Río, Cienfuegos, Trinidad, Santa Clara, and Camaguey. We arrived in Havana a month after Hurricane Irma, a Category 5 storm that struck Cuba's north coast and two weeks after the Department of State warned Americans against travel to the island because our diplomatic personnel had been attacked and "U.S. citizens may also be at risk." This advisory was put out though no visitors to the island had been affected and it is unknown who perpetrated the attacks, most of which occurred from November 2016 to February 2017. At the urging of Cuban American Senator Marco Rubio, the State Department reduced the American staffing at the U.S. embassy by more than half and ordered an equivalent drawdown of Cuban diplomats resident in Washington DC.

I can unequivocally affirm that the Cuba I knew when I left the island after a three-year tour as head of our diplomatic mission in 2002 is far different from the Cuba of 2017. There have been substantial changes that have improved the lives of many Cubans. On July 20, 2015, the U.S. Interests Section was upgraded to the level of an embassy. After fifty-four years, the elegant glass building located along Havana's seafront Malecón was restored to its rightful place in the long, painful, history of our two governments. The most remarkable change I observed, however, was in the numbers of American visitors in Havana's streets, and the city's transformation as its lovely historic buildings that had long been falling into disrepair have been turned into elegant new hotels.

After Raúl Castro officially assumed power in 2008 from his ailing brother Fidel, more than a half million Cubans entered the private sector. The repressed entrepreneurial instincts of Cubans were unleashed resulting in a profusion of private enterprises, such as family-owned restaurants, rooms-for-rent, and Cuba's ubiquitous fifties American cars, have been waxed, polished, and repaired, to serve as taxis for American visitors.

Cubans have also gained a number of freedoms. They can now travel outside the country without the government's permission, returning from visits to Miami with all manner of consumer goods, including computers, radios, and televisions. Cuban artists, are acclaimed throughout the United States and the world for their painting, photography, dance, and musical performances. In central Havana, people on the streets were better dressed and those with wealthy relatives or some money of their own were staying in hotels and frequenting restaurants that formerly catered only to foreign tourists.

What has not changed is that a Castro still leads Cuba's Communist government, but as stated earlier in this book if Raúl fulfills his promise, he will step down as president on February 24, 2018. The Cuban government remains authoritarian and socialist, providing free education and health care and making decisions from the top down. The government continues to restrict individual freedoms, especially those of opposition groups such as the "Ladies in White," and dissidents like Elizardo Sánchez, Marta Beatriz Roque, Guillermo Farinos, and the noted blogger Yoani Sánchez. Unauthorized public gatherings and publication of opposition manifestos is still illegal, although the government now tolerates gentle criticisms of its policies in state-run media.

The Cuba that has emerged in the last fifteen years is filled with energy, initiative, and hope. But what shocked and saddened me during my recent visit was that Cubans were frightened and worried that their newly found prosperity and greater freedom would be lost. This was in stark contrast to my visit in May 2016, when Cubans were excited and enthusiastic about their growing economic prosperity. I was then part of a visit by the Board of Directors of *Finca Vigía* (Lookout House), which has helped the Cuban Ministry of Culture preserve Ernest Hemingway's documents and his gracious home— *Finca Vigía*—set on a small hill in San Francisco de Paula about thirty minutes from Havana. Then, Cubans believed that their long years of suffering and deprivation were coming to a close, as a result of the emerging détente between our countries. They never imagined that on June 16, 2017 their hopes would be shattered by President Donald Trump, when he cancelled President Obama's opening and a few months later took measures that have sent relations into a Cold War freeze. In 2016 the name on every Cuban's lips was "Obama," now I heard President Trump's name spoken by Cubans in sadness and despair.

Here is what I learned during my visit in October 2017 with the Philadelphia World Affairs Council. After watching an amazing performance of dance and percussion by the Havana Compás Dance company, a young man eyes, brimming with tears, whispered to me that "Trump's policy" has hurt the dance company; he explained that fewer American tour groups are coming to see their performances and sales of the company's souvenirs are down. In Pinar del Rio, we fell in love with Down's Syndrome children and the members of the community who voluntarily run the center where the children come to socialize with each other, paint, and dance. We also were impressed by an organic farm with a popular restaurant created and managed by a family who've made a great success of their new business. But the children, the dancers, and the farm are all threatened by the stricter embargo regulations that took effect on November 9, 2017. The organic farm won't be hurt as much because other foreign tourist will continue to visit. But as people-to-people tours—like the one I was on—become less frequent, there will be fewer visits to Havana Compás Dance and to the Down's Syndrome center, and the Europeans won't fill the gap. American tour groups that provide people-to-people visits were authorized under the Clinton administration in order to allow Americans to visit without violating US law, which had long prohibited tourism to Cuba. The impact of strained relations and the travel warning has already had a negative impact on these groups. Alaska Airlines is the fourth regional airline—the other are Spirit, Frontier, and Silver—in the last year to cancel its flights to Cuba, and American, JetBlue, and Southwest Airlines have cut capacity, confirming a downturn in American travel that will result in fewer donations, less customers, and less revenues for Cuba's children, its private entrepreneurs, and its artistic community.

I had not been outside Havana since I left in 2002, so I was impressed to see numerous Cubans selling trinkets in small stands set up along several streets in Cienfuegos. But then I had long ago realized that Cubans are natural capitalists—after all they practically built Miami! I struck up a conversation with two women selling post cards in the Plaza de Armas. Both said they hoped that the consular section of the American embassy would soon reopen so they could apply for visas to visit family in Miami. Later our group had lunch at the family-run Casa Prado where the mother cooks, father does the books, and the son and daughter-in-law serve the diners. Business was off, and we were the only customers. In the afternoon, we visited the Cienfuegos Botanical Gardens that before the Cuban Revolution had a close relationship with Harvard University, but even with improved relations it has not reestablished its ties with Harvard. The garden, which is more like a forest, with its lush vegetation, massive trees, and endemic species is only minimally maintained. Its small and dedicated staff do their best, but resources are scarce.

The manager of the Classic Ballet of Camaguey where we viewed a very professional performance lamented that he had to cancel their upcoming performances in the States because the consular section is not issuing visas. In Trinidad, a UNESCO World Heritage site, we saw young people—proudly dressed in black-and-white uniforms—headed for work as servers in the numerous new restaurants catering to tourists. They were still hopeful, but how long before these establishments begin to close and they lose their jobs?

Change has come to Cuba. Its youth was beginning to believe that they had a future in their own country, rather than in the United States. The dream I have held close to my heart that Cuba's youth would some-day prefer Havana to Miami seemed to be coming true, until conserva-tive Cuban Americans—people with the same roots as these young people—convinced President Trump to extinguish their dreams. I hope this shuttering of improved relations will be reversed soon.

NOTES

PROLOGUE

"I may go back again one day," James A. Michener and John Kings, *Six Days in Havana* (Austin: University of Texas Press, 1989), 99.

CHAPTER 1

"The Cuban people hold a special place . . . ," Nelson Mandela, quoted in Isaac Saney, "When Africa Called, Fidel and Cuba Answered," *Telesur*, November 29, 2016.

"[Any fears] have dissipated today," Jorge Mas Canosa, quoted in Larry Rohter, "The 1992 Campaign: Florida; Clinton Sees Opportunity to Break G.O.P Grip on Cuban Americans," *New York Times*, October 31, 1992.

William M. LeoGrande and Peter Kornbluh, "Clinton's Campaign Calculus," in *Back Channel to Cuba: The Hidden History of Negotiations between Washington and Havana* (Chapel Hill: University of North Carolina Press, 2014), 269–71.

CHAPTER 2

Lily Prellezo and José Basulto, "Shoot-Down," in *Seagull One: The Amazing True Story of Brothers to the Rescue* (Gainesville: University Press of Florida, 2010), Chapters 27 and 28.

"Frankly, this is not cojones . . . ," Madeline Albright, quoted in "Players: Madeline Albright," CNN, http://www.cnn.com/ALLPOLITICS/1997/gen/resources/players/albright/.

Peter Kornbluh, "Posada Carriles Built Bombs For, and Informed On, Jorge Mas Canosa, CIA Records Reveal." October 6, 2009, National Security Archive.

Notes

Gaeton Fonzi, "Jorge Who?," 1993, Document 0063, Cuban Information Archives, cybab0exuke,com/doc_051-075doc0063, p7-8.

Ann Louise Bardach and Larry Lohter, "A Bomber's Tale: Decades of Intrigue: Life in the Shadows, Trying to Bring Down Castro," *New York Times*, July 13, 1998.

CHAPTER 3

William M. LeoGrande and Peter Kornbluh, "Kissinger's Cuba Initiative," in *Back Channel to Cuba*, pp 126–28.

William M. LeoGrande and Peter Kornbluh, "García Márquez's Mission" and "The FBI Delegation," in *Back Channel to Cuba*, 334–337 and 337–338.

CHAPTER 4

Claiborne, William, "Illinois Governor Defends Visit to Castro; Ryan Says U.S. Should End Trade Embargo," *Washington Post*, October 28, 1999, [Huddleston papers].

Currie, Bennie M., "Illinois Governor: Cuba Visit Success," Associated Press, October 28, 1999, [Huddleston papers].

"The trouble with Cuba is Fidel Castro," George Ryan, quoted in Associated Press, "Cuba Criticizes U.S. Interests Section for Having Politician Meet Dissident," *Wall Street Journal*, October 29, 1999, [Huddleston papers].

"Gobierno de Castro Amenaza Sección de Intereses de EEUU" [Cuban Government Threatens the US Interests Section], *Diario Las Americas*, October 28, 1999, [Huddleston papers].

CHAPTER 5

"Many days of mourning . . . ," Rafael Díaz-Balart, quoted in Abby Goodnough, "All in the Family: Brothers Wage War on Uncle Fidel," *New York Times*, March 8, 2006.

Michener and Kings, *Six Days in Havana*, 63–64.

"(Fidel's) endless rule seemed like some powerful vine," Arthur Miller, "My Dinner with Castro," *Guardian*, January 24, 2004.

CHAPTER 6

"Elián González Defeated Al Gore," William Schneider, *Atlantic*, May 1, 2001, https://www.theatlantic.com/politics/archive/2001/05 /elian-gonzalez -defeated-al-gore/377714/.

Notes

"Elián Says Dolphins Saved His Life," March 27, 2000, IOL, https://www
.iol.co.za/mercury/world/elian-says-dolphins-saved-his-life-33676.

Douglas Montero, "Castro Threatens "Battle" for Raft Boy: Gives U.S.
3 Days to Return Refugee," *New York Post*, December 6, 1999.

"The question is . . . ," Bill Clinton, quoted in Steven Mufson, "Clinton
Warns Against Politics in Cuban Boy's Case," *Washington Post*, pp A41,
December 9, 1999.

Haberman, Clyde, "NYC; A Tug of War as Complex as War," *New York
Times,* January 14, 2000.

"No one has the right to make him an American citizen," Mariela Quintana, quoted in Mcfadden, Robert D. "Grandmother Make Plea for Cuban
Boy's Return," *New York Times*, January 22, 2000.

Chapter 7

"The Capital's Assault on Injustice," *Juventud Rebelde*, July 27, 2000,
[Huddleston papers].

"The law has been upheld," Bill Clinton, quoted in Bragg, Rick, "The
Elian Gonzalez Case: The Overview; Cuban Boy Seized by U.S. Agents and
Reunited with his Father, *New York Times*, April 23, 2000.

Lizette Alvarez, "The Elian Gonzalez Case: The Overview; Raid in
Miami Opens New Front in Struggle over Cuban Boy," *New York Times*, April
24, 2000.

Chapter 8

"Please, Mr. President, forgive me . . . ," Arthur Miller, quoting himself
in "My Dinner with Castro," *The Guardian,* January 24, 2004.

"Your presence here helps," Fidel Castro, quoted in Ginger Thompson,
"Cuba, Too, Felt the September 11 Shock Waves, with a More Genial Castro
Offering Help," *New York Times*, February 7, 2002.

Cathleen McGuigan, "Saving Havana: Restoring the Old Cuban Capital
Is Good for Tourism. But What About the Fabulous Modern Buildings?"
Mcguigan, Cathleen, *Newsweek*, International Atlantic Edition 54 July 1,
2002, pp 1-4.

Chapter 9

"Dear Mr. Powell," Fidel Castro, "Letter to General (Ret.) Colin Powell," November 11, 1995, [Huddleston papers].

CHAPTER 10

"Distinguida Señora Vicky [sic] . . . ," Amalia Castro quoted in "Letter to Sra. Vicky Huddleston," Asociación Nacional de Lebreles Afganos [National Association of Afghan Hounds], February 6, 2001, [Huddleston papers].

Kamen, Al, "In the Loop: And your Little Dog, Too!" Washington Post, February 13, 2001, [Huddleston papers].

"We've always known that Fidel Castro's bark . . . ," senior State Department official, quoted in Agence France-Presse, "U.S. Diplomat Hounded Out of Cuban Dog Club," Reuters, February 13, 2001, [Huddleston papers].

"Well, I hope so." Vicki Huddleston quoted in Rene Montagne, *Morning Edition*, February 16, 2001, National Public Radio, [Huddleston papers].

DeYoung, Karen, "Message Sent Via Diplomatic Pooch, Cuba Dog Club Boots U.S. Mission Chief," *Washington Post*, February 17, 2001, Page C01, [Huddleston papers].

"I'm not going to stoop so low . . . ," Charles Shapiro quoted in Karen DeYoung, "Message Sent via Diplomatic Pooch," *Washington Post*, February 17, 2001, [Huddleston papers].

"[Havana had been]'slandered,'" Cuban Afghan Hound Association quoted in Mark Fineman, "It's a Dog's Life for U.S. Envoy in Havana," *Los Angeles Times*, March 23, 2001.

CHAPTER 11

"Guantanamo Bay [GTMO] "Gitmo," Global Security.org, *https://www.globalsecurity.org/military/facility/guantanamo-bay.htm*

"Dagger pointed at Cuba's heart," Fidel Castro quoted in "Castro Does 'Not Oppose US Prison," BBC News, 22:38 GMT January 4, 2002, ws.bbc.co.uk/2/hi/Americas/1743562.

"We hope that one day . . . ," Felipe Perez Roque, quoted in Ginger Thompson, "Cuba, Too, Felt the Sept. 11 Shock Waves, with a more Genial Castro Offering Help," *New York Times*, February 7, 2002.

Dalia Acosta, "Cuba-U.S.: Conflicting Interests Affect Incipient Thaw," February 18, 2002, Inter Press Service, [Huddleston papers].

"Shackled Detainees Arrive in Guantanamo," January 11, 2002, CNN, http://edition.cnn.com/2002/WORLD/asiapcf/central/01/11/ret.detainee.transfer/index.html

Dalia Acosta, "Cuba-U.S.: Conflicting Interests Affect Incipient Thaw," February 18, 2002, Inter Press Service, [Huddleston papers].

Notes

CHAPTER 12

"You cannot say there is change in Cuba . . . ," Vicki Huddleston quoted in Marc Frank, "U.S.'s Top Cuban Diplomat Denies Warming Trend," February 7, 2002, Reuters, TR_TNS 3 f CU LATAM DIP LDC NEWS 621 NO7139580

"The problem for us is that nothing has fundamentally changed," Vicki Huddleston quoted Anita Snow, "U.S. Diplomat Says Cuba Must Do More Than Charm Americans if It Wants Sanction to Fall," Associated Press, Thursday, BC cycle, International news, February 7, 2002, Associated Press, [Huddleston papers.

"Cuba has reacted in as positive manner," Vicki Huddleston quoted by Marc Frank, "U.S.'s Top Cuban Diplomat Denies Warming Trend," Reuters February 7, 2002, RTR_TNS 3 f CU LATAM DIP LDC NEWS 621 NO7139580

"Debe hacer mas [Ought to do more]" Vicki Huddleston quoted by *Agencia EFE*, "Cuba 'Debe Hacer Mas' En Lucha Anititerrorista, Segun Diplomatica," *Agencia EFE* ICXMUN EXG, February 7, 2002, [Huddleston papers].

"No hemos visto una Buena cooperación de Cuba sobre el terrorismmo [We have not seen good cooperation on terrorism from Cuba]" Vicki Huddleston, quoted by Oscar Madrid, "No Ve Cooperacion Cubana' sobre Terrorismo [No Cuban Cooperation on Terrorism]" EFE News Service, Cuba-EE.UU-Terrorismo, February 7, 2002. [Huddleston papers].

"Cuba should do more," Vicki Huddleston, quoted by EFE News Service, Cuba-US: U.S. Diplomat Says Cuba Should Do More to Fight Terrorism," EFE News Service February 8, 2002, [Huddleston papers].

"Cuba should do more," Vicki Huddleston, quoted by EFE News Service, "Cuba-US: U.S. Diplomat Says Cuba Should Do More to Fight Terrorism," February 8, 2002, EFE News Service, paraphrased in Financial Times Information, JOURNAL-CODE: WEFE, LOAD-DATE: February 8, 2002 [Huddleston papers].

"They cannot imagine how much we do not care," Fidel Castro, quoted in Vivian Sequera, "Fidel Castro Says He Doesn't Care if Cuba Is Included or Not on the U.S. State Department's Terrorism Watch List," Associated Press, February 16, 2002, [Huddleston papers].

"In Miami, there's extraordinary confusion . . . ," Roberto de Armas a Cuban official quoted by Tracey Eaton, "American Diplomat in Havana Says Cuba Can't Charm U.S. into Easing Embargo, *Dallas Morning News*, Knight Ridder/Tribune News Service, KR-ACC-No: K3341, February 8, 2002, [Huddleston papers].

Notes

"There is not a country in the world where diplomats don't interfere…," Fidel Castro quoted by Vivian Sequera, "Fidel Castro Says He Doesn't Care if Cuba Is Included or Not on the U.S. State Department's Terrorism Watch List," Associated Press, February 16, 2002, [Huddleston papers].

"We are in the ninth year of Clinton policy," Joe Garcia quoted in Vivian Sequera, "Fidel Castro Says He Doesn't Care if Cuba Is Included or Not on the U.S. State Department's Terrorism Watch List," Associated Press, February 16, 2002, [Huddleston papers].

"For 43 years they've been saying the same thing," Fidel Castro quoted by Dalia Acosta, "Cuba-U.S.: Conflicting Interests Affect Incipient Thaw, Inter Press Service, February 18, 2002, [Huddleston papers].

Thompson, Ginger, "Fox: Cuban Relations 'Solid,'" New York Times News Service, HGTV, *Miami Herald*, 2601413.htm, February 4, 2002.

"Goering, Laurie, "Fox Meets with Cuban Dissidents; Mexican Leader Says Human Rights a Chief Concern," *Chicago Tribune*, February 5, 2002 [Huddleston papers].

Elaine De Valle, "Radio Martí Boss Creates Lots of Static," *Miami Herald*, March 31, 2002, [Huddleston papers].

David Gonzalez, "Cuba Arrests Asylum Seekers in Mexican Embassy," *New York Times*, March 2, 2002.

Tim Weiner, "Castro's Attack on Fox Place Cuban-Mexican Ties in Danger," *New York Times*, April 24, 2002.

Chapter 13

"I think it's a terrible idea." Wayne Smith quoted in Kevin Sullivan, "In Havana, U.S. Radios Strike Note of Discord—to Cuba Gift are Arrogant Meddling," *Washington Post*, May 5, 2002, p A21 [Huddleston papers].

"In this country…" Felipe Pérez Roque, quoted in Tracy Easton, "U.S. Radio Handots Irk Cuba - Officials trade criticism over Political Tactics, human-rights practices. *Dallas Morning News*, April 9, 2002. [Huddleston papers].

Chapter 14

Kevin Sullivan, "In Havana, U.S. Radios Strike Note of Discord," *Washington Post*, May 5, 2002, [Huddleston papers].

John Bolton, quoted in Judith Miller, "Washington Accuses Cuba of Germ-Warfare Research," *New York Times*, May 7, 2002.

Lincoln Díaz-Balart, quoted in Judith Miller, Ibid.

Notes

David Gonzalez, "Cuban Dissidents Put Hope in a Petition and Jimmy Carter," *New York Times*, May 14, 2002.

"Articles 63 and 88 of your constitution allows citizens . . . ," quoted in "remarks by former U.S President Jimmy Carter at the University of Havana, Cuba, Tuesday, May 14, 2002," The Carter Center, "President Carters' Trip Report, May 20, 2002.

Oswaldo Payá, "Osvaldo Paya to Vicki Huddleston," Havana, May 18, 2002. [Huddleston papers].

Chapter 15

"Freedom sometimes grows step by step," George W. Bush, quoted in David Stout, "Bush Hews to Cuban Hard Line, but Holds Out a Carrot or Two," *New York Times*, May 20, 2002.

"One hundred years ago Cuba declared her independence," George W. Bush, "Remarks on the 100th Anniversary of Cuban Independence in Miami, Florida," May 20, 2002, The American Presidency Project, http://www.presidency.ucsb.edu/ws/index.php?pid=63117

"On May 20, 2002 President Bush delivered . . . , Jorge I. Dominguez in "Reshaping Relations Between the United States and Cuba," in *Debating U.S.-Cuban Relations: Shall We Play Ball?*, ed. Jorge I. Dominguez, Rafael M. Hernández, and Lorena G. Barberia (New York: Routledge, 2012), pp 38- 41.

"Don't be Foolish Mr. W.," Fidel Castro, quoted in Lucia Newman, "Castro: 'Don't Be Foolish, Mr. W,'" June 1, 2002, Posted: 6:30pmCNN.

Fidel Castro, "Speech Given by Dr. Fidel Castro Ruz, President of the Republic of Cuba, at the Public Rally Held at the 'Abel Santamaría Cuadrado' Revolutionary Square in Ciego de Avila on the Occasion of the 49th Anniversary of the Attacks on the Moncada and Carlos Manuel de Céspedes Barracks," July 26, 2002, Ministerio de Relaciones Exteriores de la República de Cuba, http://anterior.cubaminrex.cu/English/Speeches/FCR/fcr2002/FCR_at%20public%20rally%20on%2049%20anniversary%20moncada%2026072002.asp

Hammer, Joshua, *The Bad-Ass Librarians of Timbuktu: And Their Race to Save the World's Most Precious Manuscripts* (New York: Simon and Schuster, 2016).

Jean-Guy Allard, "Bon Voyage, Mrs. Huddleston," *Granma*, July 2002. [Huddleston papers].

Letter from Colin L. Powell, Secretary of State, to Vicki Huddleston, (not dated but presumably September 2002), [Huddleston papers].

Notes

Chapter 16

Fred Bernstein, "Lighting Matches in Cuba on the 4th," *New York Times*, July 4, 2002.

Allard, "Bon Voyage, Mrs. Huddleston."

Roger Noriega, quoted in Saul Landau and Nelson P. Valdes, "The Confessions of Roger Noriega," *Counterpunch*, September 17, 2010.

Colin L. Powell, *Commission for Assistance to a Free Cuba*, May 2004, https://pdf.usaid.gov/pdf_docs/Pcaab192.pdf.

Carlos Gutierrez, interview with the author, May 8, 2017, Skype to Mr. Gutierrez's office.

Vicki Huddleston and Carlos Pascual, *Learning to Salsa: New Steps in U.S.-Cuban Relations* (Washington, DC: Brookings Institution Press, 2010).

Barack Obama, "Statement by the President on Cuban Policy Changes," December 17, 2014, White House, https://obamawhitehouse .archives.gov /the-press-office/2014/12/17/statement-president-cuba-policy-changes.

Barack Obama, quoted in Matt Spetalnick and Jeff Mason, "Obama's Trip Aims to Make Cuba Opening 'Irreversible,'" March 16, 2016, Reuters, http://www.reuters.com/article/us-usa-cuba-address-idUSKCN0WI32P.

Ryan Teague Beckwith, "Cuba: Read President Obama's Speech to the Cuban People," *Time*, March 22, 2016, http://time.com/4267933 /barack-obama-cuba-speech-transcript-full-text/.

Ben Rhodes, interview with the author, May 16, 2017, by cellphone.

Donald J. Trump, "Remarks by President Trump on the Policy of the United States towards Cuba," June 16, 2017, The White House, https:/ /www.white house.gov/the-press-office/2017/06/16/remarks-president-trump-policy-united -states-towards-cuba.

White House Office of the Press Secretary, "Presidential Policy Directive—United States–Cuba Normalization," October 14, 2016, White House, https://obamawhitehouse.archives.gov/the-press-office/2016 /10/14/presidential-policy-directive-united-states-cuba-normalization.

Guillermo Grenier and Hugh Gladwin, "The 2016 FIU Cuba Poll: How Cuban Americans in Miami View U.S. Policies toward Cuba," Steven J. Green School of International and Public Affairs, Florida International University, https://sipa.fiu.edu/academics/video-archive/2016 /the-2016-fiu-cuba-poll/.

Chapter 17

. . . a longer story of family and friendship," Remarks by President Obama to the People of Cuba, Office of the Press Secretary, March 22, 2016,

Marc Caputo, "Inside Marco Rubio's Campaign to Shape Trump's Cuba Crackdown," *Politico*, June 16, 2017, https://www.politico.com /story/2017 /06/15/marco-rubio-donald-trump-cuba-plan-239597.

Rebecca Nelson, "Ted Cruz: Obama's New Cuba Policy 'Will Be Remembered as a Tragic Mistake,'" *Atlantic*, December 17, 2014, https://www .theatlantic.com/politics/archive/2014/12/ted-cruz-obamas-new-cuba-policy-will-be-remembered-as-a-tragic-mistake/451260/.

Gutierrez interview.

"hostile rhetoric," Cuban officials quoted in Hatzel Vela, Madeleine Wright, Andrew Perez, and Andrea Torres, "Cuban Diplomats Respond to President Donald Trump's 'Hostile Rhetoric,'" June 17, 2017, Local 10 News (Miami-Dade, Florida), https://www.local10.com/news/cuba/cuban-diplomats -respond-to-president-donald-trumps-hostile-rhetoric.

"Cuba and the United States can cooperate . . . ," Raul Castro quoted by Reuters in Havana, "Raúl Castro: Cuba Won't Compromise Sovereignty to Normalize US Relations," *Guardian*, January 25, 2017.

"But it should not be hoped . . . ," Associated Press, "Castro: Cuba Can Work with Trump if Sovereignty Respected," *Politico*, January 26, 2017, *https://www.politico.com/story/2017/01/castro-cuba-trump-if-sovereignty -respected-234210.*

Diedrich, Lisa and Tausig, Benjamin, "Mysterious Sounds and Scary Illnesses as Political Tools," *New York Times*, October 10, 2017.

"I do believe Cuba's responsible." President Trump quoted in "Trump Says Cuba 'responsible' for Alleged Sonic Attacks, but Offers No Evidence," *Guardian*, October 16, 2017.

"There is no evidence . . . ," Minister Bruno Rodriguez, quoted in Nicole Gaouette, "Cuban Minister Rejects US Sonic Attack Claims, Washington (CNN), November 2, 2017.

"Even 'Star Wars' didn't contain such fantasies," Mariela Castro quoted in "Star Wars' Fantasy? Cubans Doubt US Sonic Attacks claims," *AP News*, October 13, 2017.

"We are not much further ahead than we were in finding out why this occurred," Undersecretary of State Steve Goldstein quoted in "The Latest: Cuban Diplomat Slams Senate Hearing," *AP News*, January 9, 2018

Williams, Abigail and Connor, Tracy, "U.S. and Canada Baffled by Health 'Attacks' on Diplomats in Cuba," *NBC News*, January 10, 2018.

Marc Frank and Sarah Marsh, "Cuban Parliament Approves Communist Party Roadmap," June 1, 2017, Reuters, https://www. reuters.com/article/us

-cuba-parliament/cuban-parliament-approves-communist-party-roadmap
-idUSKBN18S5KL.

Gámez Nora Torres, "'There Are Several People with Qualities' to Re-place Raúl Castro, Says Cuba Leader's Daughter," *Miami Herald*, May 1, 2017.

Acosta, Nelson and Marsh, Sarah, "Cuba Delays Historic Handover from Castro to New President, Reuters, December 21, 2017.

Gamez Torres, Nora and Delgado, Antonio Maria, "Goodbye, Venezuela; Hello, Russia. Can Vladimir Putin save Cuba? *Nation & World*, December 27, 2017.

Marc Frank, "China Piles Into Cuba as Venezuela Fades and Trump Looms," February 14, 2017, Reuters, http://www.reuters.com /article/us-cuba
-china-analysis-idUSKBN15T2PE?il=0.

"China and Cuba Agree to Strengthen Military Cooperation," *Telesur*, March 31, 2017.

Franco Ordoñez, "Russia Considers Opening Military Base in Cuba," *Miami Herald*, October 11, 2016, http://www.miamiherald .com/news/nation
-world/world/article107473897.html.

Rhodes interview.

BIBLIOGRAPHY

Anderson, Jon Lee. *Che Guevara: A Revolutionary Life.* New Work: Grove, 1997.

Bardach, Ann Louise. *Cuba Confidential: Love and Vengeance in Miami and Havana.* New York: Random House, 2003.

Castro, Fidel, and Ignacio Ramonet. *Fidel Castro: My Life: A Spoken Autobiography.* New York: Scribner's, 2008.

Chomsky, Aviva. *A History of the Cuban Revolution.* Malden, MA: Wiley-Blackwell, 2011.

Dominguez, Jorge I. "Cuba's National Security vis-à-vis the United States: Conflict or Cooperation?" In *Debating U.S.-Cuban Relations: Shall we Play Ball?,* edited by Jorge I. Dominguez, Rafael M. Hernández, and Lorena G. Barberia, pp 38 -41. New York: Routledge, 2012.

Eire, Carlos. *Waiting for Snow in Havana: Confessions of a Cuban Boy.* New York: Simon and Schuster, 2003.

English, T. J. *Havana Nocturne: How the Mob Owned Cuba and Then Lost It to the Revolution.* New York: Harper, 2009.

Erikson, Daniel P. *The Cuba Wars: Fidel Castro, the United States, and the Next Revolution.* New York: Bloomsburg, 2010.

Feinberg, Richard. *Open for Business: Building the New Cuban Economy.* Washington, DC: Brookings Institution Press, 2016.

Frank, Marc. *Cuban Revelations: Behind the Scenes in Havana.* Gainesville: University Press of Florida, 2013.

García, Cristina. *Dreaming in Cuban.* New York: Ballantine, 1992.

Gardner, Mark Lee. *Rough Riders: Theodore Roosevelt, His Cowboy Regiment, and the Immortal Charge up San Juan Hill.* New York: Harper-Collins, 2016.

Bibliography

Geyer, Georgie Anne. *Guerrilla Prince: The Untold Story of Fidel Castro.* Boston: Little, Brown, 1991.

Gjelten, Tom. *Bacardi and the Long Fight for Cuba: The Biography of a Cause.* New York: Viking, 2008.

Green, Graham. *Our Man in Havana.* New York: Penguin, 1958.

Hemingway, Ernest. *The Old Man and the Sea.* New York: Scribner's, 2002.

Huddleston, Vicki, and Carlos Pascual. *Learning to Salsa: New Steps in U.S.-Cuban Relations.* Washington, DC: Brookings Institution Press, 2010.

LeoGrande, William M., and Peter Kornbluh. *Back Channel to Cuba: The Hidden Story of Negotiations between Washington and Havana.* Chapel Hill: University of North Carolina Press, 2015.

Michener, James A., and John Kings. *Six Days in Havana.* Austin: University of Texas Press, 1989.

Pérez-Sable, Marifeli. *The United States and Cuba: Intimate Enemies.* New York: Routledge, 2010.

Prellezo, Lily, and José Basulto. *Seagull One: The Amazing True Story of Brothers to the Rescue.* Gainesville: University Press of Florida, 2010.

Puzo, Mario. *The Godfather.* New York: Signet, 1969.

Rathbone, John Paul. *The Sugar King of Havana: The Rise and Fall of Julio Lobo, Cuba's Last Tycoon.* New York: Penguin, 2011.

Rytz, Henriette M. *Ethnic Interests Groups in U.S. Foreign Policy-Making: A Cuban-American Story of Success and Failure.* New York: Palgrave Macmillan, 2013.

Sainsbury, Brendan, and Luke Waterson. *Lonely Planet Cuba.* Melbourne: Lonely Planet, 2017.

Sweig, Julia. *Cuba: What Everyone Needs to Know.* Oxford: Oxford University Press, 2016.

Szulc, Tad. *Fidel: A Critical Portrait.* New York: HarperCollins, 1990.

Thomas, Hugh. *The History of Cuba.* New York: Penguin, 2010.

ACKNOWLEDGMENTS

Our Woman in Havana would not have been written without the tireless encouragement, mentoring, and editing of my wonderful daughter, Alexandra. Another invaluable person to the writing of this memoir is Peter Corsell, who served with me in Havana and is both a great friend and superb editor.

A new friend, Carol Byerly, author of *Fever of War: The Influenza Epidemic in the U.S. Army During World War I*, also did a superb job of editing and helping me to organize my ideas. My son Robert also edited an early version several years ago and has given me excellent advice throughout the process.

I found the information contained in two excellent books to be of great help in reviving my memory and verifying facts: Ann Louise Bardach's *Cuba Confidential: Love and Vengeance in Miami and Havana* and William Leo Grande and Peter Kornbluh, *Back Channel to Cuba: The Hidden History of Negotiations between Washington and Havana*. My story would not have been complete without the insights of former secretary of commerce Carlos Gutierrez; former deputy national security adviser Ben Rhodes, Consul General Ricardo Zuniga, and Ambassador Jeff Delaurentis.

Finally, thank you to my superb agent and editor, Philip Turner, my friends Kay and Rod Heller, and my husband Bob, whose neverending faith convinced me that I could complete this book.